IMAGES
of America

BRACKEN COUNTY

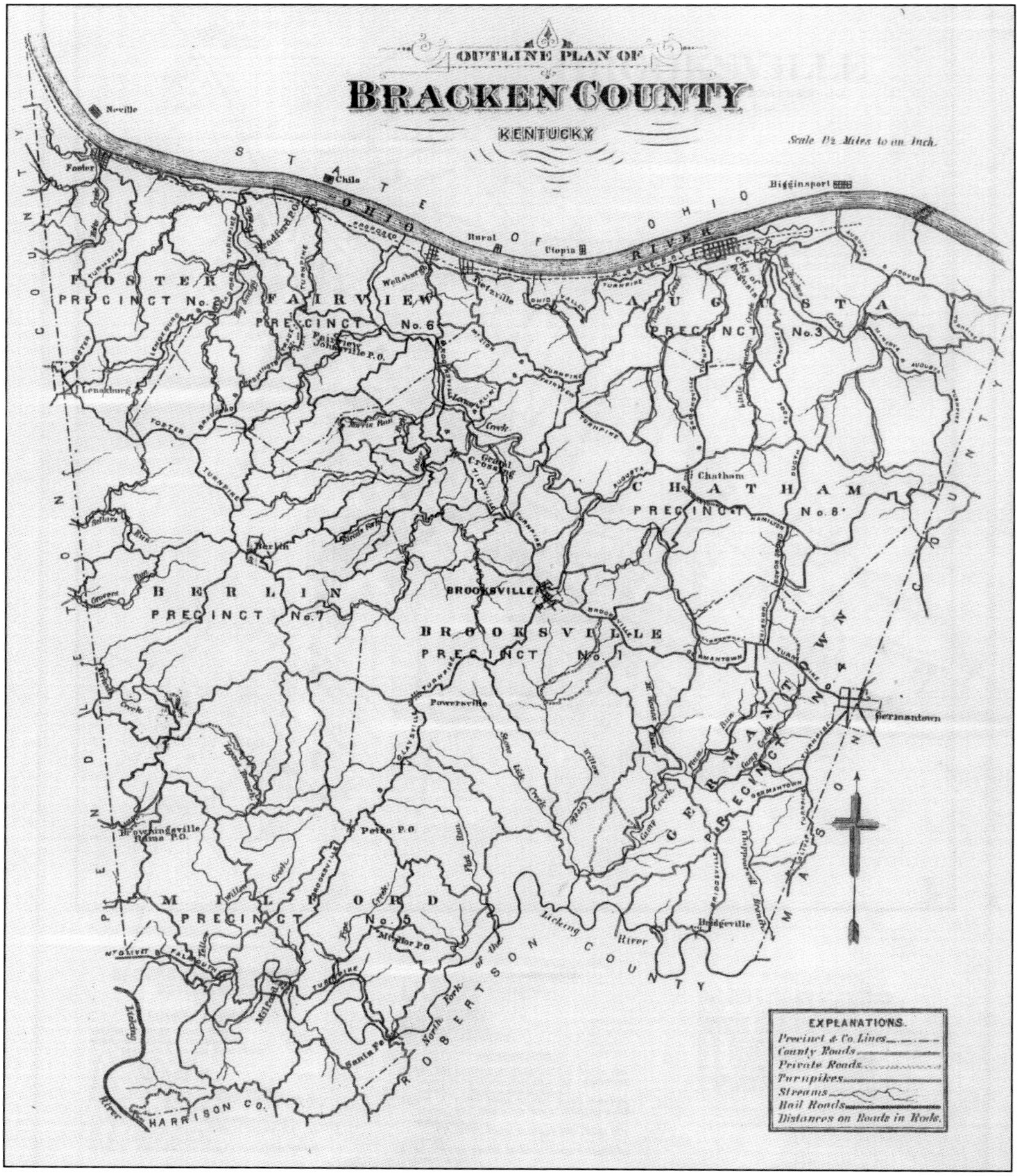

MAP OF BRACKEN COUNTY. Bracken County was formed in December 1796, and its first court was held in early 1797 in Augusta. The county was named for William Bracken, an early settler whose life was ended by unfriendly Native Americans. Portions of land from the counties of Mason and Campbell were taken to form this new county, nearly square in shape. (Courtesy of Bracken County Historical Society.)

ON THE COVER: In 1915, the Brooksville Lumber Mill was owned by Garrett Jett, and the business was located at the bottom of Depot Hill. When this photograph was taken, large granite slabs for the John Downard family mausoleum were being delivered to the Powersville Cemetery. The slabs can be seen on the wagon, which required four teams of horses to pull the load. (Courtesy of Bracken County Historical Society.)

IMAGES
of America

BRACKEN COUNTY

Bracken County Historical Society

ARCADIA
PUBLISHING

ISBN 978-0-7385-8674-8

Published by Arcadia Publishing
Charleston, South Carolina

Printed in the United States of America

Library of Congress Control Number: 2010928318

For all general information, please contact Arcadia Publishing:
Telephone 843-853-2070
Fax 843-853-0044
E-mail sales@arcadiapublishing.com
For customer service and orders:
Toll-Free 1-888-313-2665

Visit us on the Internet at www.arcadiapublishing.com

The Bracken County Historical Society is dedicating this book to the memory of our past presidents and valued researchers: Howard Bentley, George Cummins, Jacqueline Heaverin, Rose Mary Lawson, Elizabeth Parker, Jack Weiss, and Shirley Wolfe.

Contents

ACKNOWLEDGMENTS

The completion of this volume of historical photographs could not have happened without the encouragement and assistance of Bracken County residents, as well as members of the Bracken County Historical Society. Once the necessary photographs had been collected, the manuscript committee examined historical volumes and newspaper articles written by the following local historians and authors: Keith Algier, Bobbi Apking, Steve Appelman, Chester Bryant, Nick Clooney, Nina Clooney, David Crumbaugh, Judy Foster and the Bracken County Homemakers, W. Baxter Harrison, John Leming, John Lenox, Caroline Miller, Rosemary Pell, and Walter Rankins. Numerous oral traditionalists who resided in the county also did their part in keeping the county's history alive by relating their versions of the past: Jessie Bryant, J. W. Crumbaugh, Willard Fryman, Jacquelyn Heaverin, Elizabeth Parker, Claude McCracken, James "Sonny" Thompson, and Jack Weiss. Several individuals supplied the majority of images in this volume, and the society would like to express gratitude to Robert Adams, Carol Wallin Boney, *Bracken County News*, Marilyn Bryant, Greg Cummins, Diana French, Ron French, John H. Henderson, Clark Hennessey, Ruby LaMonda, Thom Lawson, John Lenox, Roberta Shepherd, Bernie Spencer, Suzanne Weaver, John White, and John Workman. Essential technical advice and support were provided by William Baker, Greg Haitz, Britton Hennessey, Connor Hennessey, Patricia Lenox, Phyllis Lenox, Mary Jane Lucas, and Susan Ratliff. The utmost appreciation is given to William Baker, Carol Wallin Boney, Roberta Shepherd, Elizabeth Taheri, and Mary Watson for proofreading and editing the text.

The Bracken County Historical Society is particularly indebted to its research historian, Caroline Miller, for her efforts formatting the photographs and coordinating the project through its completion. Miller wishes to acknowledge the persistence and encouragement of Alison Gibson and Shirley Mohrfield, who first brought Images of America to her attention. Amy Perryman of Arcadia Publishing guided Miller and the society with timely professional advice and information. With their support, this volume of Bracken County history can be readily available on bookshelves and placed into the hands of interested readers.

Introduction

The Bracken County Historical Society had its origin in 1993, and its membership is comprised of representatives from all organizations in the county, as well as members from several states. The society recognized the need for a history, which could be conveyed by photographs, postcards, and other illustrations. This compilation of images will serve as a lasting memorial to past residents and a record for future generations.

Bracken County, founded in 1797, is a high rolling land possessing abundant clear waters from the Ohio River and North Fork of the Licking River, as well as a natural watershed providing farmers and industry with the earth's most valuable resource. Plentiful forests rewarded early citizens with raw materials for shelter and animals for subsistence. Settlers arrived first from ports east on the Ohio River before wagon trains brought families over the Appalachian Mountains into central Kentucky. Once the land was safe from Native American attacks, Augusta flourished as a port city used for transportation of tobacco, hemp, grapes, and livestock. To complement this port, boats were constructed in nearby Levanna, Ohio, and flatboats were made in Claysville, near the southern border of Bracken County.

The county derived its name from two creeks, Big Bracken and Little Bracken, which were possibly named after an early hunter, William Bracken. Surveyors Robert McAfee and James McAfee charted the river lands as early as 1780, building a small surveyor's cabin at the mouth of Chalfont Creek near Rock Springs. Soon after, James Pribble established a trading post on the southeast hill above Augusta. Pribble sent for the Teegarden, Thomas, and Smith families to settle the land, and they remained at the post for several years. These pioneers became the first owners of land farther inland in the county, instead of relocating along the Ohio River. Philimon Thomas acquired land near Buchanan's Station, later named Germantown, and encouraged a group of Pennsylvania Dutch to settle in this area of relatively flat fields and bluegrass soil. The Pennsylvania Dutch were also credited with laying the first plank road in the 1870s on what is currently called Dutch Ridge Road. Trees were felled and split so they could be laid with the flat side up, enabling carriages to travel without getting stuck in ruts and mud.

Bracken County was the home of several stonemasons who quarried the stone, faced it, and constructed single and two-story homes in the eastern portion of the county. Reportedly, Abraham Baker Sr. labored with his employees and slaves to build five stone houses in the 1820s—several of them remain as residences on Dutch Ridge and Minerva Roads. Of course, log cabins predated the sturdier stone buildings, and remarkably, many of them dot the roadsides of Bracken County today. These log cabins were covered with wood siding, which makes them unrecognizable to most residents and tourists. Augusta has five cabins, some of which had been located in other parts of the county before being reconstructed, serving as summer homes and businesses.

Over the next two centuries, Augusta and Brooksville became the sites of several courthouses. Augusta trustees immediately provided educational training in legal, ministerial, and medical fields. Although the county was vastly rural, its location in relation to larger cities, within a few hours' carriage ride, gave its citizens the ability to communicate and trade in both cultures. Once river traffic slowed as a result of rail transportation, a group of local businessmen constructed its own county railroad from Wellsburg on the Ohio River to the county seat, Brooksville. "Big Windy" was a small locomotive with only a few cars that had to run forwards and backwards, with no turnaround area available. This effort continued for several decades. Brooksville and the remaining portions of the county were experiencing continued growth. Although small, this railroad was necessary for Brooksville and the remaining parts of the county to prosper.

"A Beautiful Situation" is the phrase often used to describe the streets and landscapes along the Ohio River. The sunrises and sunsets over Augusta provided the natural beauty behind numerous poems and paintings; however, these placid waters at times turn angry, flooding homes and destroying businesses. Residents had to become resilient to these dangers and have turned empty lots into green spaces and neighborhood parks. Builders became quite imaginative in designing homes that could meet FEMA (Federal Emergency Management Association) regulations, which required living space to be elevated above the 100-year flood plain.

Hollow Bracken is the title of a small collection of poems by Hanson P. Diltz aptly describing this land among small hills that rise above the Ohio. Scattered on the ridges and along its creeks were those log cabins and stone houses built by a hearty pioneer group of men and women who endeavored to leave a legacy for their descendants. Hopefully this volume of photographs offers a visual history of Bracken County.

One

Settlers Organized Land

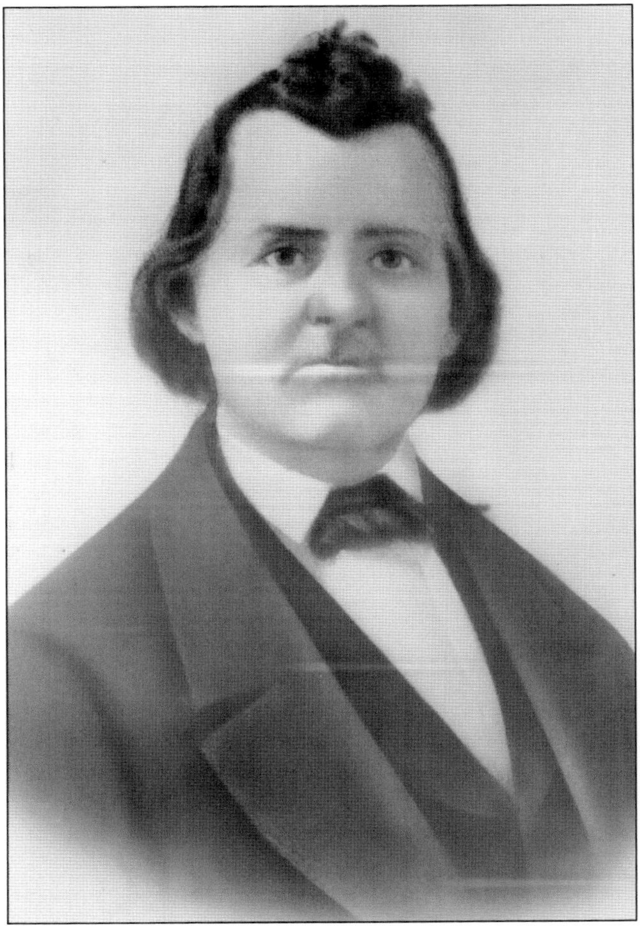

William Buckner. Buckner was the son of Philip Buckner (1747–1830), the founder of Augusta, and Tabitha Daniels Buckner. The Buckners arrived in Augusta with several families from Virginia in 1794. Although some early researchers believed this image to be Philip Buckner, there is more persuasive evidence that the illustration is of his son, William Buckner. Most of Augusta's streets were named after Phillip and Tabitha's children. The city was chartered by the Legislature of Kentucky on October 2, 1797. Land was deeded for the city by Philip Buckner. Buckner and his sons were fond of hunting and the chase, having the true pioneer spirit. When the elder Buckners chose to retire to a less-settled town, they moved to Phillip's hunting lodge at Powersville, a site of only a few cabins. William continued to lead a privileged life as the son of a powerful and prominent representative to Frankfort. (Courtesy of Knoedler Library.)

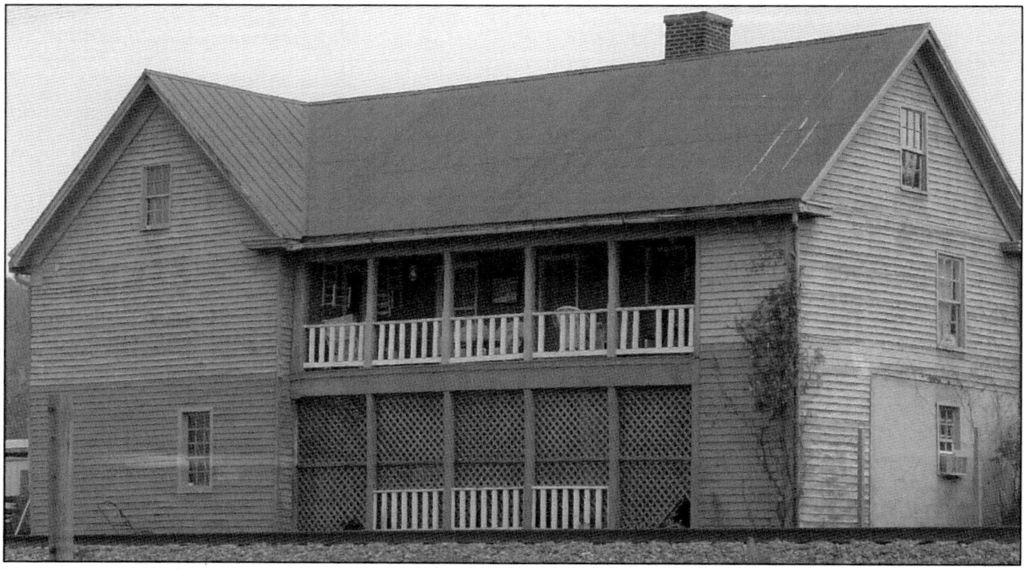

First County Court Buildings. Court was first held in 1796 in the Dickinson Morris house, pictured above, which is located on Park and Third Streets, now the home of Luciano Moral. The home was constructed as a double log cabin with siding placed over logs, allowing the structure to be maintained into the 21st century. Pictured below is the county jail, constructed in 1811 to replace a log jail built in 1803. This jail consists of 2-foot stone walls imbedded 4 feet into the ground. The jailer's quarters were located on the second floor. In his quarters, a trap door acted as the entrance to the jail cell, with prisoners having to climb down a ladder. Newspaper accounts told of boat captains placing unruly passengers or deckhands in this jail, as it was so close to the river. Located close to the jail were the necessary stocks and, at times, a quickly erected platform for hangings. (Both, courtesy of Bracken County Historical Society.)

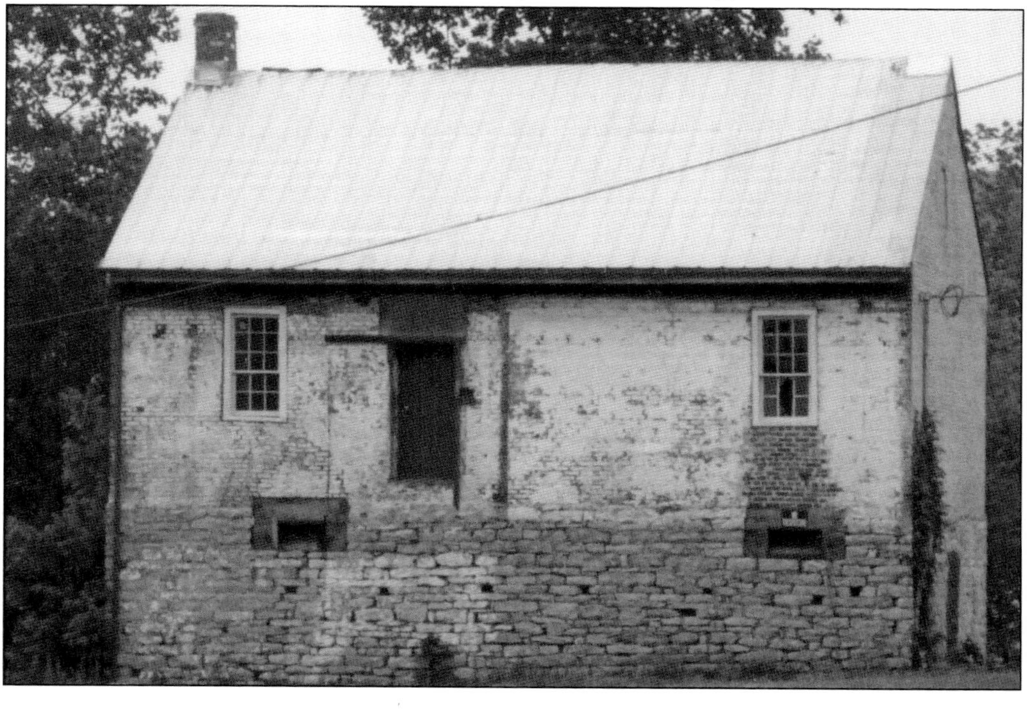

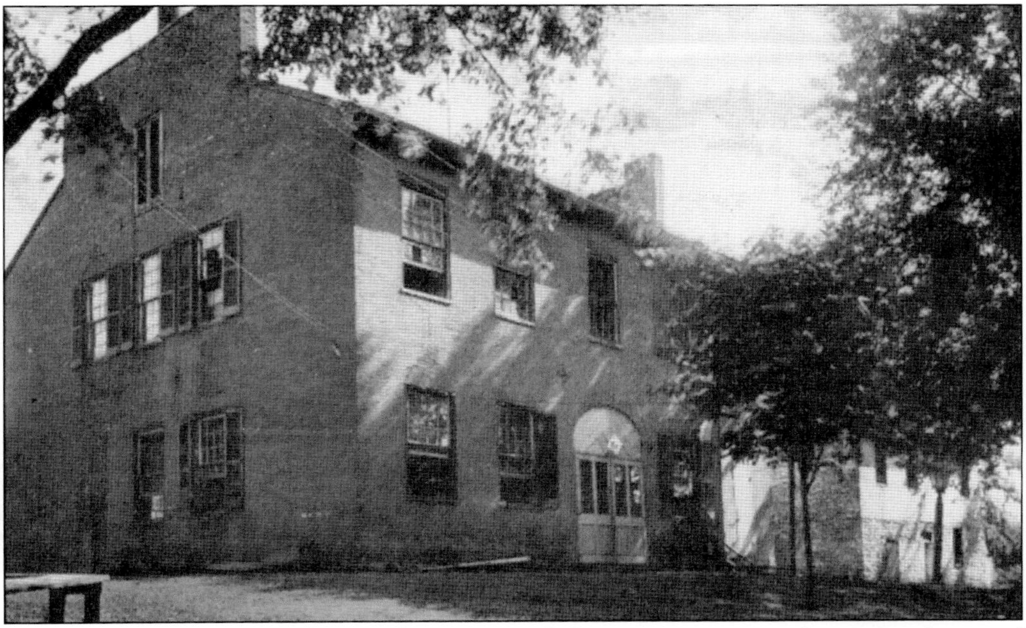

AUGUSTA PUBLIC SQUARE. The courthouse pictured above was once a grand structure that stood for nearly 80 years, until the city sold the building in 1908. After the center of government was moved to Brooksville in 1839, this structure served the city of Augusta, and it later became a center of culture and a meetinghouse for local fraternal organizations. Several noted speakers delivered orations on the stage at the west end of the first-floor hall while spectators sat on numerous green benches. Shown below is the city park, the site of stage productions and entertainment. The large gazebo has been replaced, and the park remains as a center for parades, concerts, and the ever-popular corn hole tournaments. (Both, courtesy of John and Juanita White.)

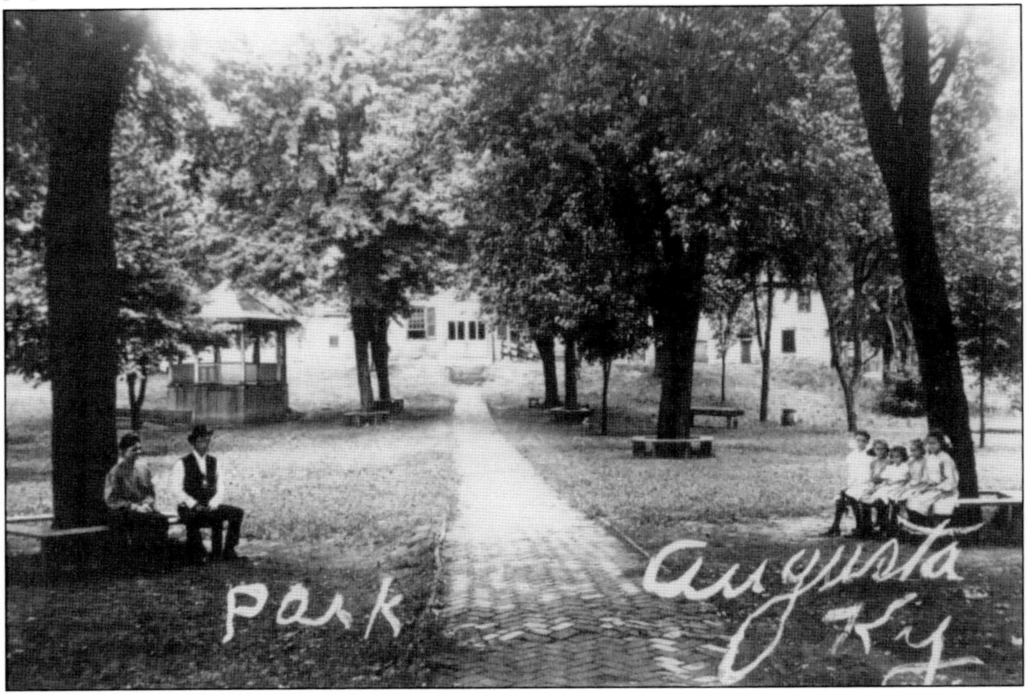

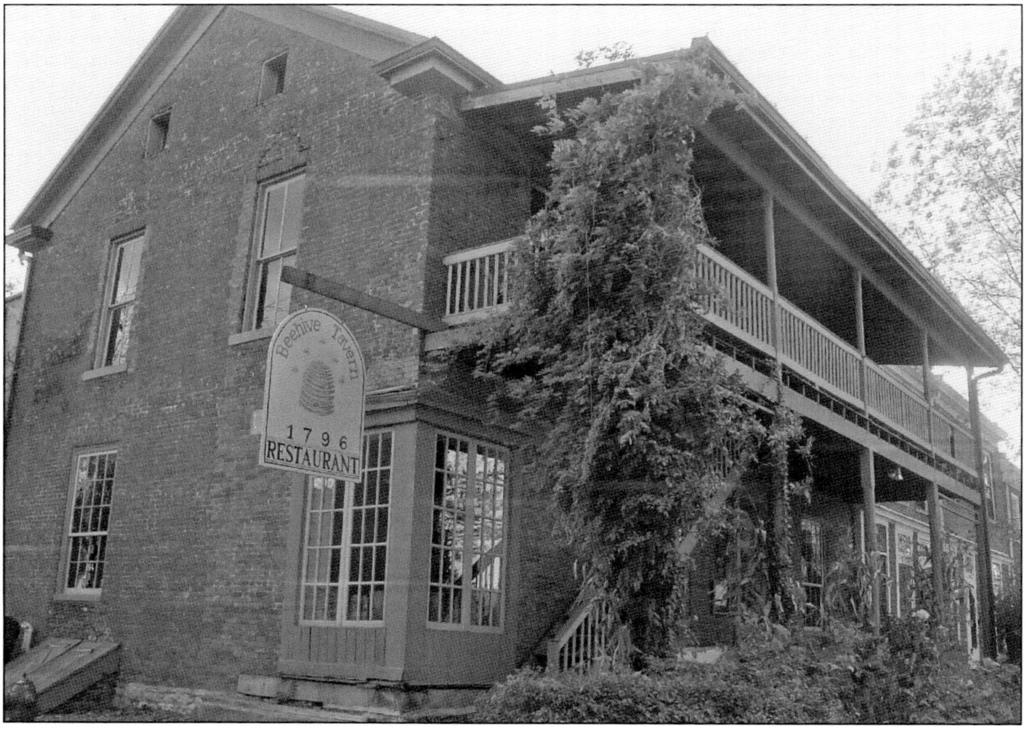

18TH-CENTURY STRUCTURES. Pictured above is a building that was erected during the late 1700s. During the Battle of Augusta on September 27, 1862, mortally wounded bodies of home front soldiers were laid beyond the counter so family members could identify their loved ones. One block west on Riverside Drive is the former home (below) of the Bradford-Marshall families. World War II general George C. Marshall's parents lived in this home prior to their move to Uniontown, Pennsylvania. (Both, courtesy of Marilyn Bryant.)

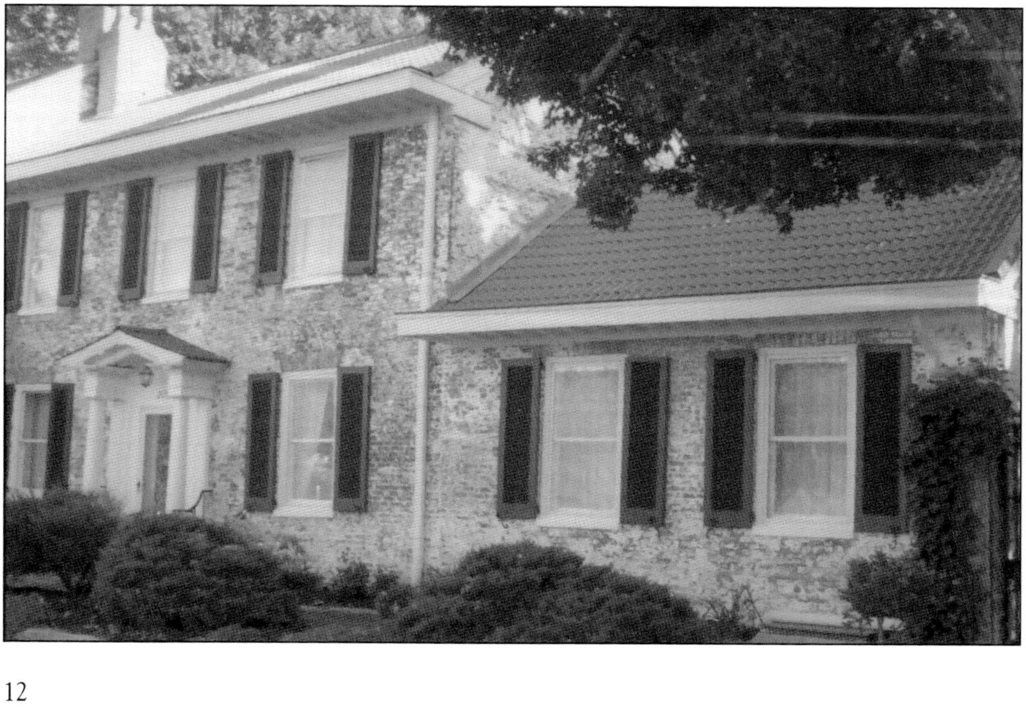

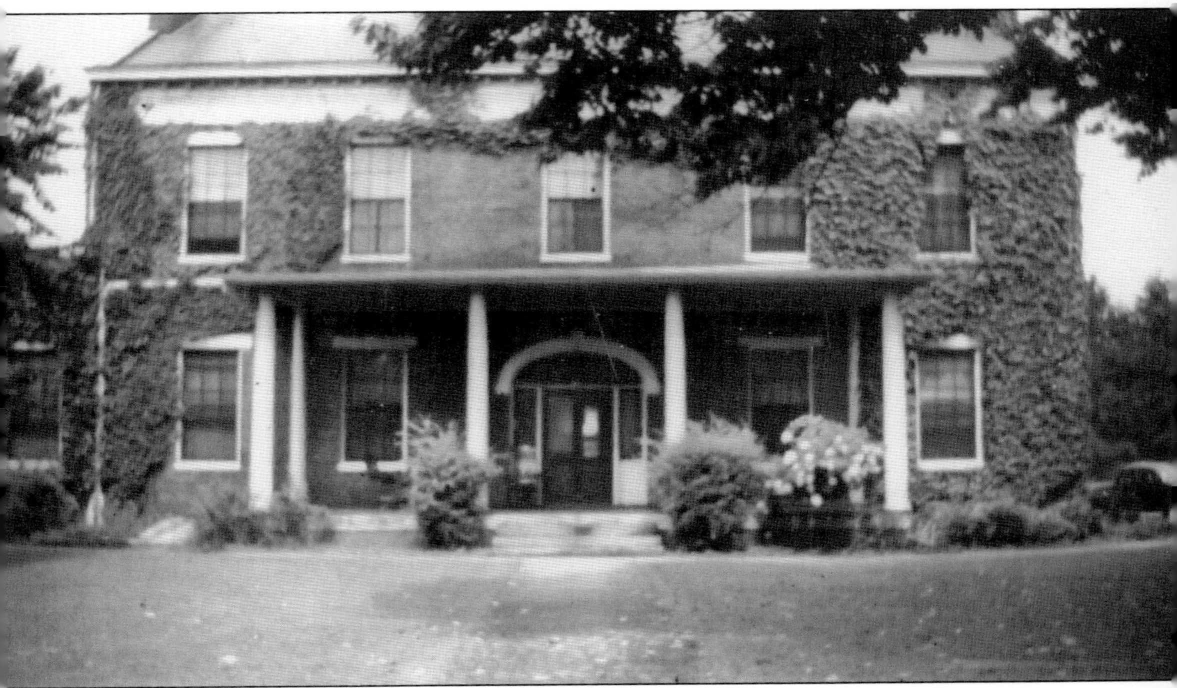

White Hall, Designed by Thome. Arthur Thome, an early settler of Augusta, was a trustee of Bracken Academy, the preparatory school that eventually became Augusta College. Thome soon constructed a flour mill and operated other enterprises in the fledgling town. In 1809, he designed and began construction on White Hall, a three-story antebellum mansion on west Third and Elizabeth Streets. Thome was a master woodworker and planed boards for the walnut trimmings and furniture. After emancipating his slaves, it was revealed that he was a conductor of fugitive slaves on the Underground Railroad. One freed slave recalled that Thome would awake in the night, feed and clothe fugitive slaves, and transport them across the Ohio River to freedom. For three decades, he was a close friend of Rev. John Rankin, the famed abolitionist of Ripley, Ohio. Many historians suspect that he was conducting slaves from Augusta to Rankin's Underground Railroad system. In 1815, Thome began building the Presbyterian church at the southeast corner of Upper and Third Streets. (Courtesy of Marilyn Bryant.)

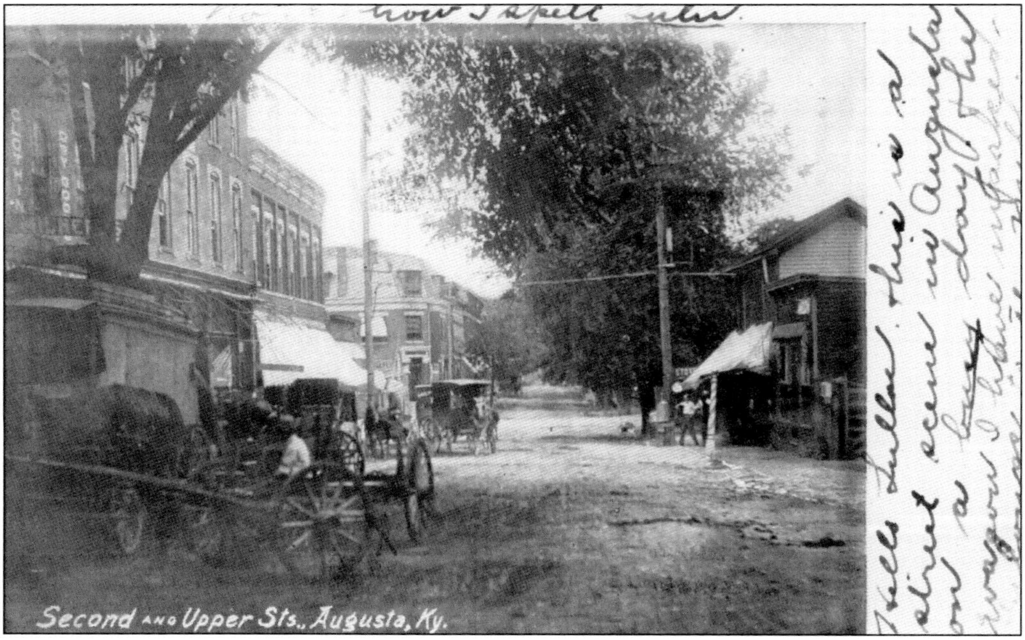

Upper Street Bustled. The street lined with businesses in Augusta was first named Upper, and this name is noted in most historical references; however, it has maintained the name Main Street into the 21st century. Although the street was covered with dirt and possessed few sidewalks, it was durable enough for carriages and wagons delivering goods to merchants and riverboats. Pictured above in the early 1900s are numerous carriages and what appears to be a barber's pole at the far right. The bottom picture is North Upper Street with Augusta German Bank, which no longer remains, on the left. (Above, courtesy of Bernie Spencer; below, courtesy of Roberta Shepherd.)

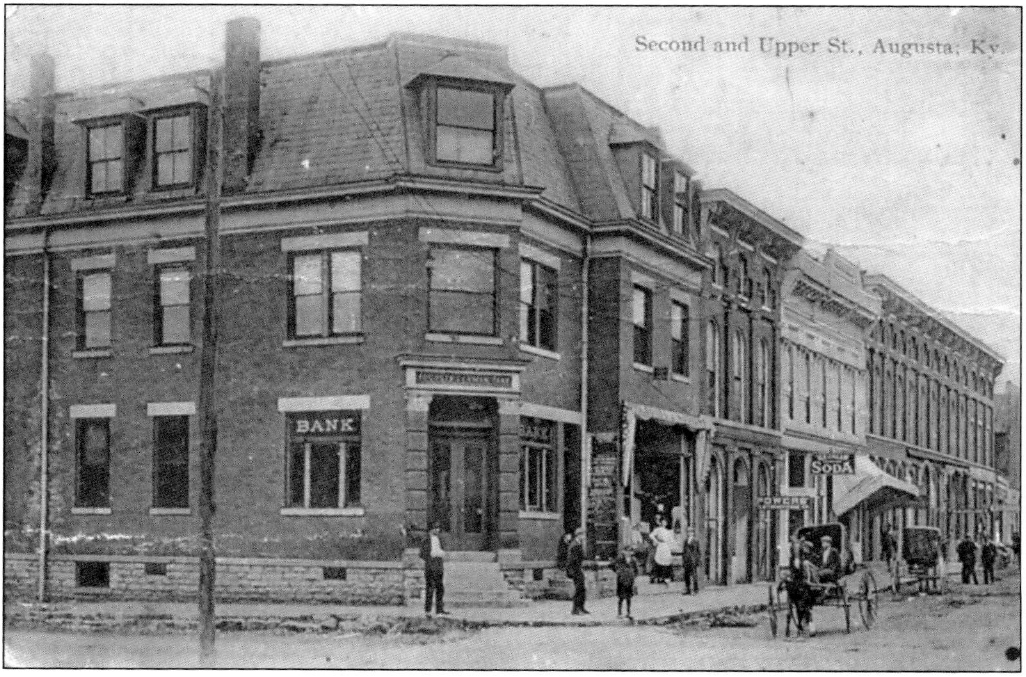

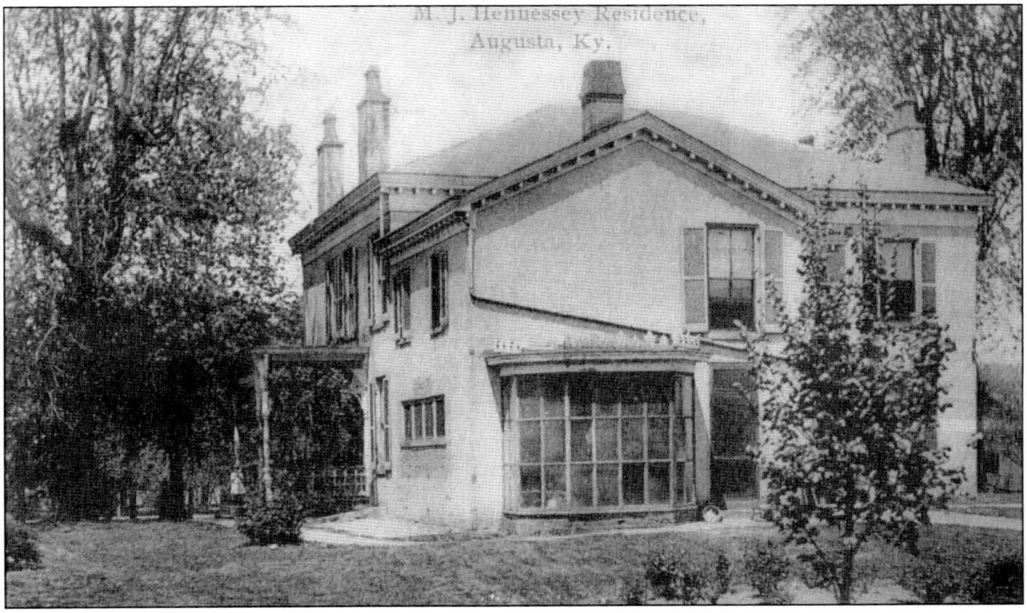

Mansions and Inns Dotted Augusta. The mansion above, located at Third and Elizabeth Streets, was built in the early 1800s and later owned by the Wells, Ryan, Hennessey, and Appelman families. During the Battle of Augusta, a wounded soldier was carried there for treatment; however, he lived only a few days. Decades later, when visitors or traveling statesmen required a stay overnight, the most acceptable accommodations would have been found at the Parkview Inn, which is pictured below. This inn has welcomed guests who were delivered by stagecoach, carriages, crank-engine cars, and the finest limousines in the area. For over 150 years, guests of Augusta have been able to rely on quality lodging and fine dining at the Parkview Inn. (Both, courtesy of Robert Adams.)

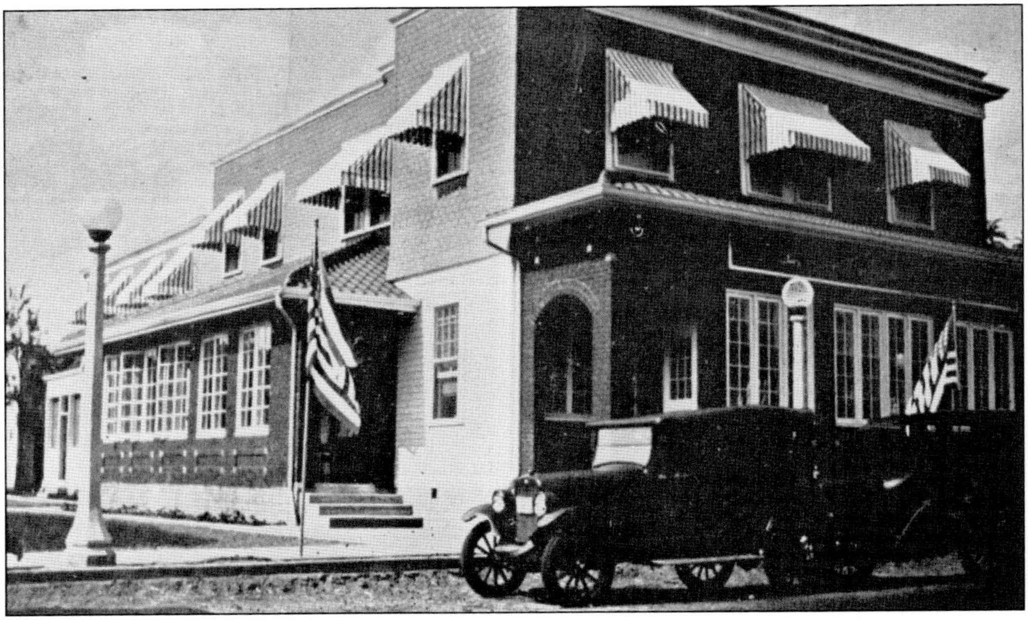

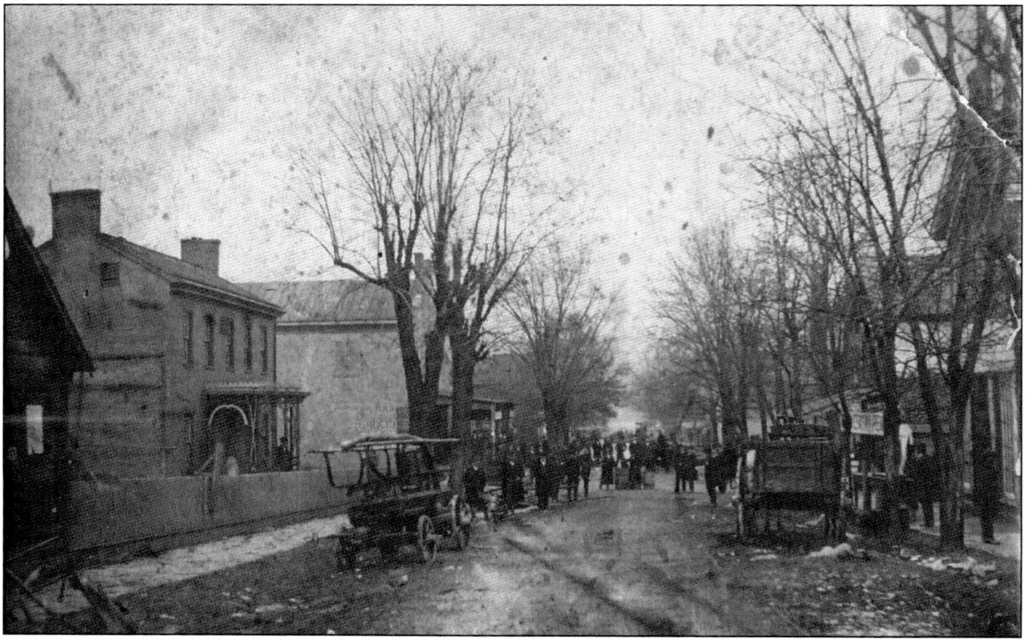

Carriages and Buckboards. In the 1890s, there were scenes of buckboards and carriages getting stuck in the muck after heavy rains on the dirt roads of Augusta and Brooksville until plank or graveled streets were available. On market days, business owners feared that clients could not get through the muddy passages. Pictured below is another means of travel that was not as common—travel on the frozen Ohio River. This seemingly unafraid lady and her lone horse appear well protected for their ride over the frozen water to Boude's Landing or Thomas' Resort on the Ohio side. What is not apparent in the picture is how they were able to get down the steep bank without upsetting the carriage. (Both, courtesy of Marilyn Bryant.)

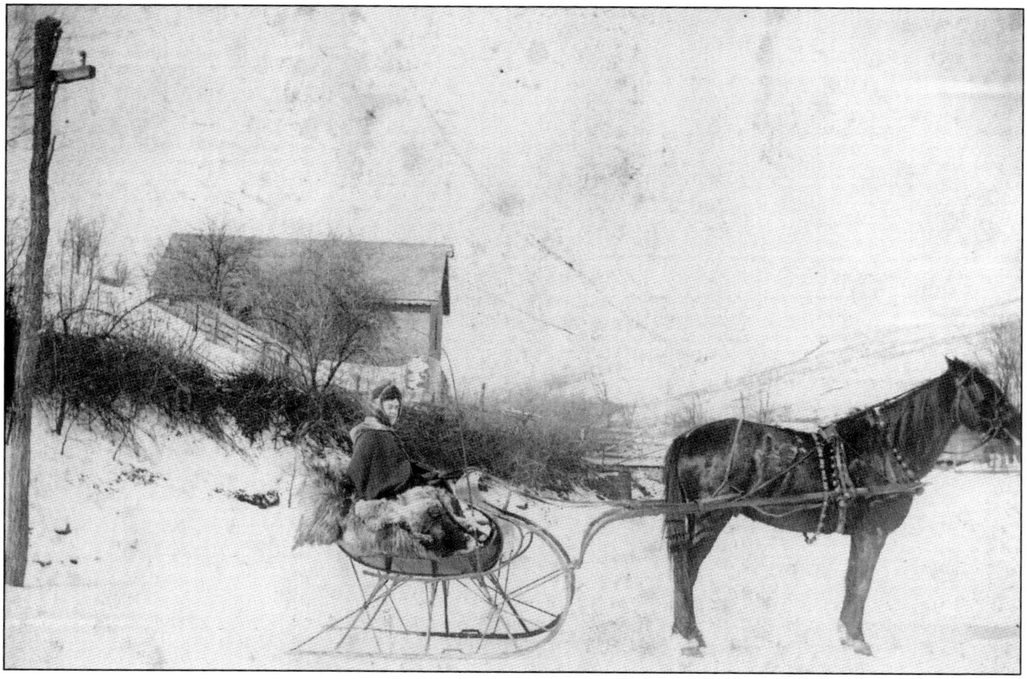

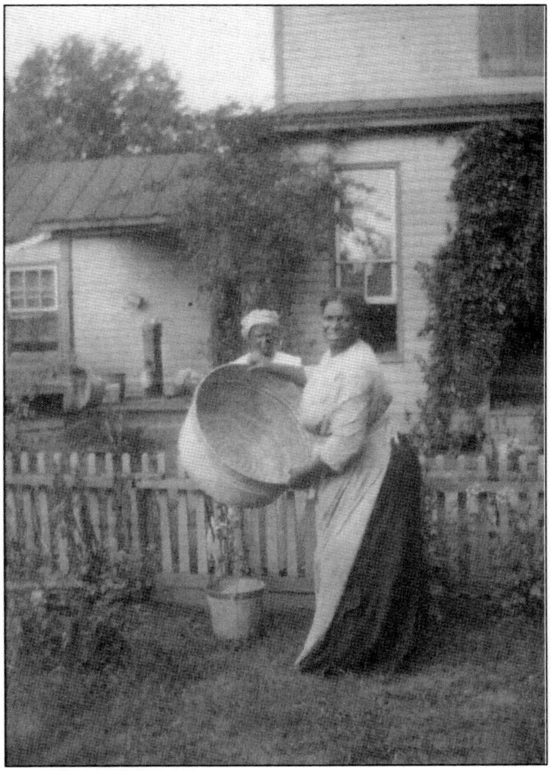

African Americans Employed. Older newspaper accounts list the names of worthy African American citizens in Bracken County. Perhaps most well known in Augusta was Nace Simmons, caner of chair bottoms. Ben and Rachel Beckett were employed in the Wells-Ryan mansion, and Roderick made his home with the Powers families of Elizabeth Street. John Pattie, a brick mason from Dover, laid brick on several Augusta mansions and churches. Moses Preston was the first African American photographer in the U.S. Navy and head photographer of the *Louisville Herald*. Grant Laughlin was best known as the porter at Smith Hotel, and "Aunt" Harriet's cakes were always the first selected at church gatherings. The names of the women and children pictured are unknown. (Both, courtesy of Marilyn Bryant.)

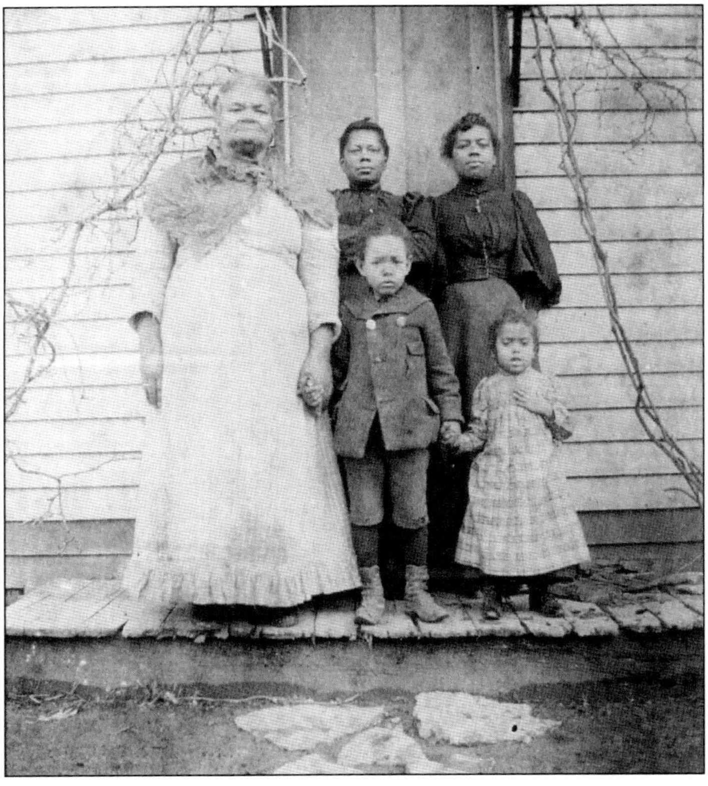

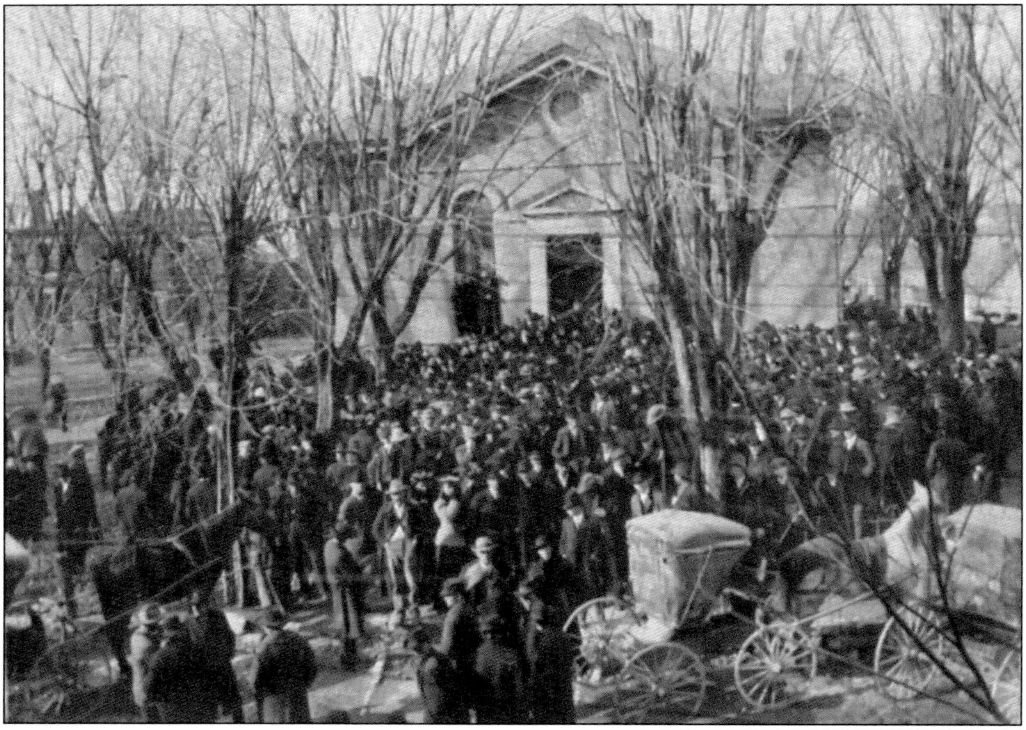

Courthouses Reveal Secrets. The one-story building pictured above in Brooksville was erected in 1839, and the first court term was convened that year. However, it and its additions were condemned and ordered dismantled on July 22, 1913, and $50,000 was raised for construction of the present building. Historians believe this crowd picture was taken at the Robert Laughlin hanging in 1897. (Courtesy of Bracken County Historical Society.)

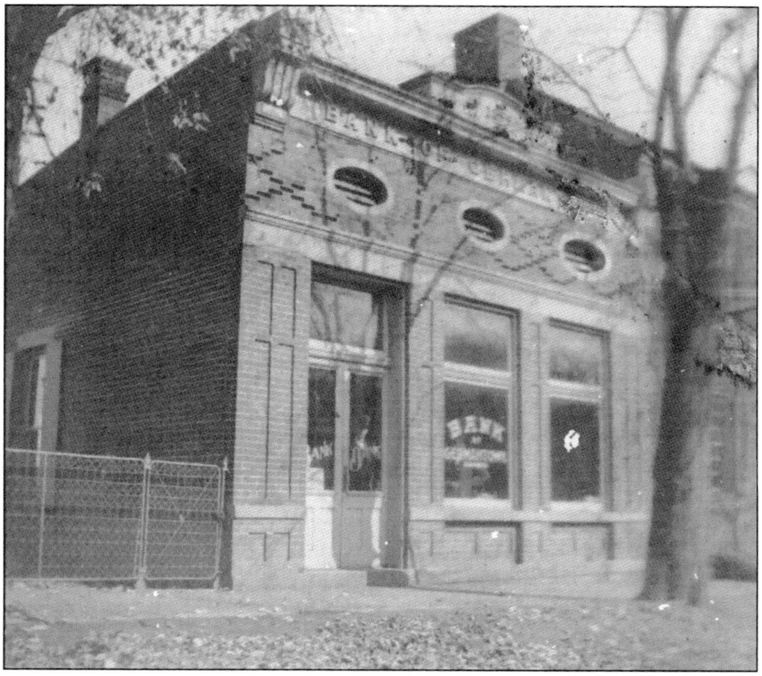

Bank of Germantown. This mid-20th-century building served as the site of the Germantown Bank. This bank and the Farmers and Traders Bank merged in 1930. Before it was purchased by another banking facility in the early 1990s, Manville Fryman was the president and operation officer. (Courtesy of John H. Henderson.)

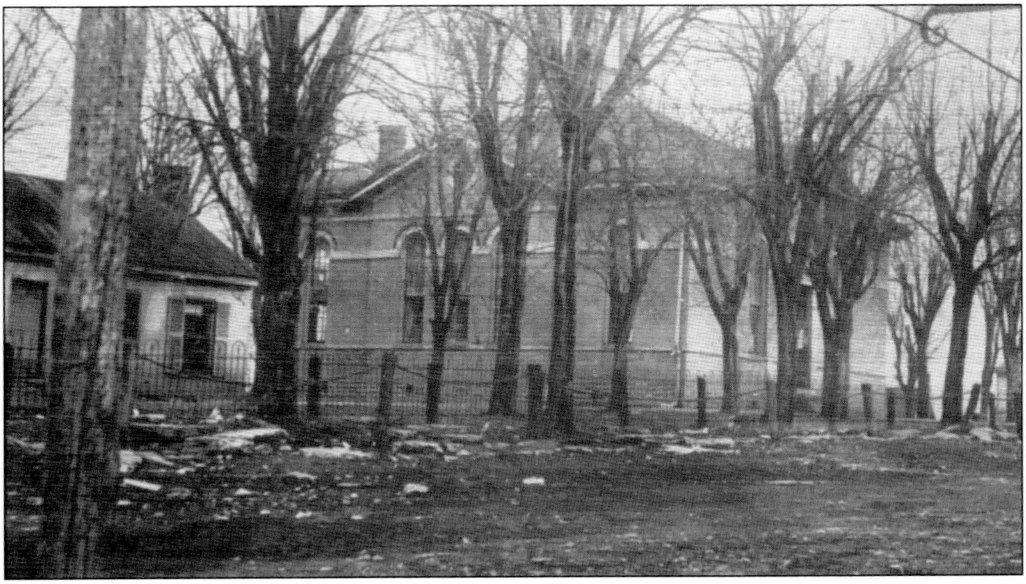

Brooksville Courthouses. The earliest courthouse in Brooksville was erected around 1839. Additions were constructed between 1862 and 1864 to allow for additional court departments, as seen in this exceptional picture. This courthouse served the citizens until the 1930s. (Courtesy of Marilyn Power Sandy.)

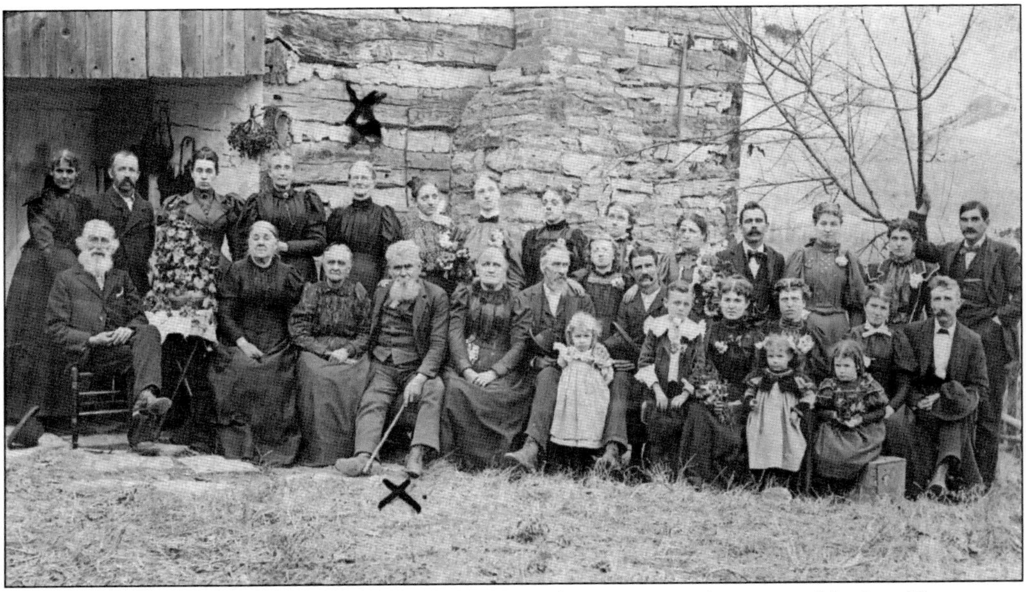

Boude–Diltz Families of Augusta. This photograph represents what is possibly the oldest image of an extended family in Bracken County. Most of those pictured lived in or near Augusta and were descendants of Watson and Rebecca (Veach) Diltz and Samuel and Susan (Payne) Boude. (Courtesy of Carol Wallin Boney.)

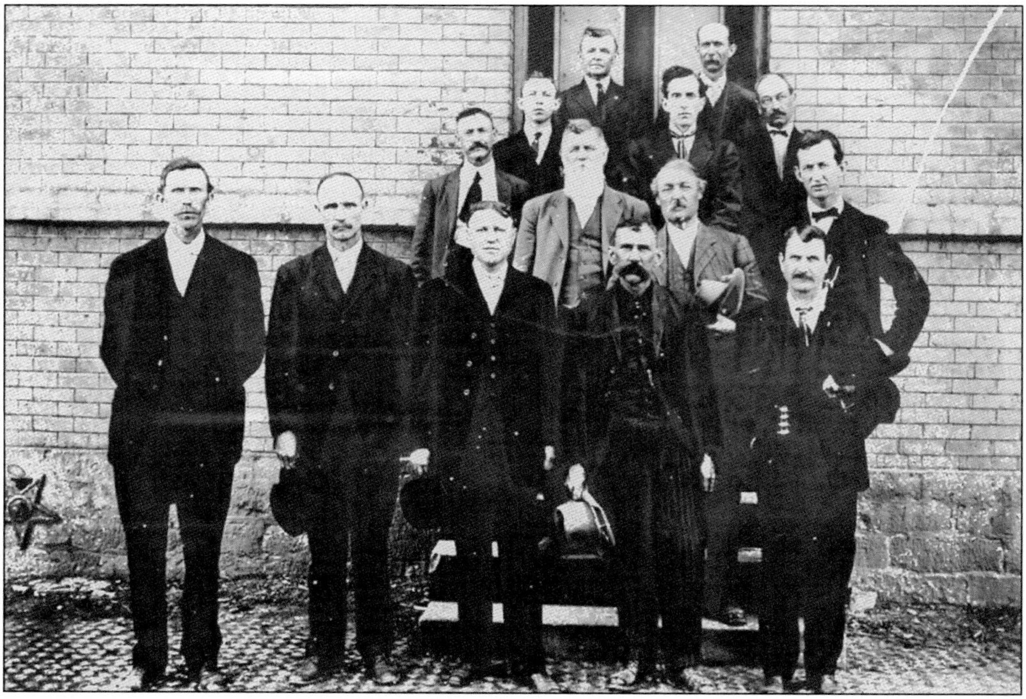

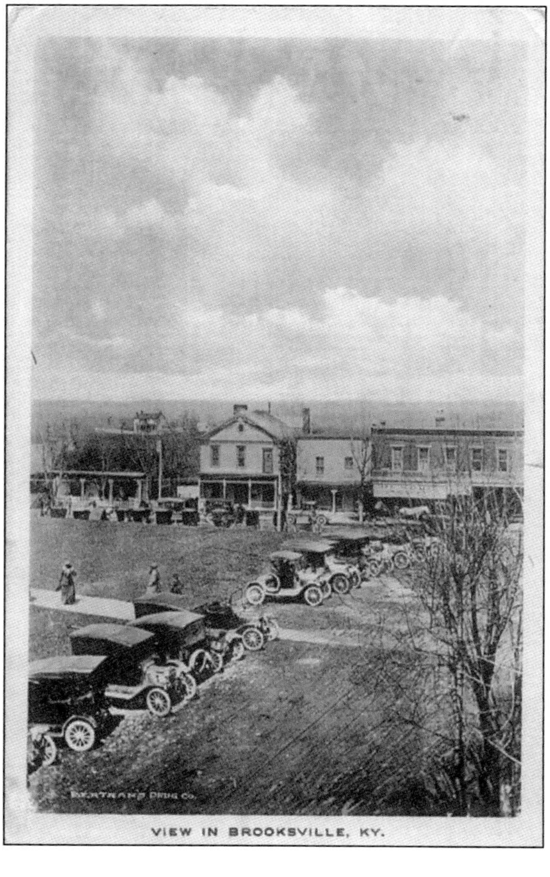

CENTER OF GOVERNMENT AND TRADE. This photograph was taken at the back entrance of the old courthouse in the late 1800s. Pictured are, from left to right, (front row) Milford magistrate John Woodward, Johnsville magistrate Albert Sroufe, county judge William Gibson, Germantown magistrate Charles Kurtz, and Foster magistrate John Morris; (second row) Berlin magistrate O. L. Grigson, Brooksville magistrate P. T. Cook, sheriff B. F. McAtee, and magistrate James Thompson; (third row) county clerk Thomas Cummins, county attorney George Kinney, and master commissioner James Ware; (fourth row) Chatham magistrate Asbury H. Brooks and jailer Charles Kinney. Since Brooksville was the center of government, streets were often crowded with early Ford Model A cars, as well as horses and wagons. (Both, courtesy of Bracken County Historical Society.)

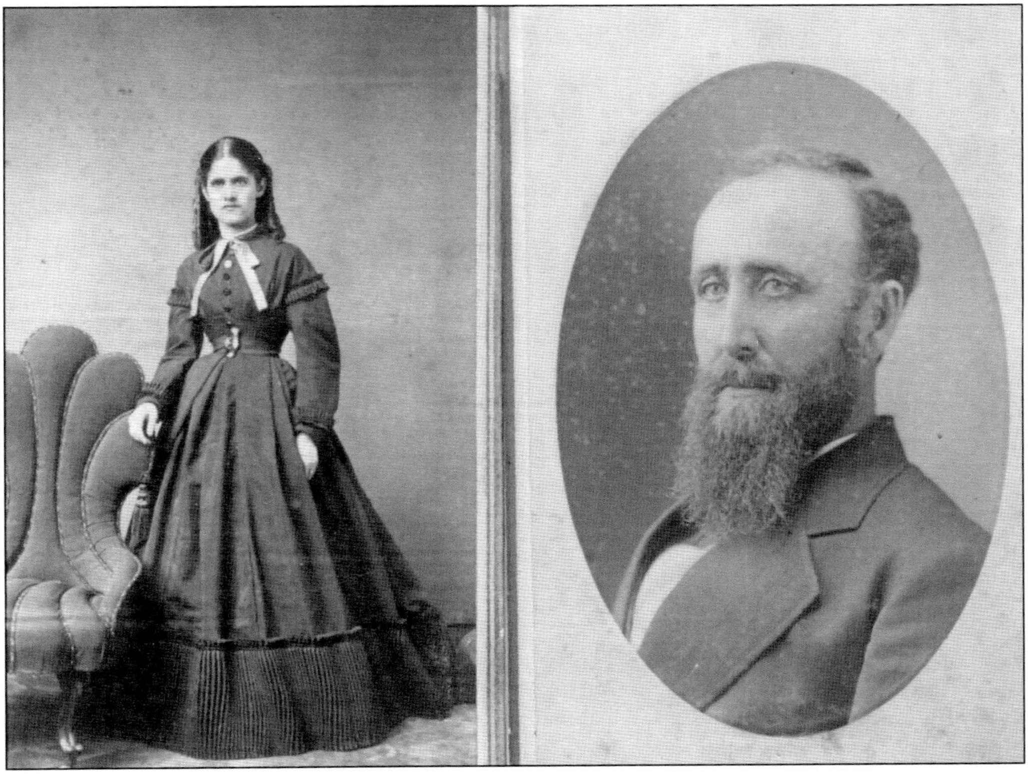

THREE GENERATIONS OF DOCTORS. When the first Dr. Wallin, shown here, was completing his studies in the 19th century, he most likely did not think that he was beginning a medical tradition. Son Corlis Wallin and grandson W. B. Wallin also pursued medical careers. Pictured above with Dr. David Jackson Wallin is his beautiful wife, Mary (Corlis) Wallin. (Courtesy of Carol Wallin Boney.)

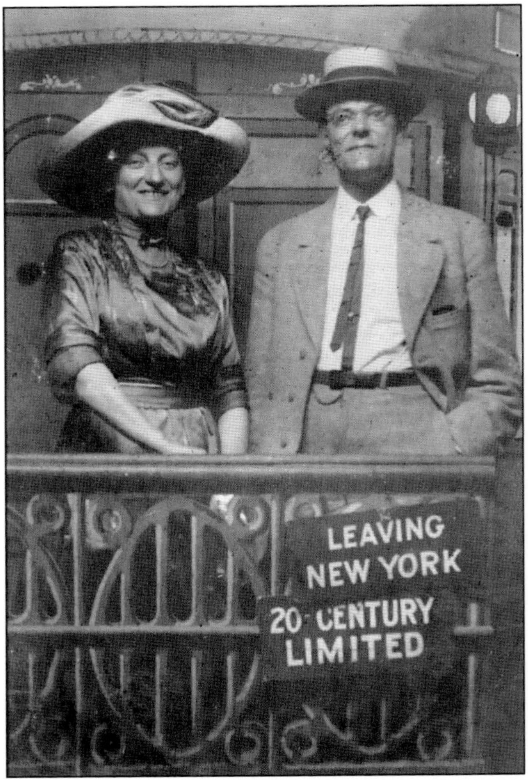

DR. NOAH COLVIN. Born in 1881, Dr. Colvin served the citizens of Bracken County through most of the 20th century. He is shown striking a handsome pose with his wife, Stella, in this early 1920s vacation picture. Whether or not the scene in the background was an actual train or just a backdrop is not known. (Courtesy of Carol Wallin Boney.)

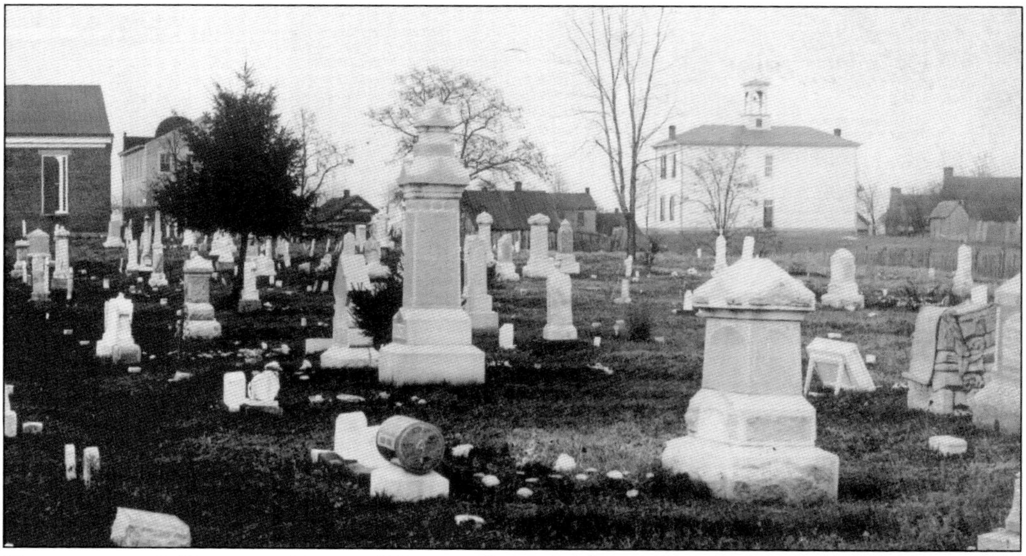

Germantown's Bustling Street. The city that straddles two county lines was quite a center of commerce and entertainment in the first decade of the 20th century. However, when the 1918 Spanish influenza pandemic hit the area, the county's doctors were overwhelmed with patients. The local doctors and nurses traveled to treat the ill or simply pronounce the patients dead. This cemetery next to the Germantown Christian Church bears the names of those lost in 1918. This particular cemetery contains the oldest tombstone in the county, dating back to the late 1700s. The photograph below provides an excellent illustration of the busy streets in Germantown during the 1910s. Perhaps a funeral was being held at the Pepper Funeral Home, as most of the carriages are tied up near his business. (Both, courtesy of John H. Henderson.)

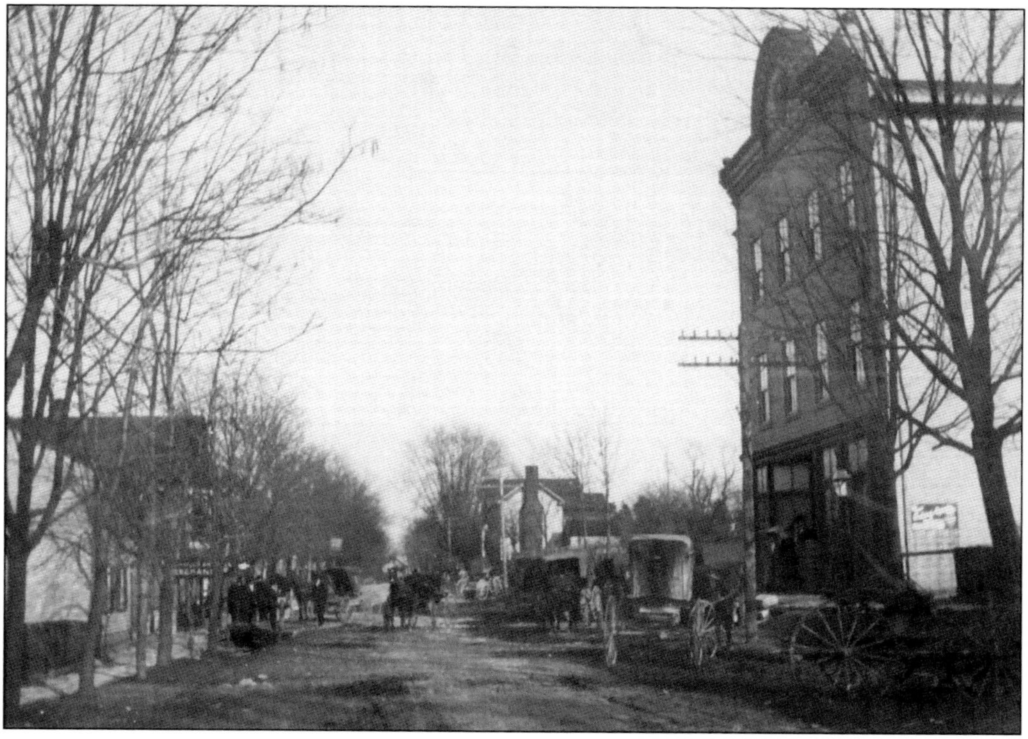

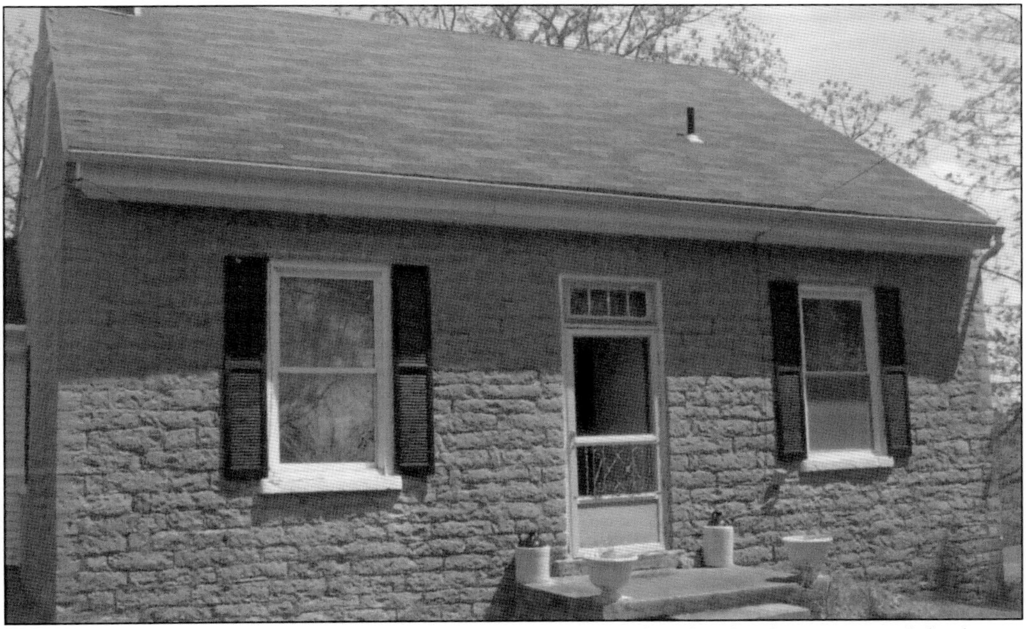

Stones Used for Construction. George Heck is believed to be the first owner of the house pictured above, which was constructed in 1821 of area stone. The stone house is one of nearly a dozen that remained in the county for the next two centuries. Charlie and Joyce Schweitzer raised their children in this home, where they are enjoying their retirement today. (Courtesy of Caroline Miller.)

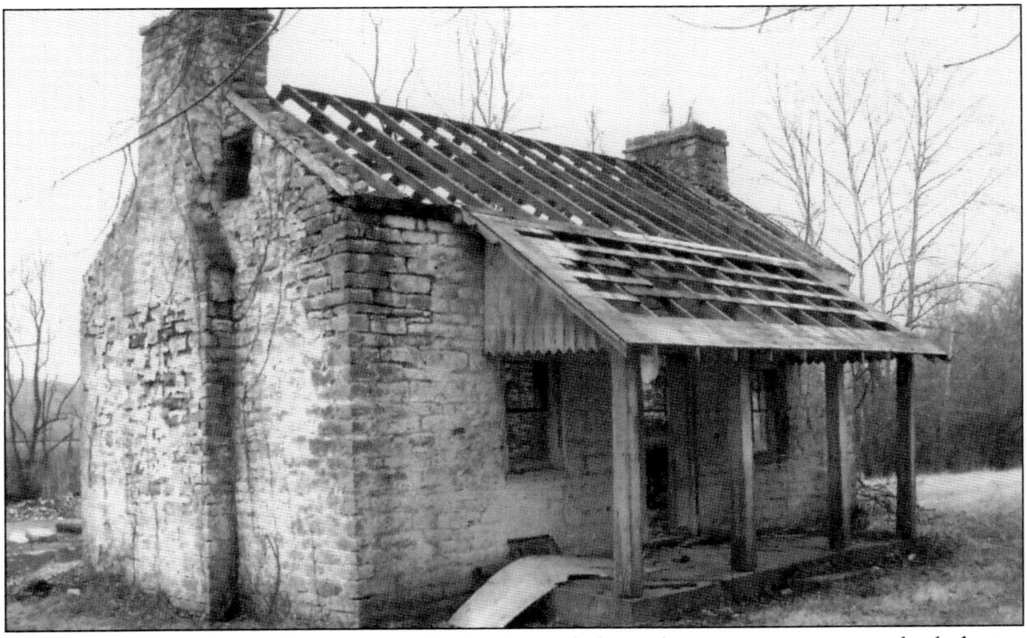

Chalfont Stone House Abandoned. Archeologists believe this stone structure was built during the first decade of the 19th century by Mordecai Chalfont. This house is located 4 miles west of Augusta on the north side of Kentucky Route 8. Bracken County Historical Society was responsible for replacing the roof and boarding the windows. There are plans underway to have the structure moved to Augusta and restored. (Courtesy of Bracken County Historical Society.)

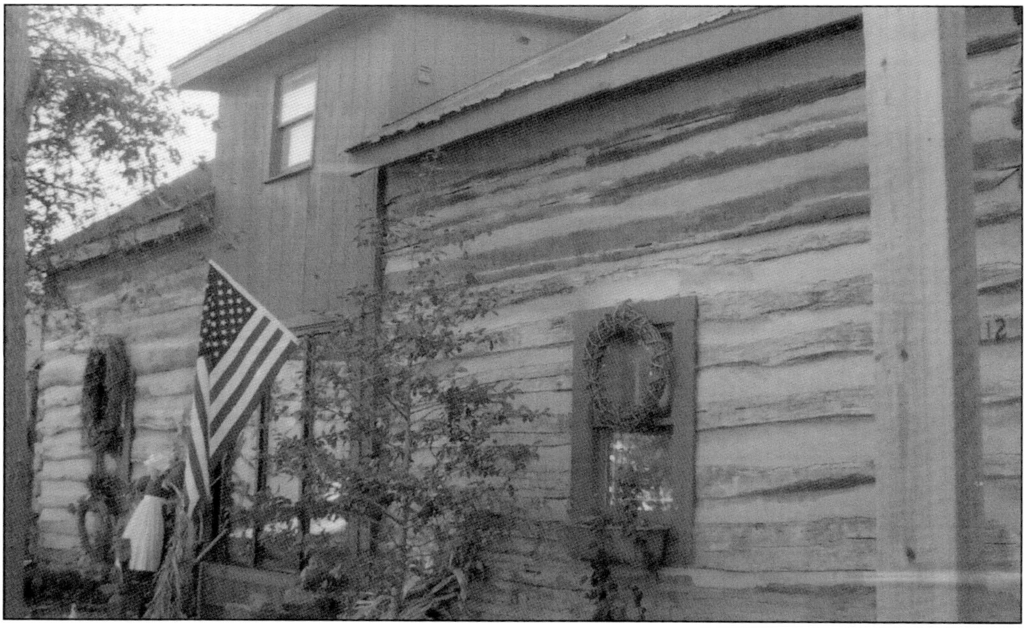

Log Cabins Converted into Businesses. Augusta is home to several log cabins, some of which are original to the city. Others, like those pictured here, have been reassembled and appear to have always been in the city. The cabin displaying the American flag is the current site of Bertha Hough's gift shop. The other log cabin is used as a guest room for Parkview Inn. These cabins are similar to those built by the first settlers when the Teegarden, Thomas, and Pribble cabins were erected at Pribble's Fort above Hillside Cemetery in Augusta. The oldest cabin, believed to have been built around 1792, belonged to John Winter near Germantown. Of course, there are many log houses in the county that have been covered by siding and are not recognizable as log structures. (Both, courtesy of Bracken County Historical Society.)

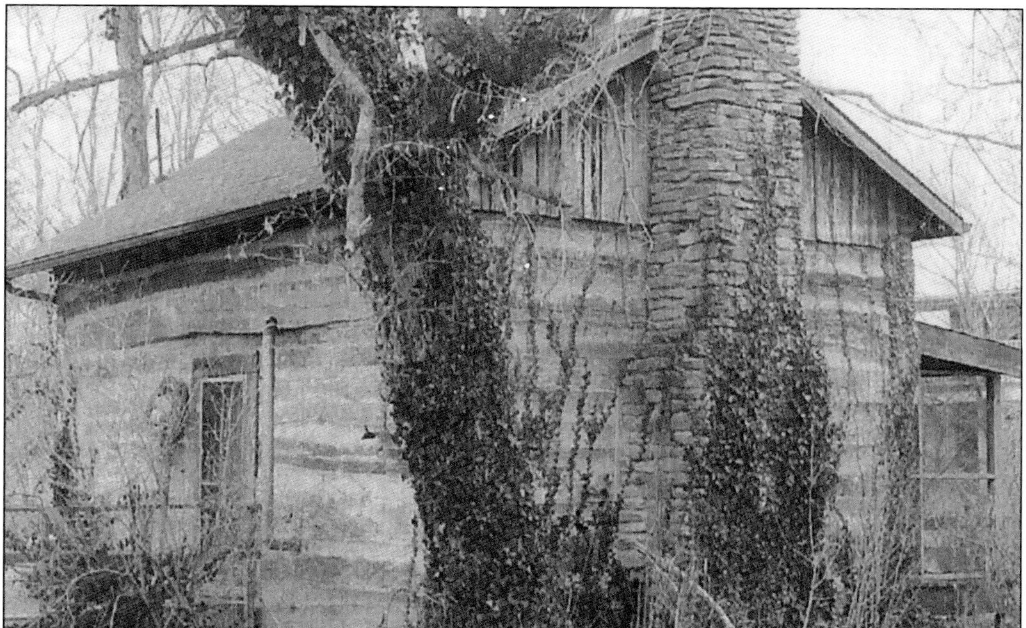

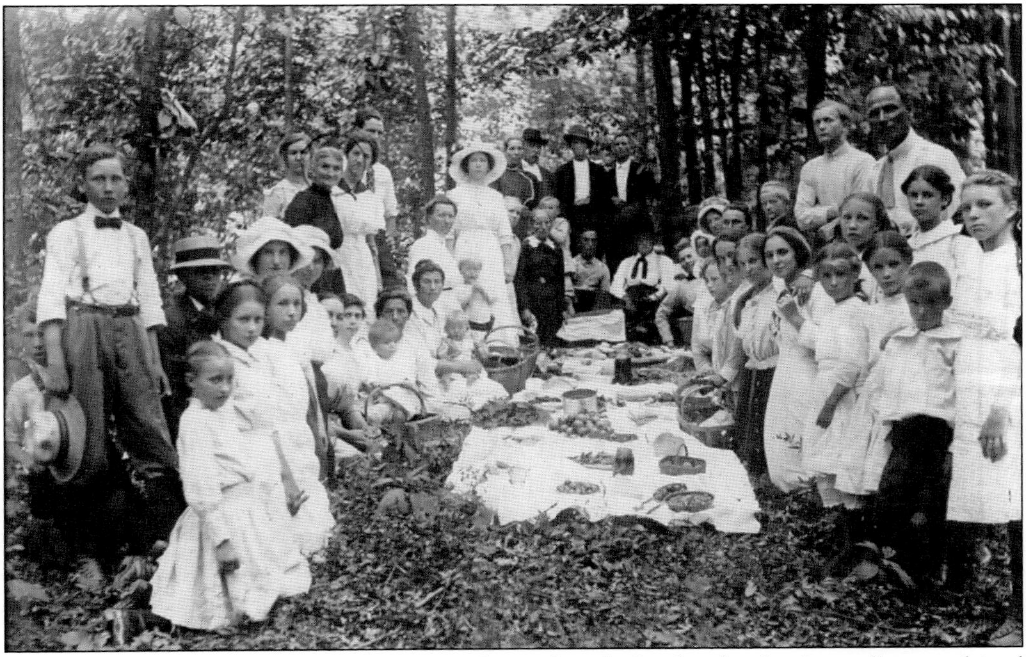

Family at Picnic. This unusual picture was located in the Locker family photo album archived at Bracken County Historical Society. This late 19th-century photograph seems to capture several families at an unknown location in Bracken County. The only person identified is Sue (Teegarden) Locker, standing on the left, dressed in black. (Courtesy of Bracken County Historical Society.)

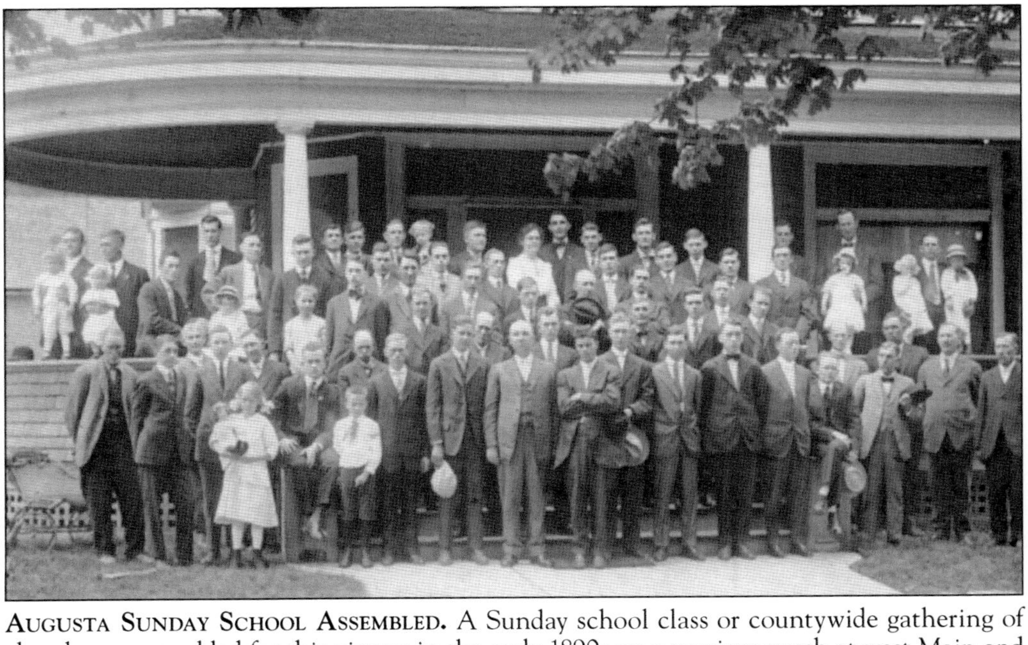

Augusta Sunday School Assembled. A Sunday school class or countywide gathering of churchmen assembled for this picture in the early 1890s on a spacious porch at west Main and Fourth Streets. What is most odd about this group is the absence of women and the presence of only a few children. Writing on the back of the postcard mentions there were 60 men in this group. (Courtesy of Bob and Betty Campbell.)

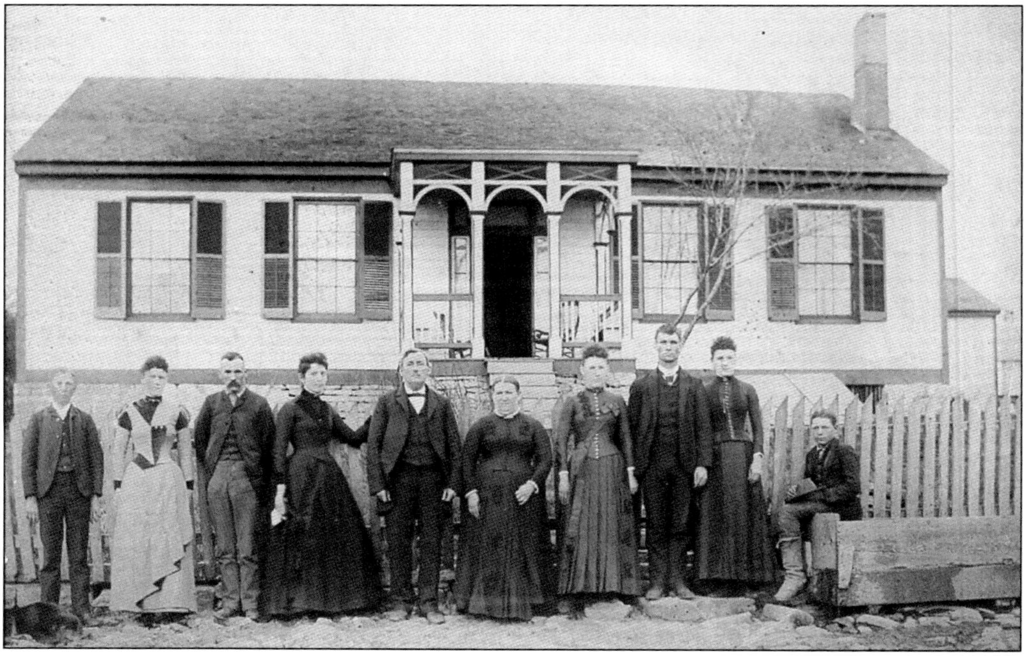

Lytle and Heaverin Families. During the late 1800s, the Lytle and Heaverin families of the Johnsville area, photographed above, were considered prominent citizens. The top picture includes, from left to right, C. F. Lytle, Carrie Lytle, Albert Lytle, Sylvia Thomas Lytle, W. T. Lytle, Martha Heaverin Lytle, Lizzie ?, Allen Pepper, Lila Lytle, and Claude Hiles. The larger group picture included several generations of the same families, perhaps posing for a large family wedding. All of the men were dressed in suits, and the children have on white. C. F. Lytle is pictured in the last row, fourth from the right, while his wife, Carrie Lytle, is shown in the last row, third from the left. (Both, courtesy of Bracken County Historical Society.)

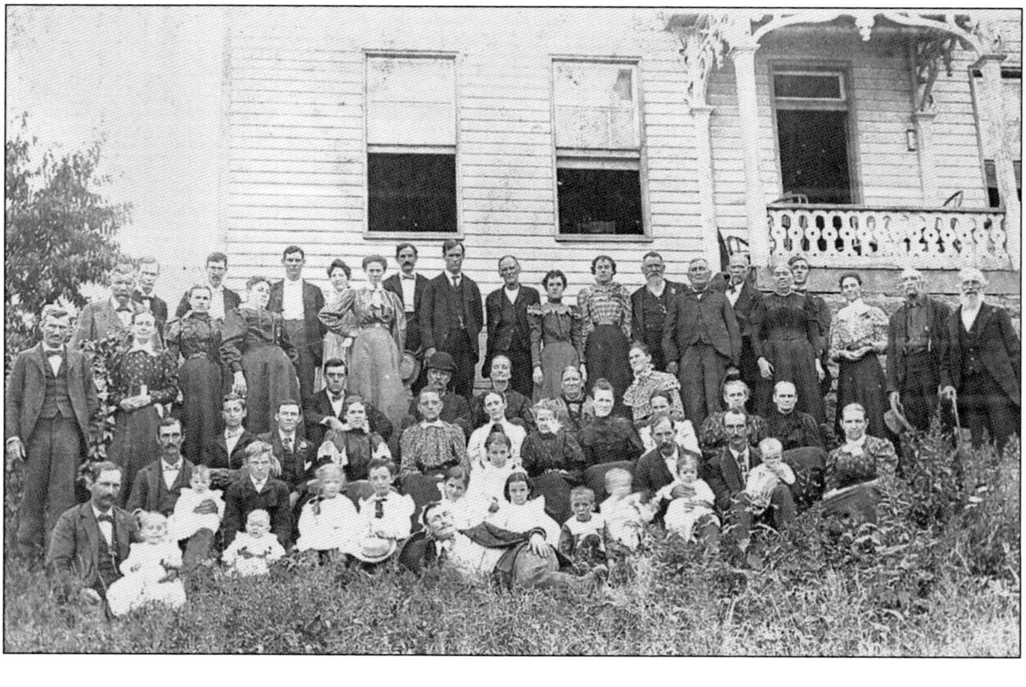

Two

Education Provided Opportunities

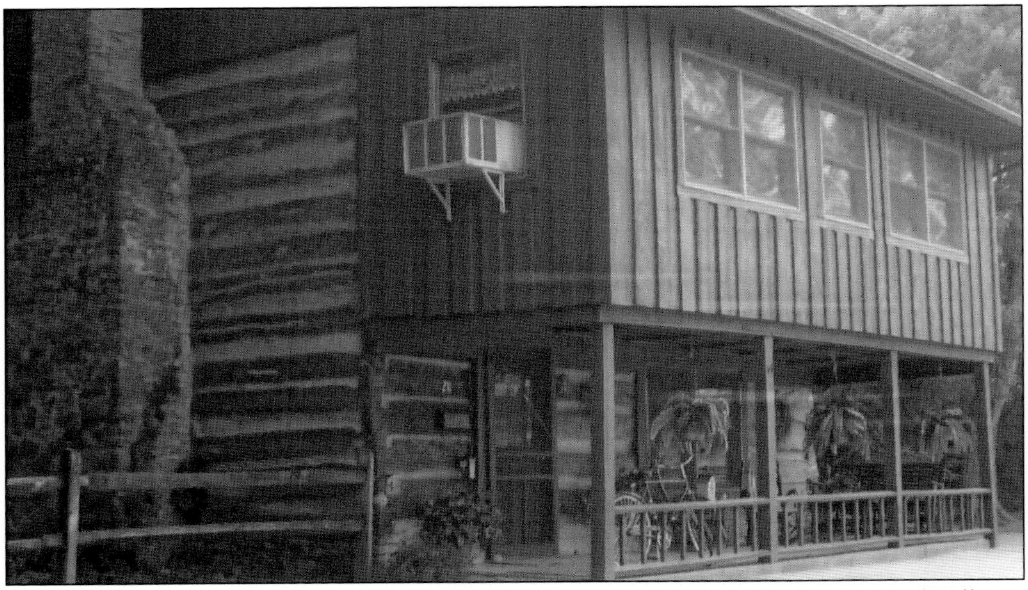

Robert Schoolfield Offered Classes. This 1797 log cabin is located on the corner of Williams Street and Riverside Drive in Augusta and was once home to Schoolfield Preparatory School. Robert Schoolfield taught the first classes recorded in the history of Bracken County. The settlers from Virginia, Maryland, and Pennsylvania were educated, and they wanted schools for their children to attend. Local students probably sat on wooden benches, used quills or slate boards, and were taught lessons by older students, as well as Schoolfield. If male students found the distance to walk was lengthy, they had the option of renting a room within a family's home in Augusta. This log structure was renovated after the television miniseries *Centennial* was filmed on this street in 1978. Universal Studios placed a facade on the front to appear as if it were a silversmith's shop in St. Louis, Missouri. Once the film crew finished their work, the front appearance was remarkable, encouraging a local resident to restore the cabin. (Courtesy of Bracken County Historical Society.)

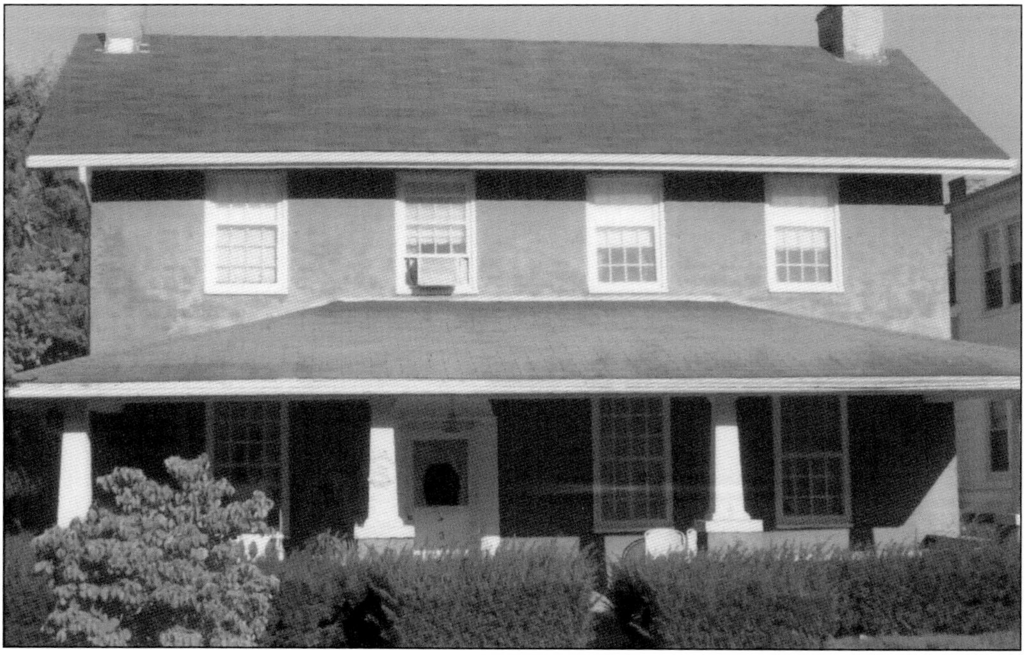

Bracken Academy. Bracken Academy was chartered by an act of the Kentucky Legislature in 1798. Academy classes were held for male students in the rear portion of this home, located at the corner of Third and Elizabeth Streets in Augusta. The Kentucky Legislature awarded the institution 6,000 acres of land in western Kentucky to be sold for income to support the school. Among the earliest trustees were John Pattie, Nathaniel Patterson, Philip Buckner, William Buckner, James Armstrong, James Wells, Robert Smith, Thomas Nelson, and Martin Marshall. The insignia pictured here is the official emblem for Augusta College, sometimes referred to as Augusta Methodist College. One graduate revered his college days so much he had the insignia, as pictured below, carved into his tombstone, located in the Augusta Hillside Cemetery. (Both, courtesy of Bracken County Historical Society.)

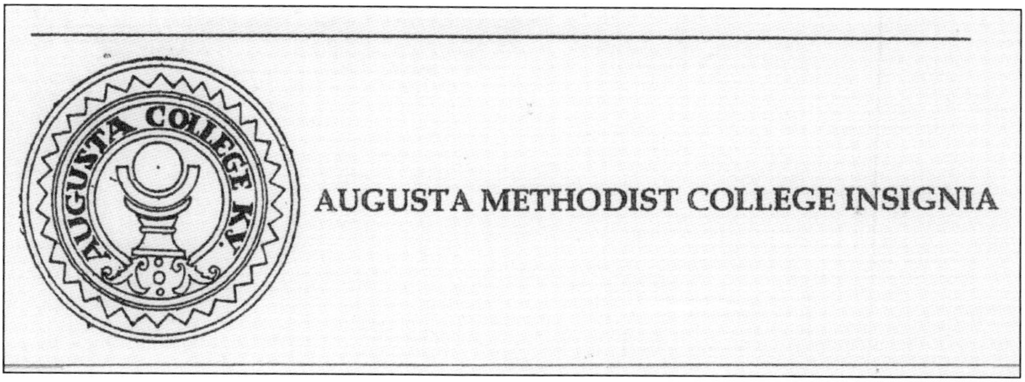

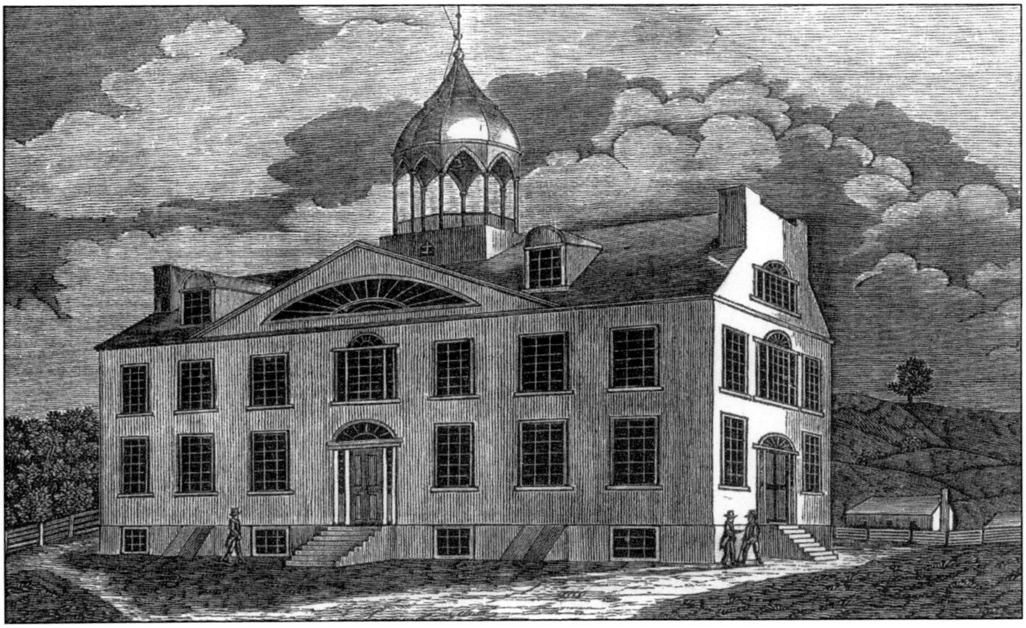

Augusta College Graduates Excelled. Augusta College was chartered in 1822 by the Ohio and Kentucky Methodist Episcopal Conferences. The college is considered the oldest Methodist-supported college in the world. The college began with six professorships and an attached primary and preparatory school. The original college was located on Augusta Independent School grounds, with boardinghouses later facing it on the east and west. Another boardinghouse was located on the Riverside Drive, later becoming the "Beannery." (Above, courtesy of William Baker; below, courtesy of Bernie Spencer.)

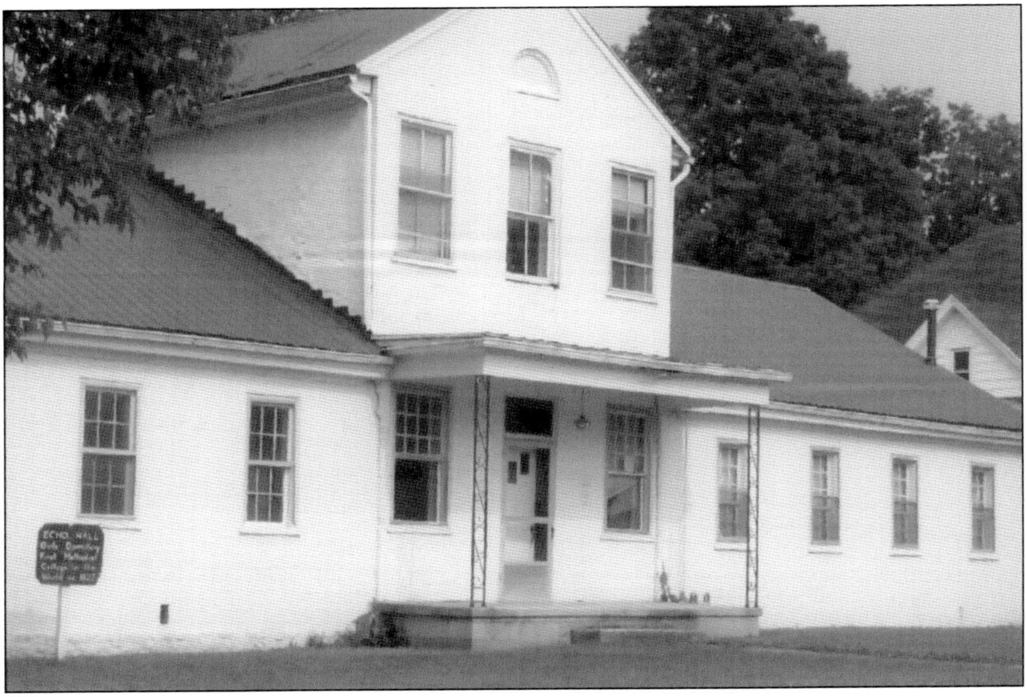

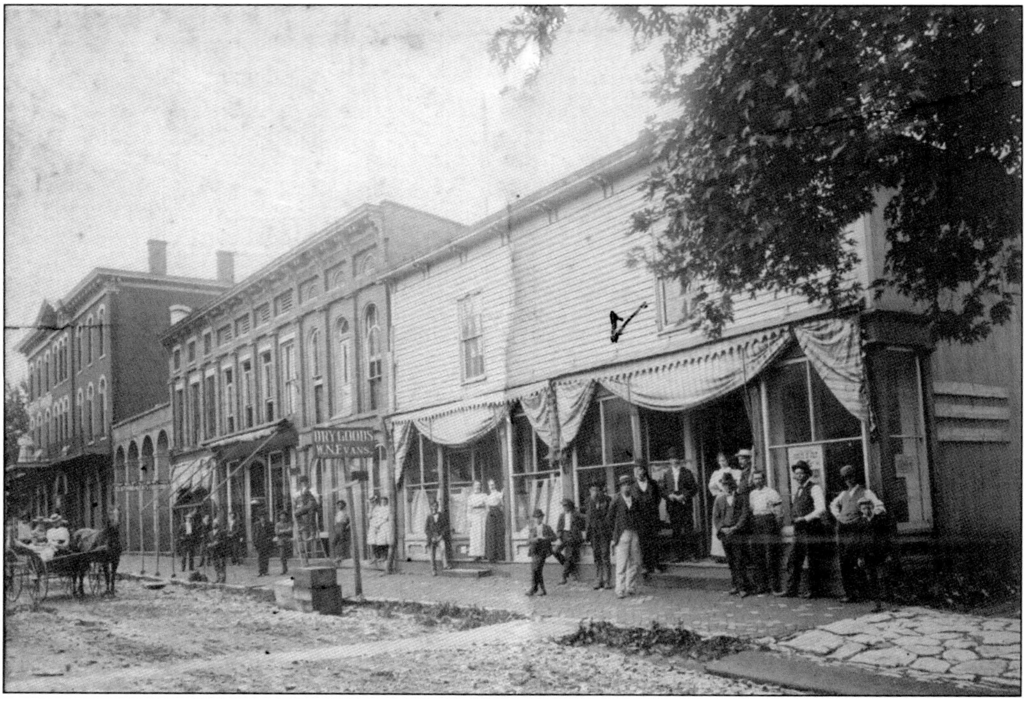

Augusta College Era. This street scene in Augusta is reminiscent of the lifestyle and activity that the college town possessed just before free and public education for whites occurred in Kentucky. Pictured below is Augusta College, which maintained classes on this site until 1887. In 1896, this structure was torn down, and later that same year, the Augusta High School was built at a cost of $20,000. In December 1899, the building was destroyed, but it was rebuilt in 1900. This building, now improved with several additions, serves as Augusta Public School. (Above, courtesy of Beverly Harber; below, courtesy of Marilyn Bryant.)

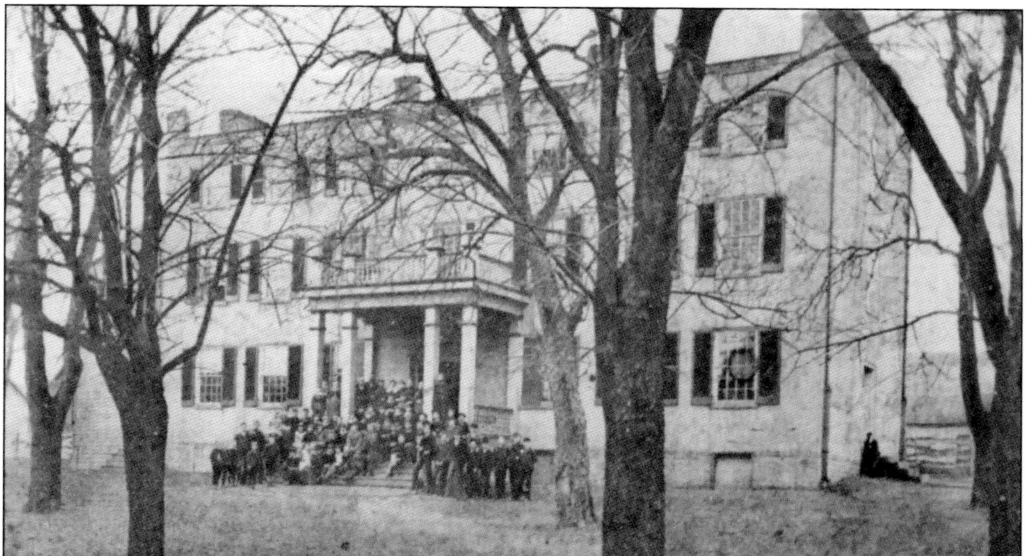

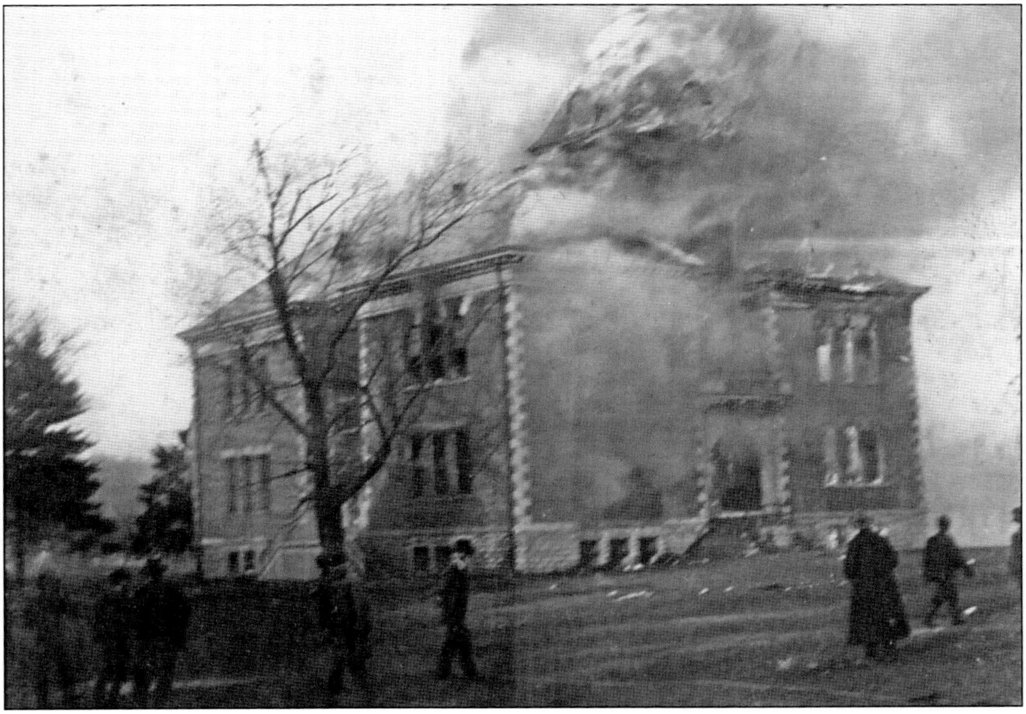

Augusta School Rises. Present and former Augusta residents have seen their schools burn at least three times. In this photograph from December 1899, smoke can be seen billowing from classrooms upstairs. A local resident noticed the smoke and notified the fire department, which kept the building from totally collapsing. The bottom picture reveals the school rebuilt at its current location soon after the gymnasium was constructed in 1926. The floods of 1913, 1937, and 1997 ruined books and equipment, but the school has been able to clean the debris and open its doors again. Recent renovations and additions have converted this proud building into a state-of-the-art education center while maintaining its historical structure. (Above, courtesy of Marilyn Bryant; below, courtesy of Beverly Harber.)

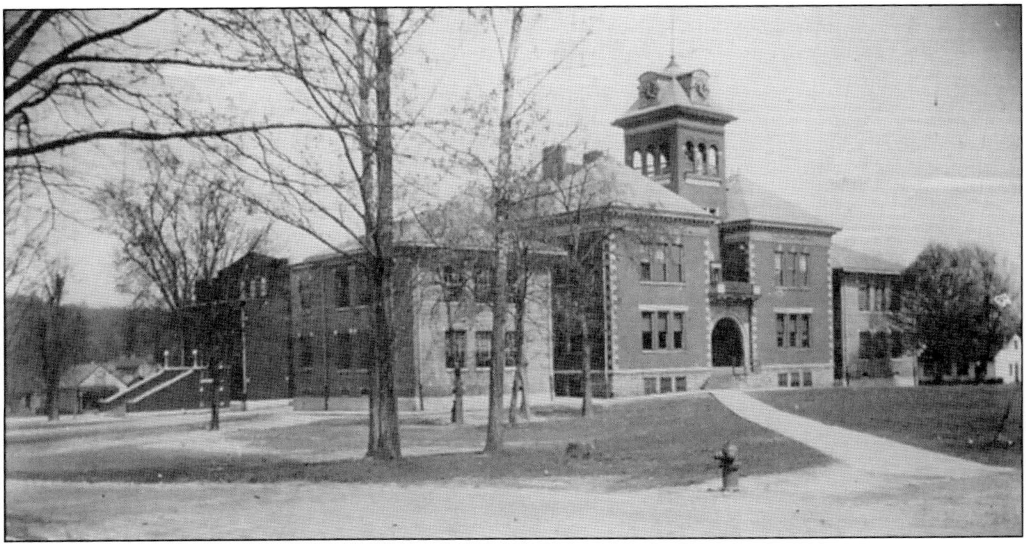

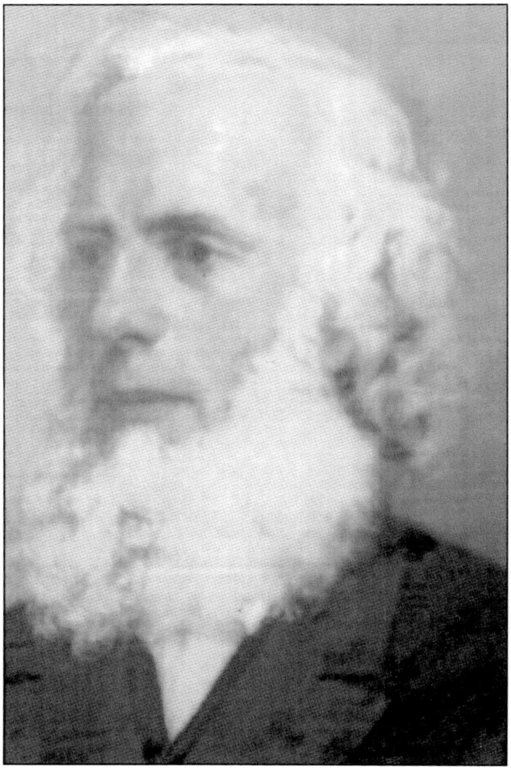

Thome and Fee, Local Abolitionists. James Armstrong Thome (1813–1873), pictured at left, was an anti-slavery society vice president who graduated from Oberlin College in the mid-1830s after leaving Cincinnati's Lane Seminary. Thome had begun his education at Augusta College before advocating anti-slavery stances and persuading his father, Arthur Thome, to emancipate his 15 slaves. Another vocal abolitionist who attended Augusta College was John Gregg Fee (1816–1901). Fee later became a missionary for the American Missionary Association, based in New York. Fee is often called the most noted abolitionist in Kentucky and is credited with the 1855 founding Berea College, the first institution in Kentucky to educate blacks and whites and males and females in the same classroom. (Left, courtesy of Oberlin College; below, courtesy of Berea College.)

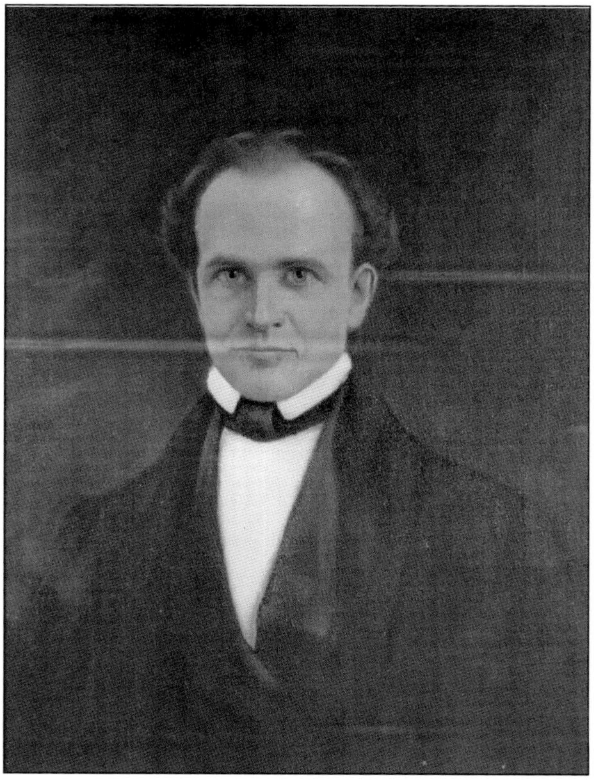

ABOLITIONISTS TREATED BY LOCAL DOCTORS. Dr. John Coburn, pictured below in a tintype, was a medical doctor in Germantown during the mid-19th century. Coburn was notified of a ruckus in Germantown, where Dr. Jonathan Bradford of Augusta and a group of men were attempting to tar and feather Rev. J. B. Mallett, an abolitionist. Coburn rescued the startled and weakened Mallett and persuaded Bradford to take his men and return to Augusta. Pictured at right are, from left to right, J. B. Mallett; John Fee; and John Gregg Hanson, Fee's cousin and architect of Berea College. These abolitionists bore the brunt of many beatings, arson, and threats. They and their families, called the "Berean Exiles," had to flee Kentucky. (Right, courtesy of Berea College; below, courtesy of John Patterson.)

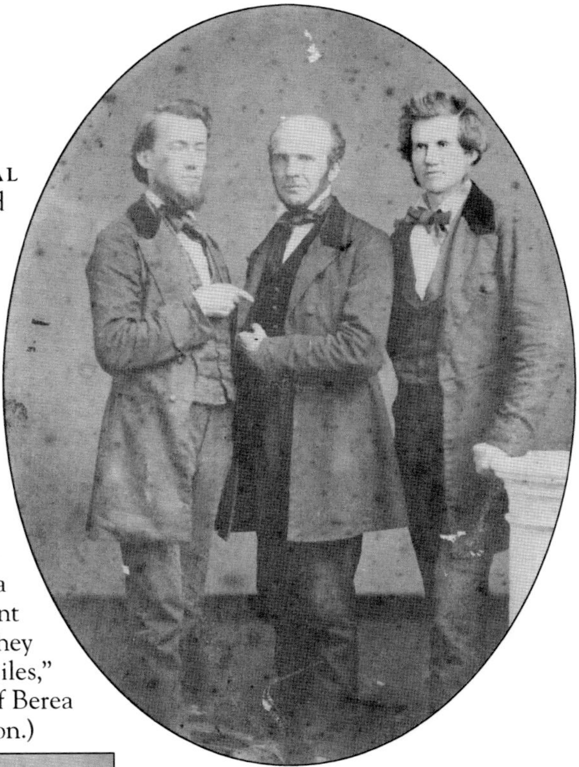

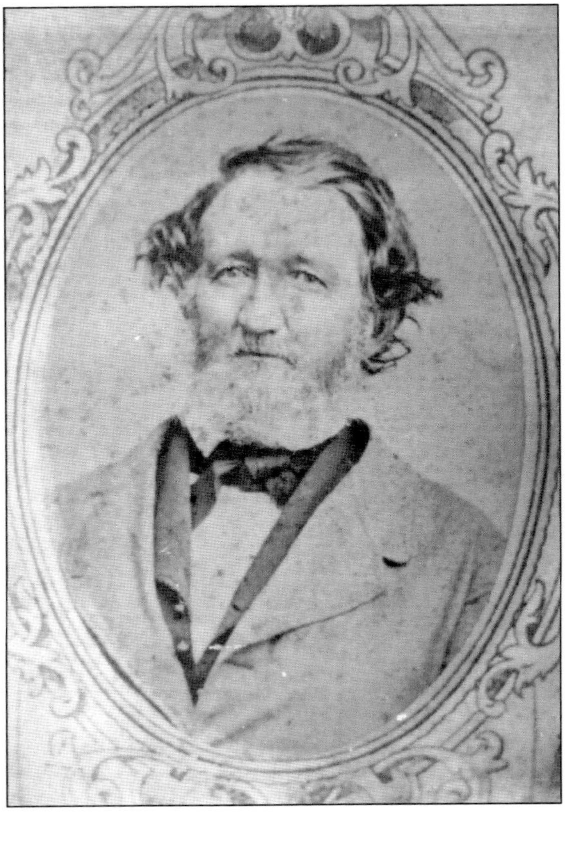

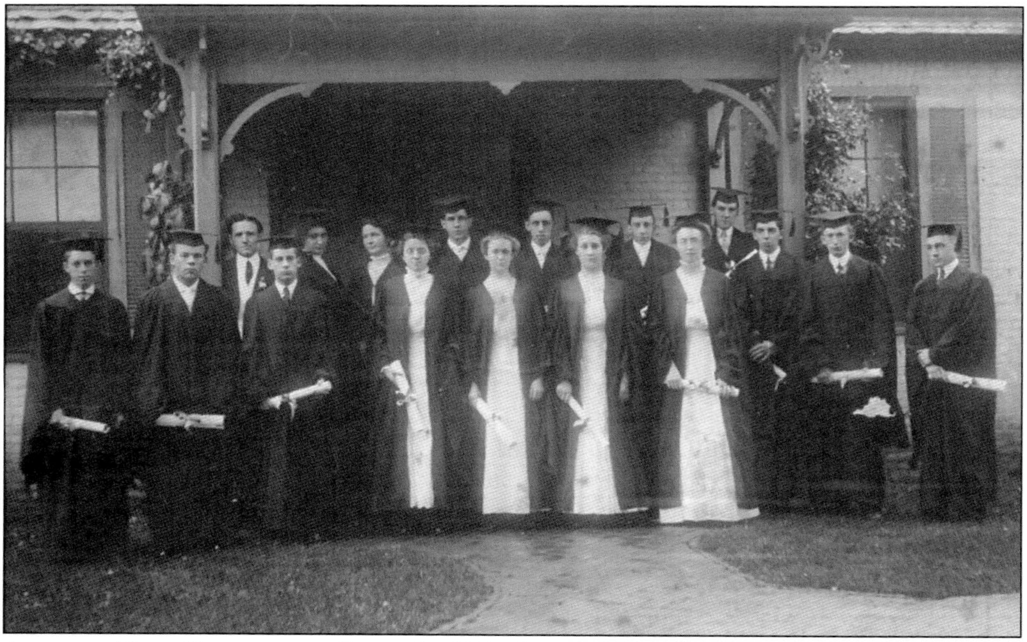

AUGUSTA HIGH GRADUATING CLASS. In 1910, Augusta School graduated Kentucky's foremost newspaper editor, James Norris. In the photograph are, from left to right, (front row) Baxter Harrison, Edward Bush, Claude Taylor, Louise Dreesback, Hattie B. Dunbar, Ada Curtis, Mary Laughlin, John Hancock, Carley Foley, and James Norris; (back row) Professor Williams, Lena Meyer, Mayme Yates, Dimmitt Ginn, Powers Robertson, J. Coughlin, and Wilber Steen. (Courtesy of Bracken County Historical Society.)

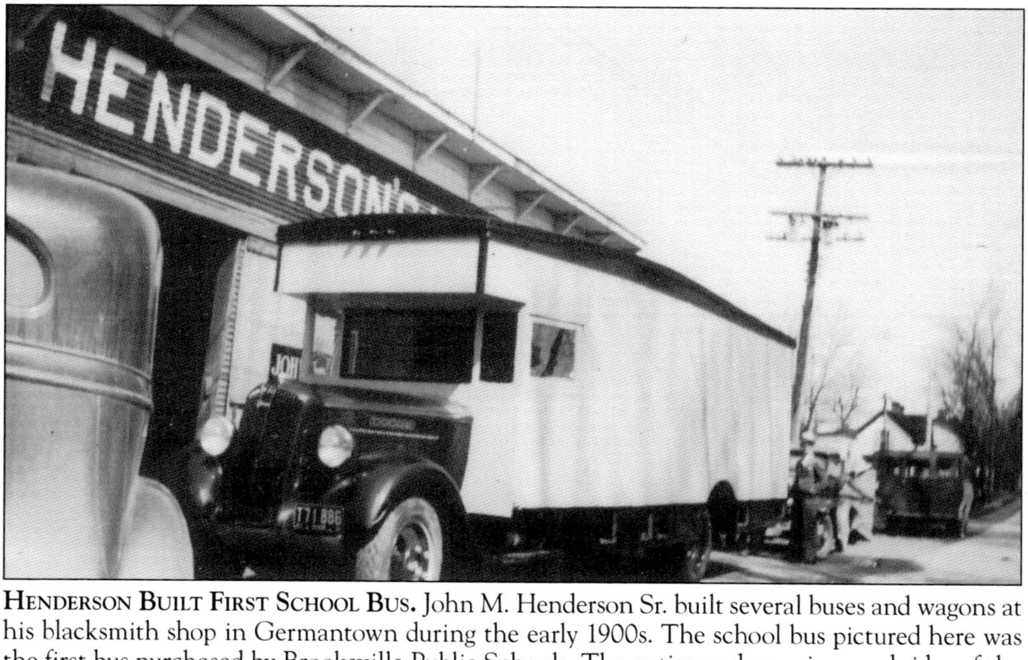

HENDERSON BUILT FIRST SCHOOL BUS. John M. Henderson Sr. built several buses and wagons at his blacksmith shop in Germantown during the early 1900s. The school bus pictured here was the first bus purchased by Brooksville Public Schools. The entire undercarriage and sides of the bus were manufactured in his shop. Only the tires and engine were purchased. (Courtesy of John H. Henderson.)

PUBLIC SCHOOLS COURSE OF STUDY. These booklets contain a listing of courses of study for two public schools in Bracken County. The Brooksville catalogue listed the requirements of primary, intermediate, grammar, and high school departments. The catalogue, adopted in 1910, was sponsored by these advertisers: Corlis Dry-Goods, Calvin's Drug Store, First National Bank, Asbury and Gray's, Coons and Gibson Grocery, John Corlis Funerals, B. F. Metcalfe Livery, Downing and Hannon Livery, Bertrams Drug Company, Staton Grocery, Farmers Equity Bank, and W. T. Breeze Hardware. The 1916–1917 Augusta Public Schools Bulletin did not list sponsors but included this list of teachers: Nancy Hancock, first and second grades; Julia Moneyhon, third grade; Loree Hagan, fourth grade; Jennie Buchanan, fifth grade; Mary Coughlin; sixth, seventh, and eighth grades; Nell Jordan, high school; and Elizabeth Ginn, A. J. Jolly, and James Norris, high school. (Both, courtesy of Bracken County Historical Society.)

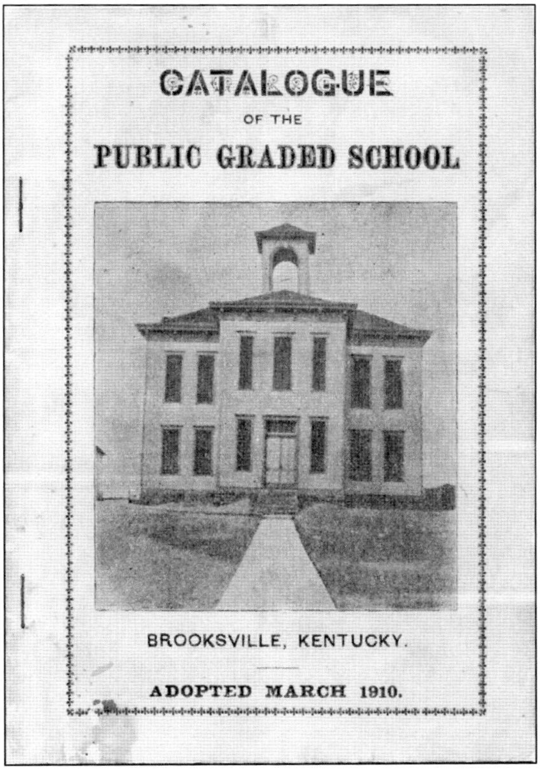

CATALOGUE
OF THE
PUBLIC GRADED SCHOOL

BROOKSVILLE, KENTUCKY.

ADOPTED MARCH 1910.

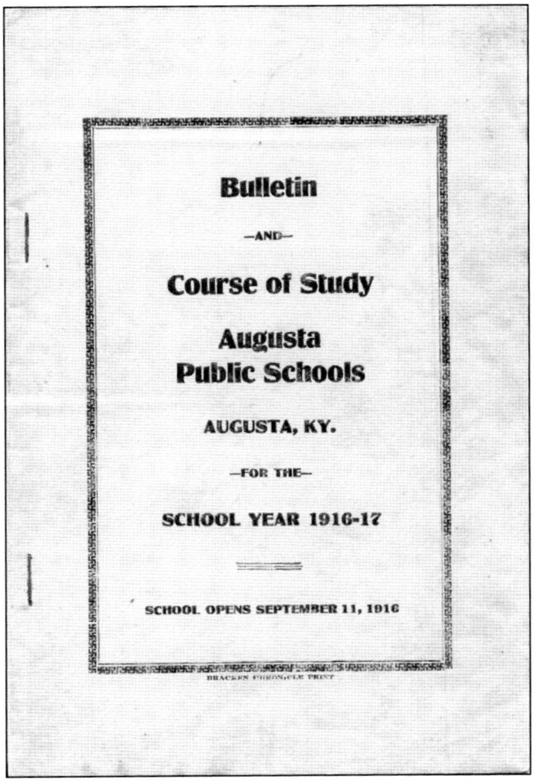

Bulletin
—AND—
Course of Study
Augusta
Public Schools
AUGUSTA, KY.
—FOR THE—
SCHOOL YEAR 1916-17

SCHOOL OPENS SEPTEMBER 11, 1916

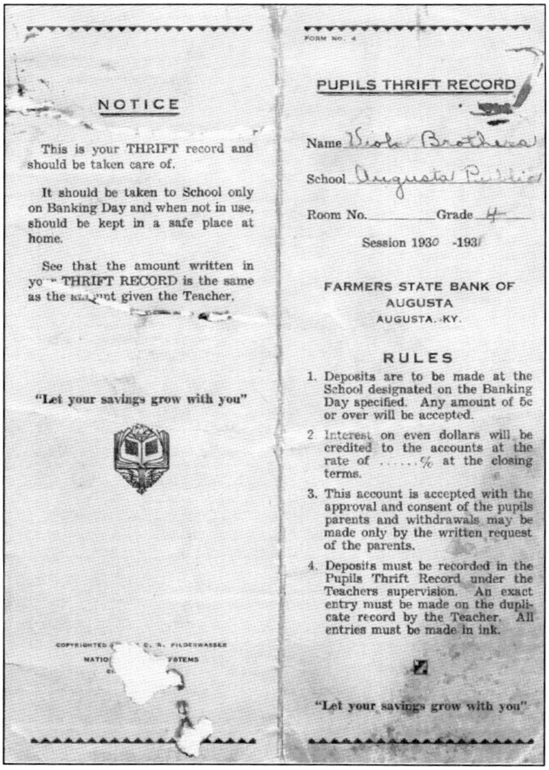

NOTICE

This is your THRIFT record and should be taken care of.

It should be taken to School only on Banking Day and when not in use, should be kept in a safe place at home.

See that the amount written in yo[illegible] THRIFT RECORD is the same as the [illegible] given the Teacher.

"Let your savings grow with you"

COPYRIGHTED [illegible] C. R. PILDERWASSER
NATIO[illegible] [illegible]YSTEMS

FORM NO. 4

PUPILS THRIFT RECORD

Name Viola Brothers

School Augusta Public

Room No. ______ Grade 4

Session 1930 -1931

FARMERS STATE BANK OF AUGUSTA
AUGUSTA, KY.

RULES

1. Deposits are to be made at the School designated on the Banking Day specified. Any amount of 5c or over will be accepted.
2. Interest on even dollars will be credited to the accounts at the rate of ......% at the closing terms.
3. This account is accepted with the approval and consent of the pupils parents and withdrawals may be made only by the written request of the parents.
4. Deposits must be recorded in the Pupils Thrift Record under the Teachers supervision. An exact entry must be made on the duplicate record by the Teacher. All entries must be made in ink.

"Let your savings grow with you"

Augusta School Thrift Card. In 1930, when Viola Brothers was in the fourth grade, she was encouraged to deposit a quarter into her "Thrift Account" at Farmers State Bank of Augusta. The small card allowed her to account for her savings throughout the school year. Deposits were made at school on the day set aside for banking, under the supervision of the teacher. Each student could deposit 5¢ or more, with interest to be credited at the closing of the term. Parents were to give permission for their children to take part in this activity and were encouraged to store the cards in a safe place. Viola had deposited $11.60 by the end of the term in the Farmers State Bank of Augusta. (Both, courtesy of Bracken County Historical Society.)

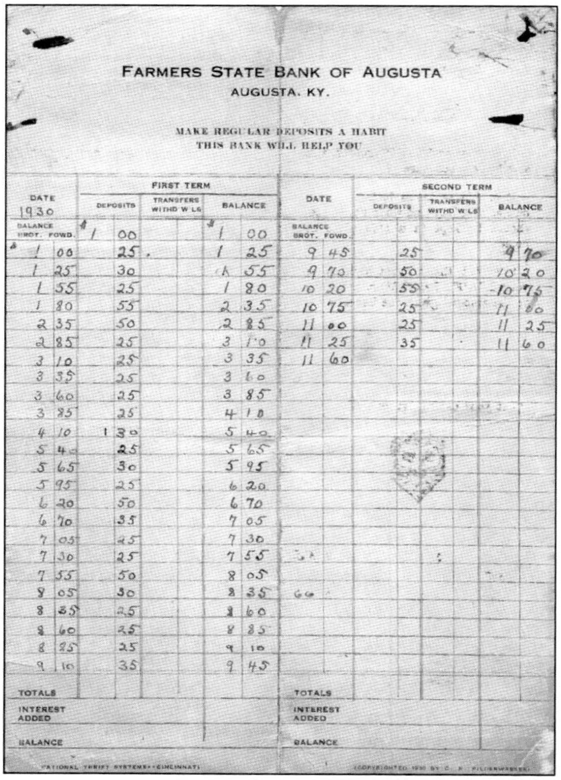

FARMERS STATE BANK OF AUGUSTA
AUGUSTA, KY.

MAKE REGULAR DEPOSITS A HABIT
THIS BANK WILL HELP YOU

DATE 1930	FIRST TERM Deposits	Transfers Withd'w'ls	Balance	DATE	SECOND TERM Deposits	Transfers Withd'w'ls	Balance
Balance Brot. Fowd.	$1 00		$1 00	Balance Brot. Fowd.			
$1 00	25		1 25	9 45	25		9 70
1 25	30		1 55	9 70	50		10 20
1 55	25		1 80	10 20	55		10 75
1 80	55		2 35	10 75	25		11 00
2 35	50		2 85	11 00	25		11 25
2 85	25		3 10	11 25	35		11 60
3 10	25		3 35	11 60			
3 35	25		3 60				
3 60	25		3 85				
3 85	25		4 10				
4 10	1 30		5 40				
5 40	25		5 65				
5 65	30		5 95				
5 95	25		6 20				
6 20	50		6 70				
6 70	35		7 05				
7 05	25		7 30				
7 30	25		7 55				
7 55	50		8 05				
8 05	30		8 35				
8 35	25		8 60				
8 60	25		8 85				
8 85	25		9 10				
9 10	35		9 45				
TOTALS				TOTALS			
INTEREST ADDED				INTEREST ADDED			
BALANCE				BALANCE			

NATIONAL THRIFT SYSTEMS—CINCINNATI (COPYRIGHTED 1930 BY C. R. PILDERWASSER)

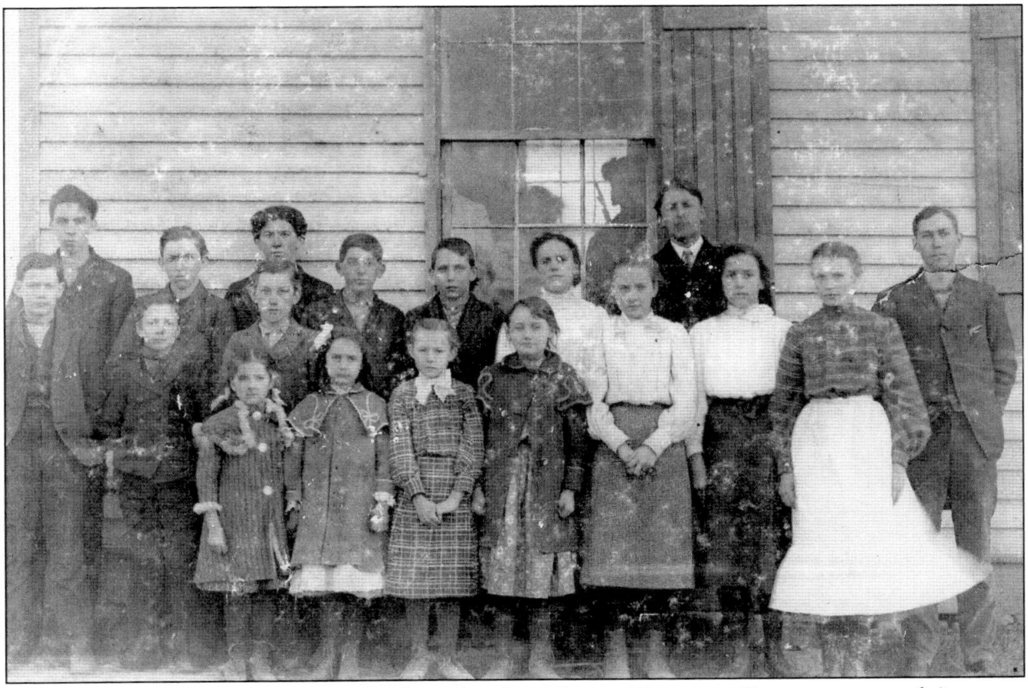

LOCUST GROVE SCHOOL STUDENTS. This school was located between Germantown and Augusta. This rare photograph is a glimpse of the local children who are now great-grandparents to hundreds of Bracken County residents. (Courtesy of Bracken County Historical Society.)

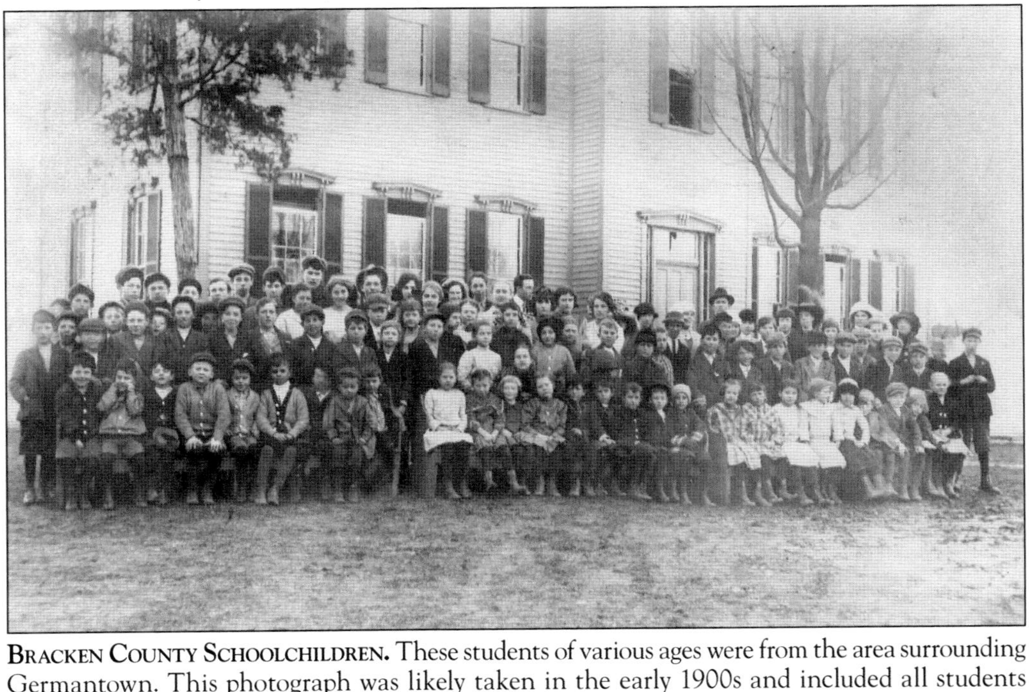

BRACKEN COUNTY SCHOOLCHILDREN. These students of various ages were from the area surrounding Germantown. This photograph was likely taken in the early 1900s and included all students attending Germantown Public School. At one time in Bracken County, there were 52 schools where classes were conducted in log structures heated by a pot bellied stove with water carried in buckets for the children. (Courtesy of John H. Henderson.)

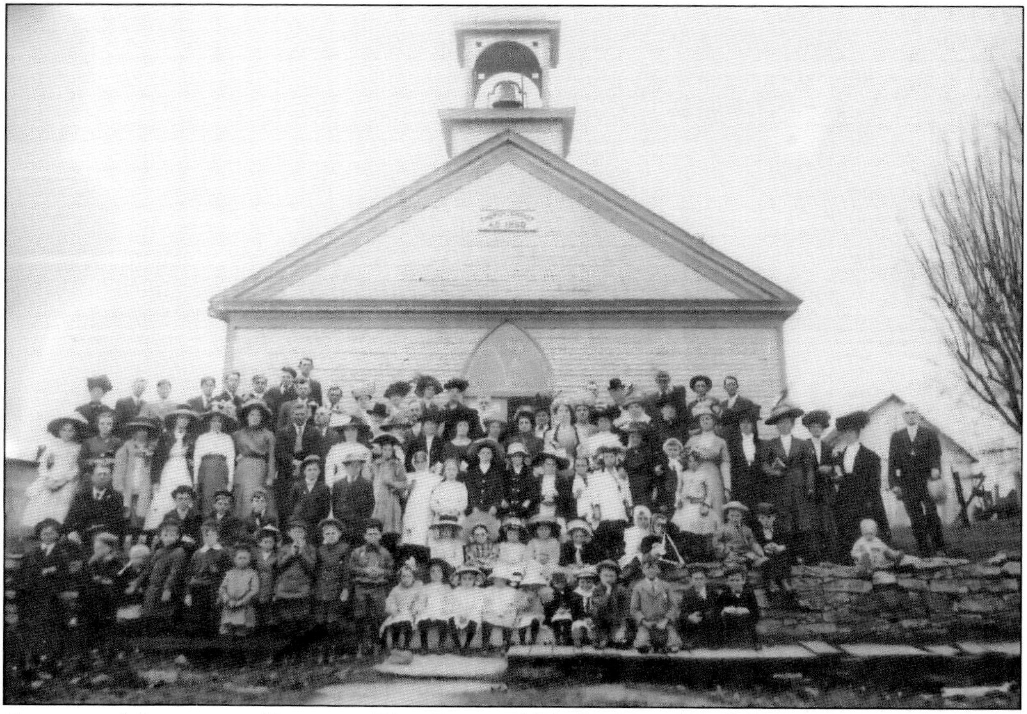

CONCORD METHODIST CHURCH. The Concord Methodist Church is pictured before it was renovated and recently expanded. The women and girls are dressed in white, and even the older boys appear to have on white shirts. Perhaps this day in the early 1900s was set aside as a spring celebration in dedication of the church. (Courtesy of Thom Lawson.)

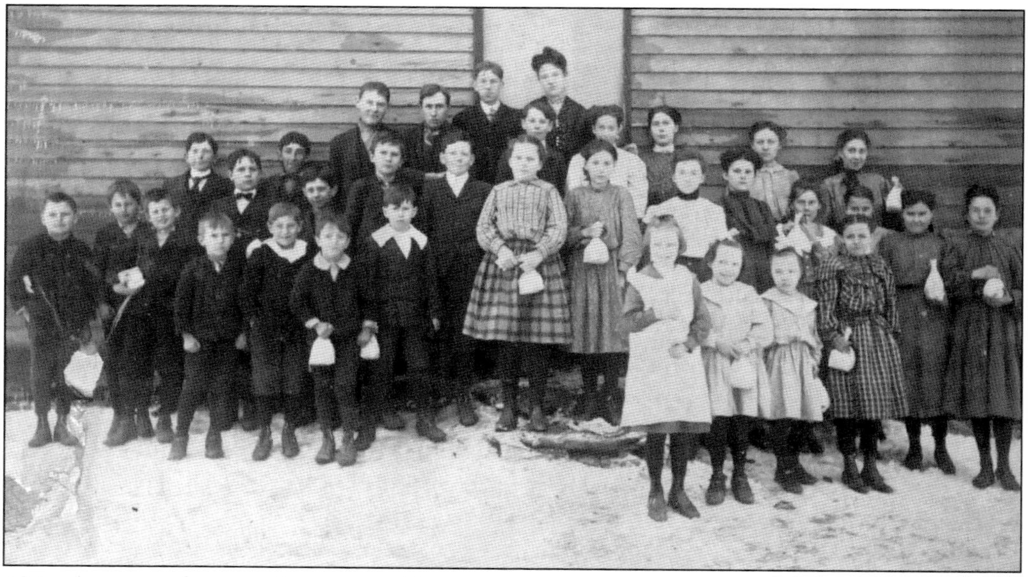

1902 AUGUSTA SCHOOL STUDENTS. The image of these young schoolchildren standing in the deep snow without coats is believed to have been taken by P. B. Power in 1902. The young teacher standing tallest in front of the window was Helen Carter Brooks. If the dating is accurate, this might be the oldest remaining photograph of a group of students in Bracken County. (Courtesy of Carol Boney.)

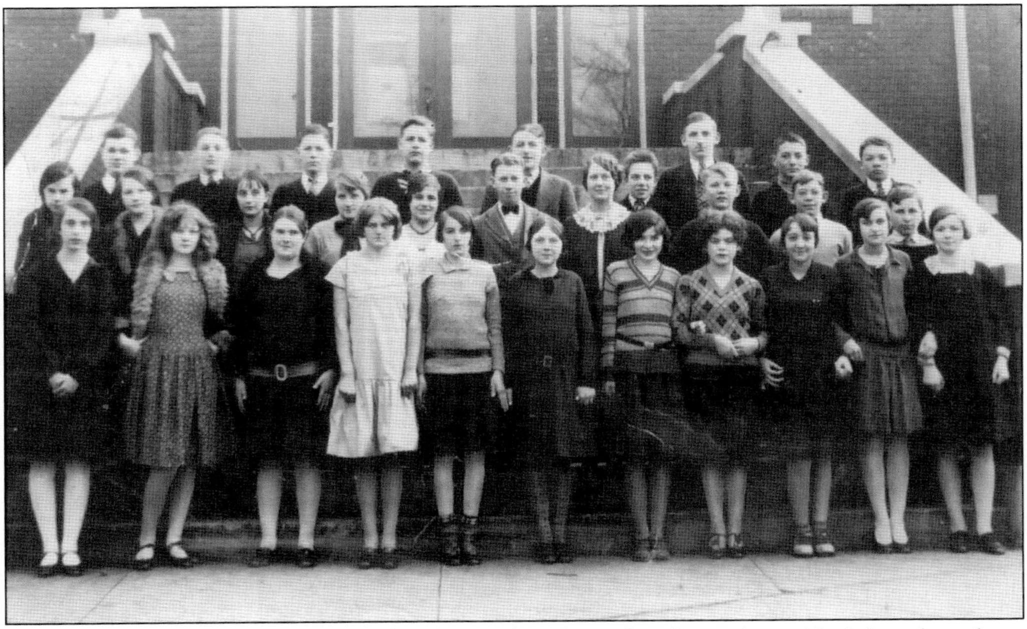

Flapper-Era Dresses Evident. The shorter hemlines far above the calf of their legs dates this picture of Augusta High School students to 1928. In that year, women were feeling more independent and demonstrated it with their dresses, skirts, and cropped or bobbed hairstyles. (Courtesy of Carol Wallin Boney.)

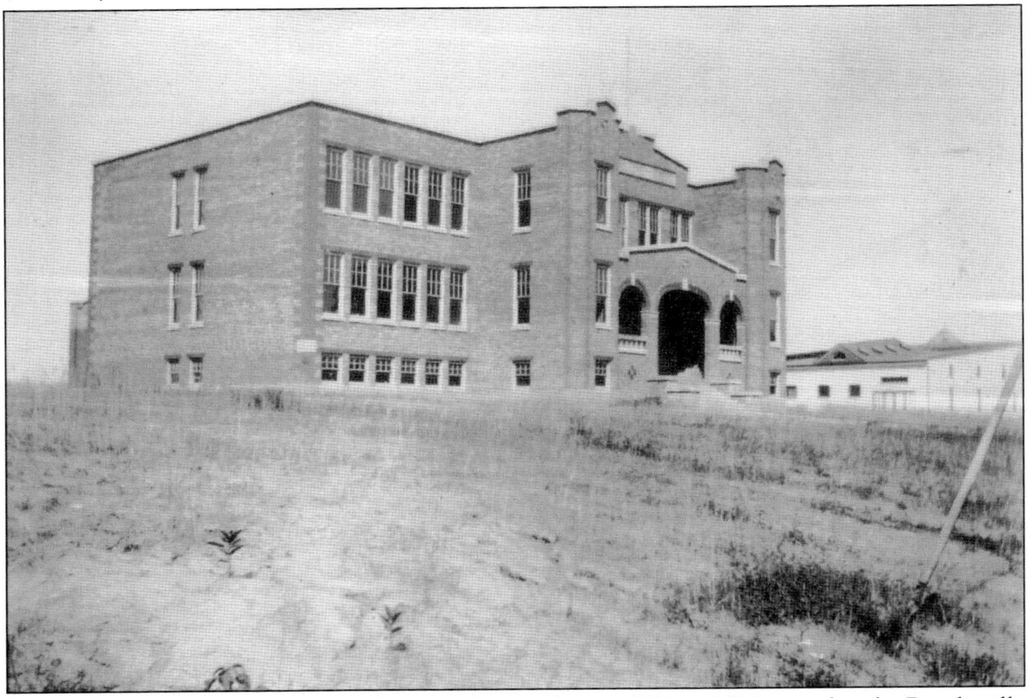

Brooksville High School. This photograph was taken in 1923 or 1924, just after the Brooksville Public School was constructed. Certainly the administrators believed the structure would last a century, but in the late 1970s, the school was demolished when larger and more modern elementary and middle schools were built. (Courtesy of John H. Henderson.)

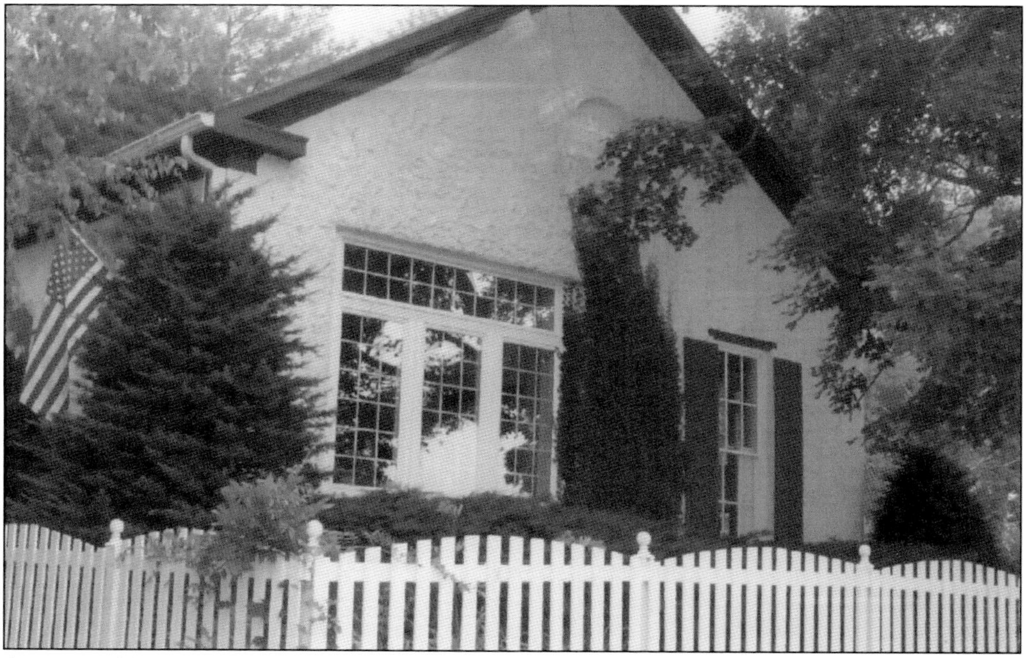

Augusta Methodist Church. This small home on Riverside Drive was once a Methodist church, built in 1819 on land donated by Augusta resident James Armstrong. Several of the college presidents were ordained ministers and invited well-known orators to deliver addresses to the students in this church. (Courtesy of Bracken County Historical Society.)

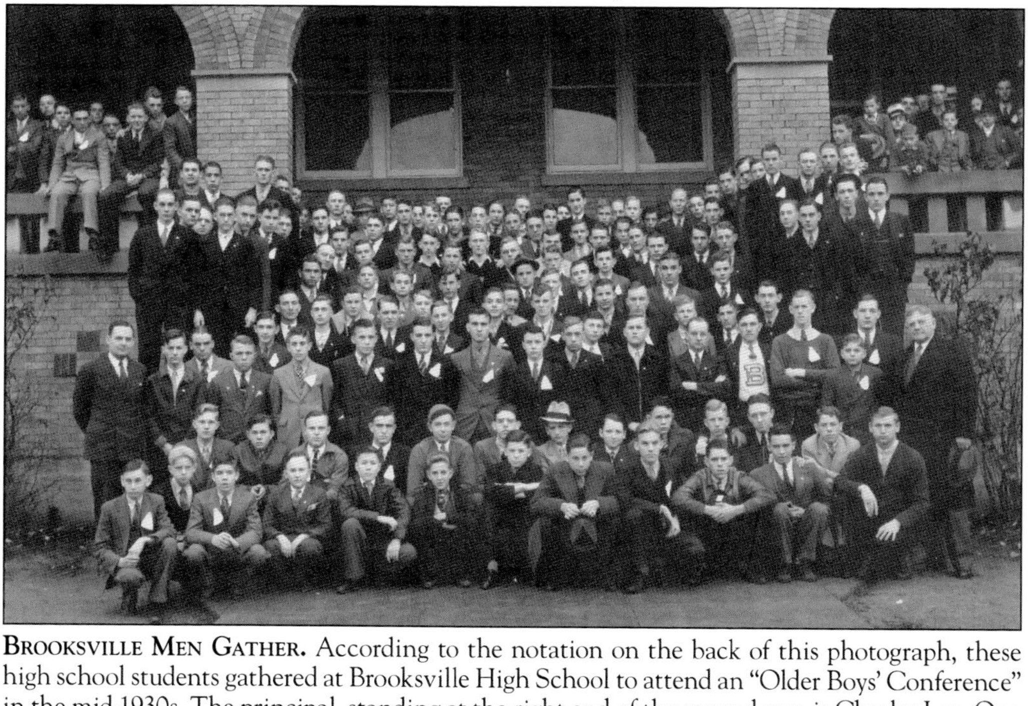

Brooksville Men Gather. According to the notation on the back of this photograph, these high school students gathered at Brooksville High School to attend an "Older Boys' Conference" in the mid-1930s. The principal, standing at the right end of the second row, is Charles Lea. One student was evidently proud of his school, as he pulled back his coat to reveal the "B" on his sweater. (Courtesy of Carol Wallin Boney.)

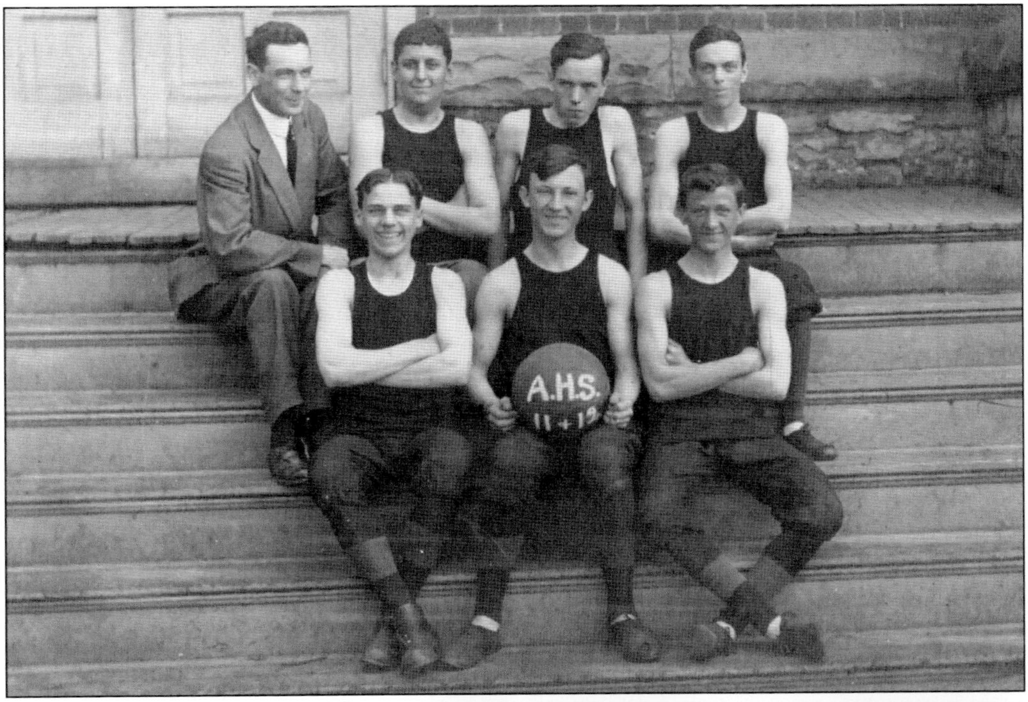

AUGUSTA HIGH BASKETBALL. The 1911–1912 team members pictured above are, from left to right, (first row) Stanley Jackson, Chester Bryant, and Dexter Thornsbury; (second row) coach Leo O'Neill, Kelly Brown, Jack Hunter, and Walter Colvin. The 1916 team was composed of, from left to right, (first row) mascot Raymond Boothe; (second row) William Asbury, John I. Ward, Bert Cline; (third row) John Brooker, William Jolly; (fourth row) coach J. T. Norris, Leo Federer, and A. J. Jolly. Boothe's senior maxim included these words: "It is a fact that I am small in stature, but a fellow must be a whopper if he is any bigger than I feel when standing on the corner shaking myself, with cap on the side of head, cigarette in my mouth, dealing out words of wisdom to the other boys. At one time I had a high opinion of my prowess among the fair sex." (Both, courtesy of William Baker.)

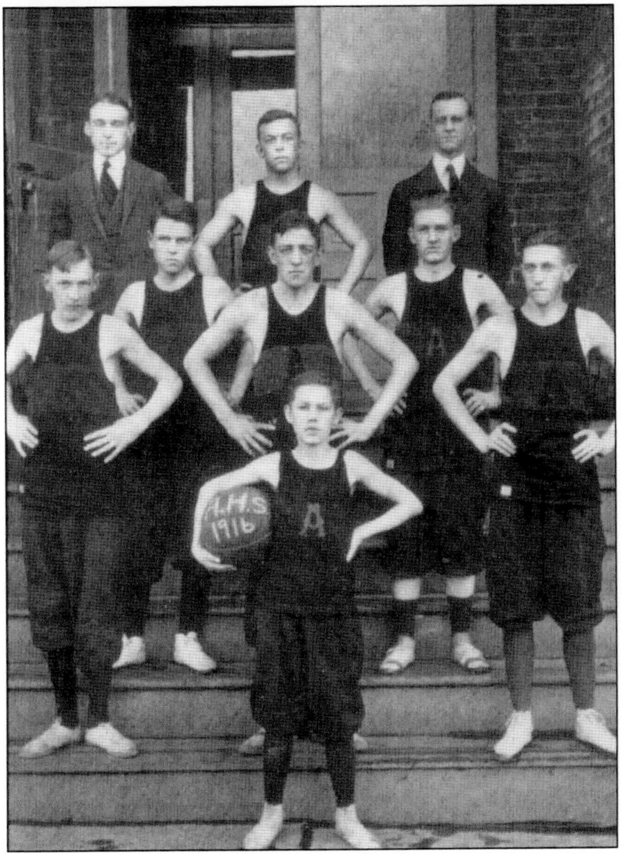

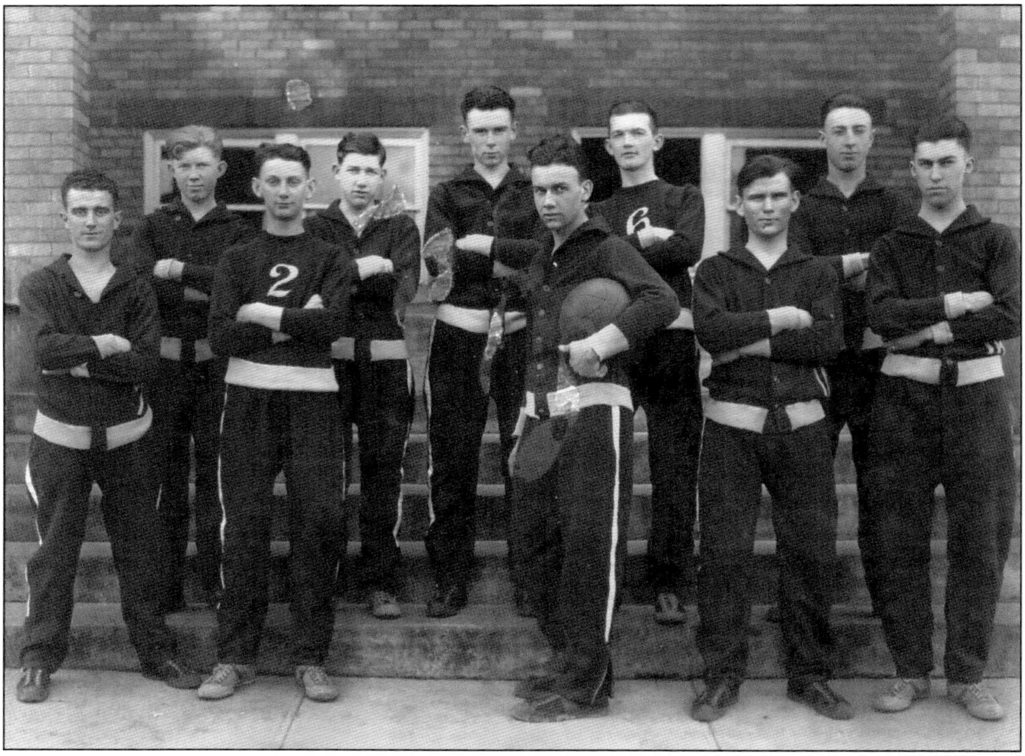

Brooksville Teams. The 1939 Kentucky State Basketball Tournament was won by Brooksville, a team from a small high school in northern Kentucky. Team members shown below are, from left to right, Vernon Kalb, Albert Power, Warren Cooper, Marvin Cooper, and John Staton. Several from this team served their nation in World War II, only a few years after claiming the top award in this sport. This outstanding feat by a local team, that once had an outdoor playing arena and a Polar Bear as its mascot, has never been repeated. (Both, courtesy of Suzanne Cooper Weaver.)

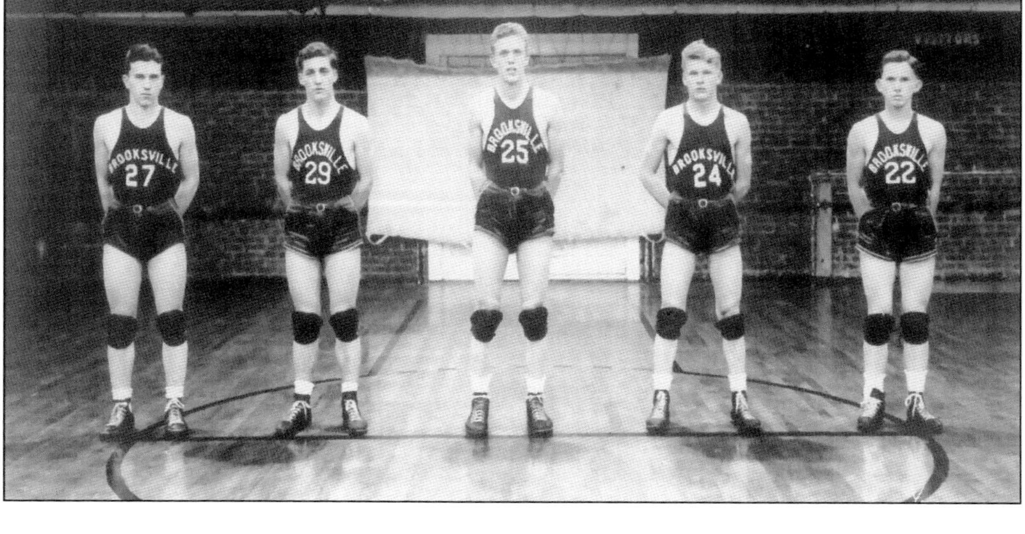

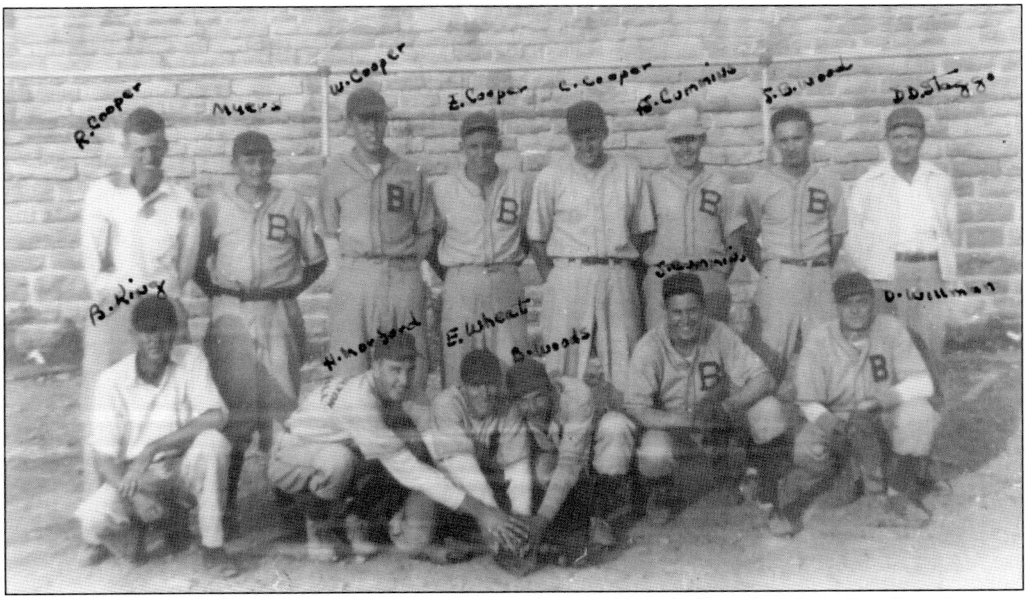

Teams Coveted State Titles. Herb Moford, a professional baseball pitcher from Bracken County, is pictured with both teams. The post–World War II Brooksville baseball team included, from left to right, (first row) Broadus King, Herb Moford, Earl White, Dutch Wood, J. Cummins, and Dennis Willman; (second row) Ralph Cooper, Bill Myers, Warren Cooper, Edward Cooper, Clyde Cooper, Albert Cummins, J. B. Wood, and umpire Demaree Staggs. Shown below is the 1945–1946 Brooksville High School basketball team; from left to right are (first row) William Hause, Ray Crawford, Joseph Meyers, Leo Moneyhon, Herbert Moford, Charles Stapleton, John Corlis, Robert Taylor, Edwin Weiss, James Hedgecock, Robert Palmer, and coach Jarvis Parsley; (second row) Sherman Shepherd, Eugene Egnew, Gaston Reese, Jack Metzger, Paul Maloney, High Moreland, Sonny Gaffin, Ray Hill, and Parker Peddicord. (Above, courtesy of Marilyn Sandy; below, courtesy of Roberta Shepherd.)

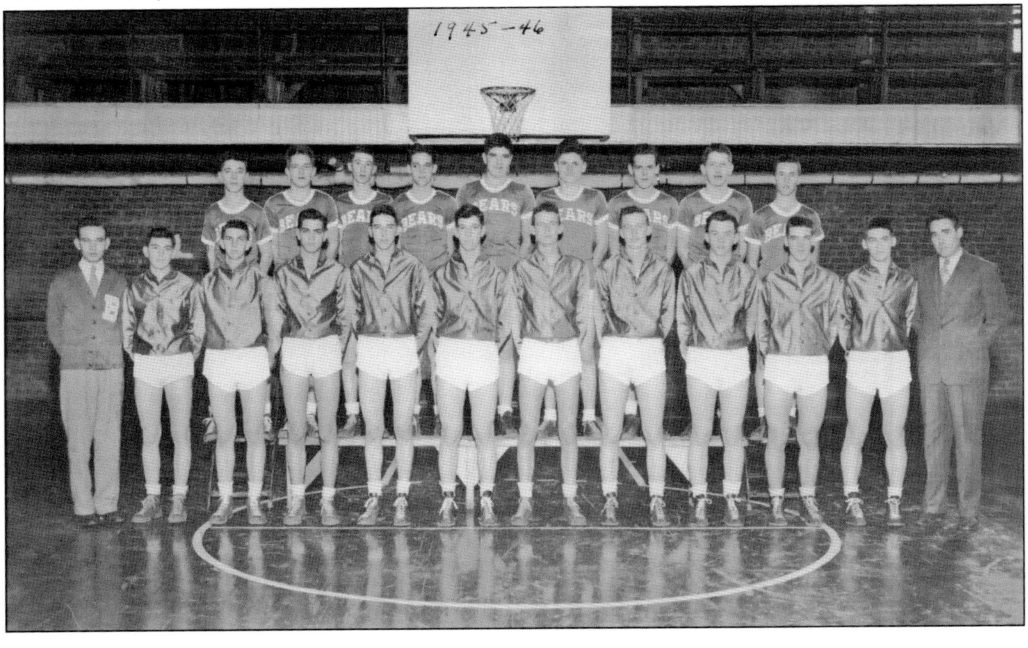

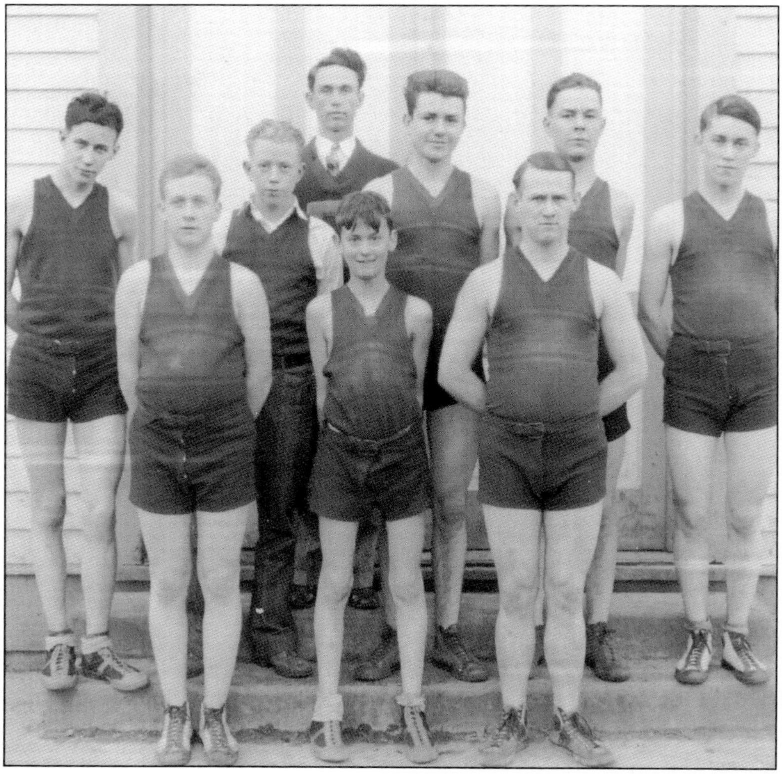

Undermanned and Undersized. The 1927 basketball team of Germantown High School was somewhat small in stature, but they certainly played with great pride for their school. Only three of these players have been identified: at right in the first row is Leonard Kennedy; at left in the second row is Leo Hinson; and second from right in back is Wood Pollock. (Courtesy of Bracken County Historical Society.)

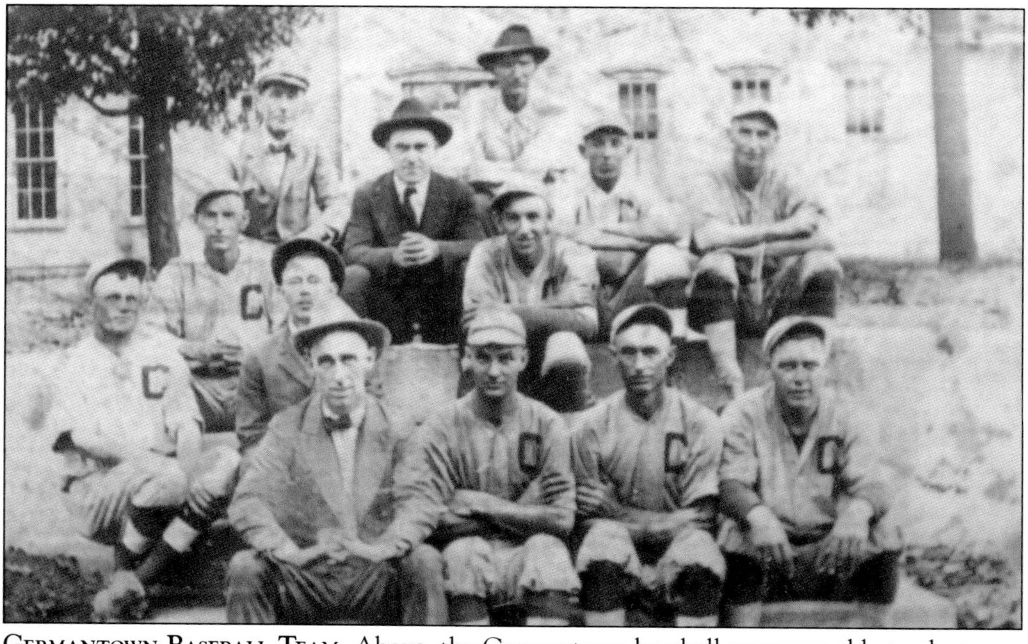

Germantown Baseball Team. Above, the Germantown baseball team was able to gloat over their win against the Cincinnati Redlegs. Pictured are, from left to right, (first row) coach Bryant Byar, Julian Pollock, ? Hatfield, and Mannen McKibben; (second row) Walt Minter and Truman Lea; (third row) Wood Pollock and Tom Hatfield; (fourth row) Charles Fox, Buck Haughaboo, and John Hatfield; (fifth row) Gene Pollock and Nate Hatfield. (Courtesy of John Henderson.)

Three

Floods and Wars Transformed Households

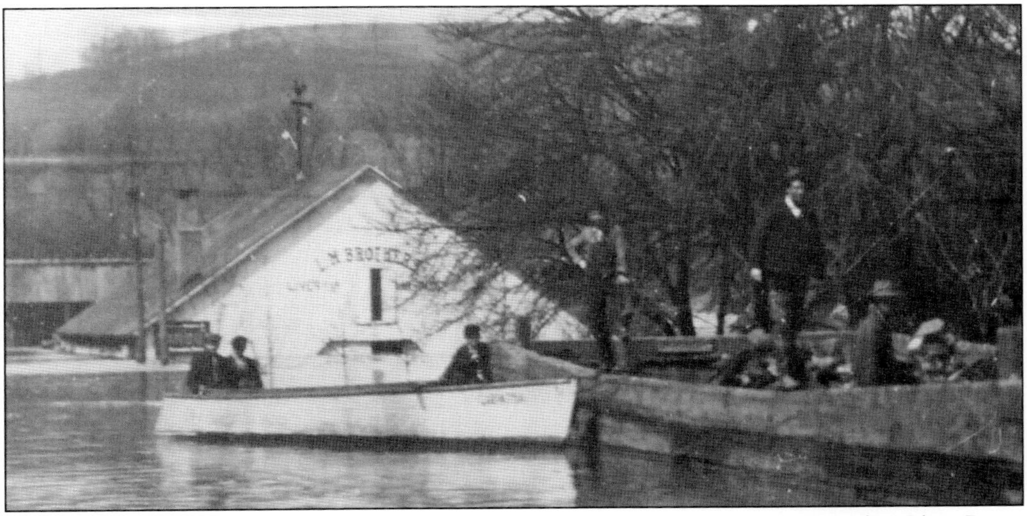

Floodwaters Immerse Augusta. The year 1913 brought extensive rains to the Ohio River Valley—the highest level of flooding in Augusta since 1884. Early in January, heavy rains fell, and by the middle of the month, widespread floods were inevitable. This constant rain caused every major river and creek in Kentucky to flood, with Cincinnati, Ohio, reaching its highest mark at 62.2 feet. The temperature helped keep flooding to a minimum, as the ground was not frozen, allowing some water to be absorbed. Seen above is Second Street, which has been engulfed. Residents were unable to return to their homes for several weeks. Such was the life of people who fought the water, mud, and disease that was brought on with each major flood. In 1883 and 1884, floodwaters destroyed the Pioneer Cemetery, pushing headstones and metal coffins down river. Some of the stones were pulled to shore and reset at Payne Cemetery on the west side of Augusta. Pictured in the background is the L. M. Brothers Livery, which was immersed in water. (Courtesy of Greg Cummins.)

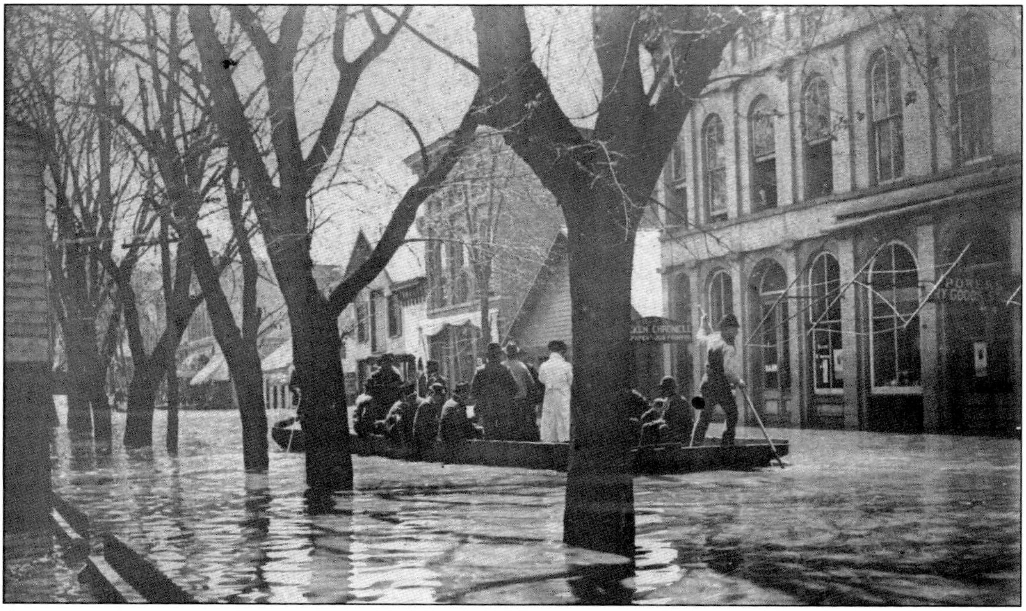

Augusta Streets in 1913 Flood. These two photographs display the desperation and energy involved with moving supplies and household items when a natural disaster strikes. When the occupants of these businesses left their doorways, they stepped onto flatboats or wagons and gazed across the muddy angry waters to Ohio. The upper picture appears to show a flatboat in at least 2 feet of water on Upper Street. The man at the front is steering the boat, making careful not to run into fences and other hidden obstacles. A horse and wagon, shown below, were backed to the doorway of a business so that employees and owners could empty their wares. With no weather bureau to predict when a crest would occur, the residents had to rely on their own wits to outsmart the rising water. (Both, courtesy of Marilyn Bryant.)

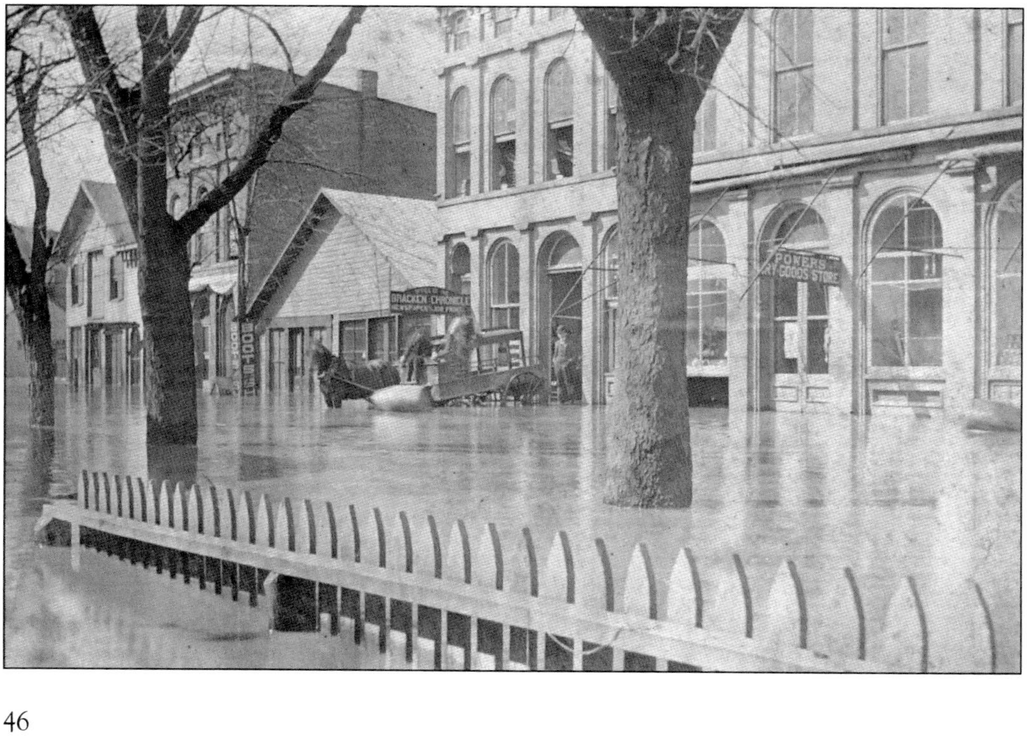

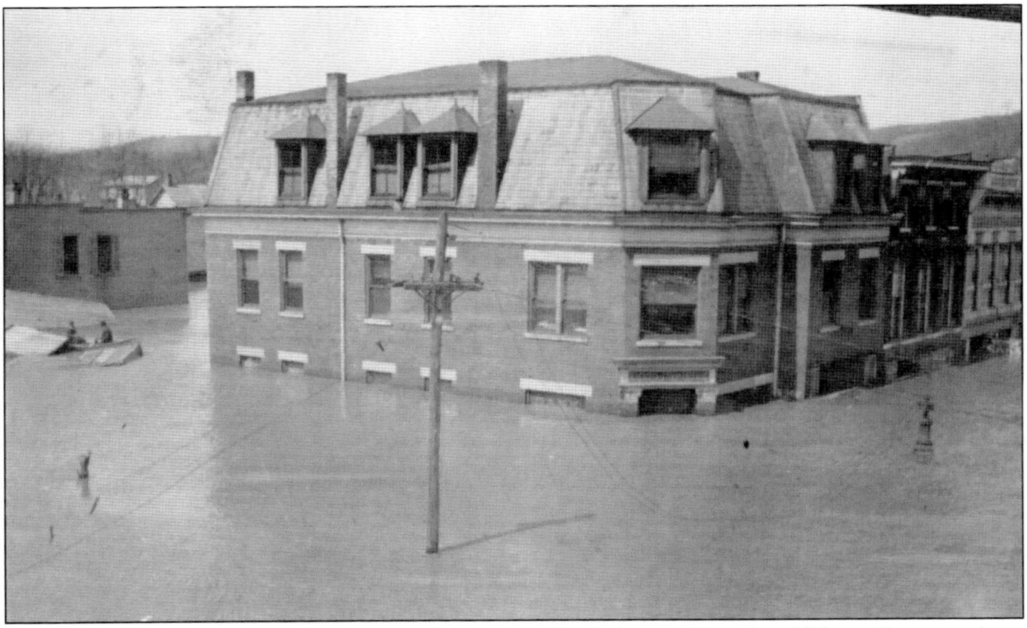

AUGUSTA'S UPPER STREET INUNDATED. The picture above shows Second and Upper Streets, where the German Bank could not keep the water from its first floor. Businesses were forced to close their doors and wait for the river to crest and water to recede. The 1913 flood was a reminder to store owners that they should always be wary of unusual weather and be prepared for the event of a flood. (Courtesy of Robert Adams.)

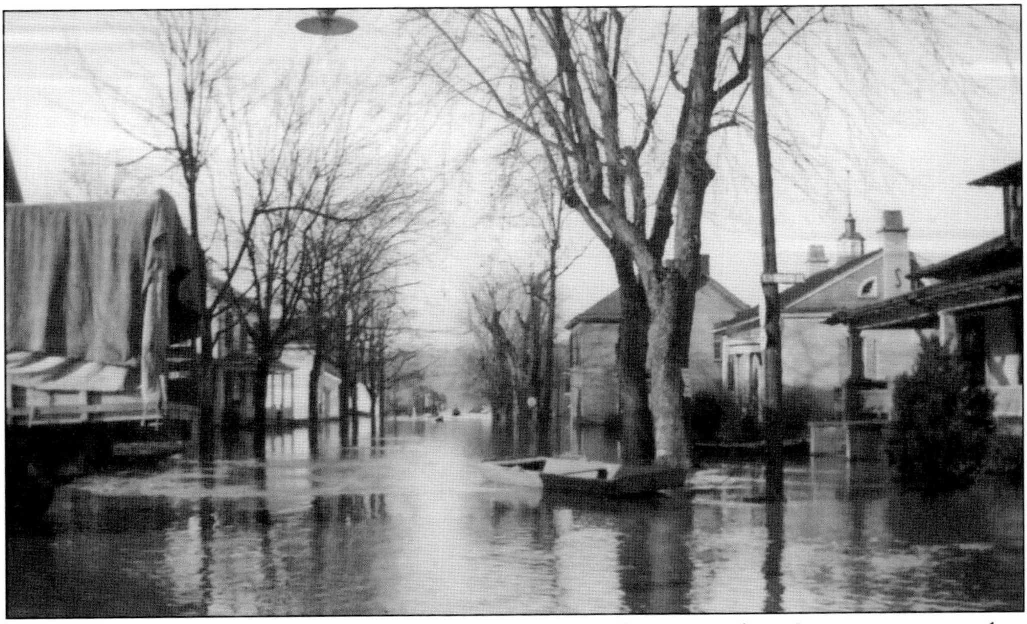

1937 FLOODWATERS. In January, heavy rains began to fall over Bracken County, causing what is known as the Great Flood of 1937. The most significant rainfall occurred from January 13 to January 24. The scene above is Fourth Street looking west past the current post office. This photograph clearly demonstrates the location where the record floodwaters crested. (Courtesy of Clark Hennessey.)

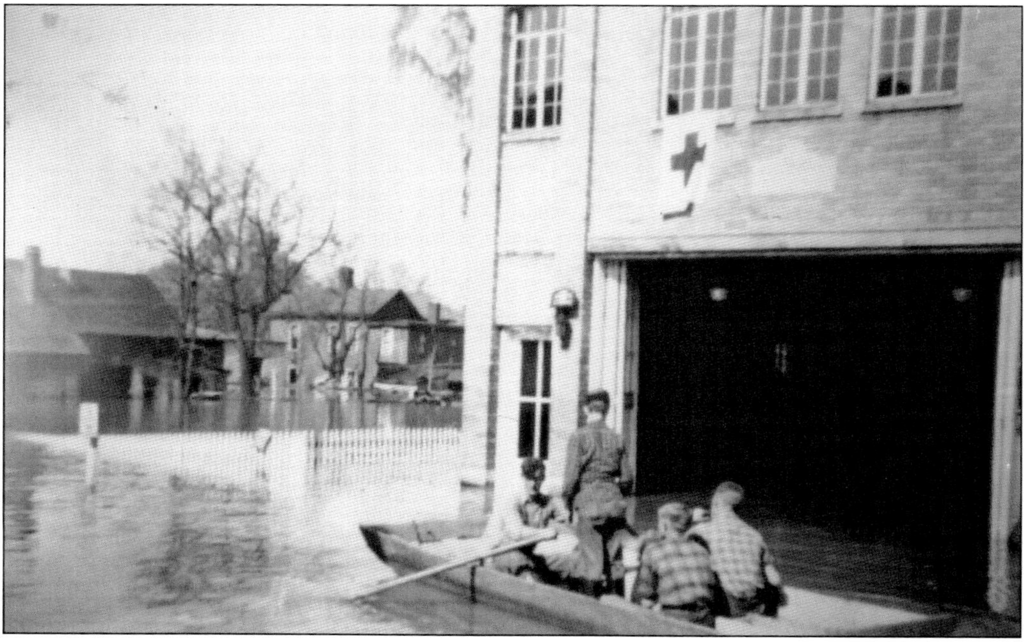

WATER REACHED FOURTH STREET. Pictured above, city hall hangs a Red Cross flag, alerting residents to apply for assistance. Library officials thought they would be spared from the rising floodwaters, since the building was several feet above the usual flood plain. However, as can be seen below, the 1937 flood reached their doors and continued to the steps of the nearby Fourth Street house of former Ohio justice Harlan Cleveland, currently owned by John and Juanita White. The fast-rising floodwaters of 1997 only threatened north Third Street and did not cross the railroad tracks. (Above, courtesy of John H. Henderson; below, courtesy of Clark Hennessey.)

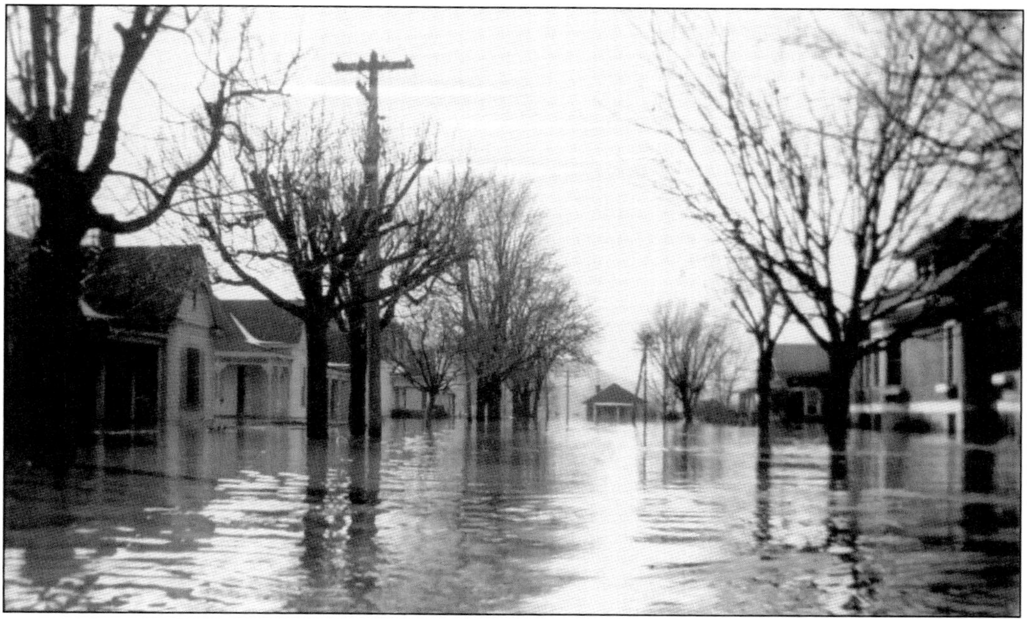

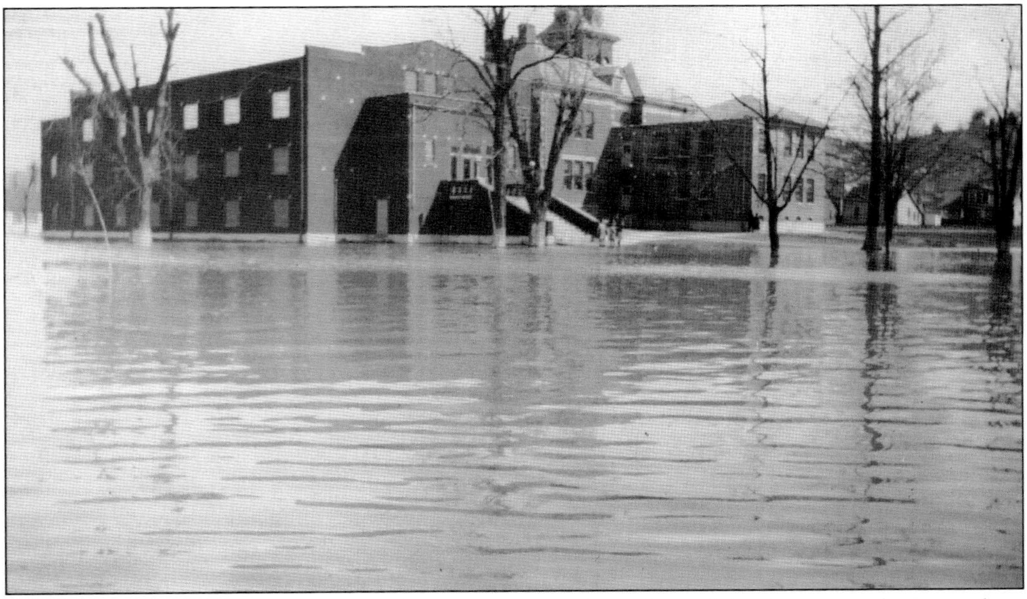

Floodwaters' Great Strength. Augusta Independent School barely escaped tremendous damage from the fast-moving floodwaters. This picture was taken after the water had somewhat receded. The Red Cross donated at least one four-room house to a local family. The cottage was built at the intersection of Second and southeast Williams Streets and remained there until torn down in the late 1990s. (Courtesy of Bernard Spencer.)

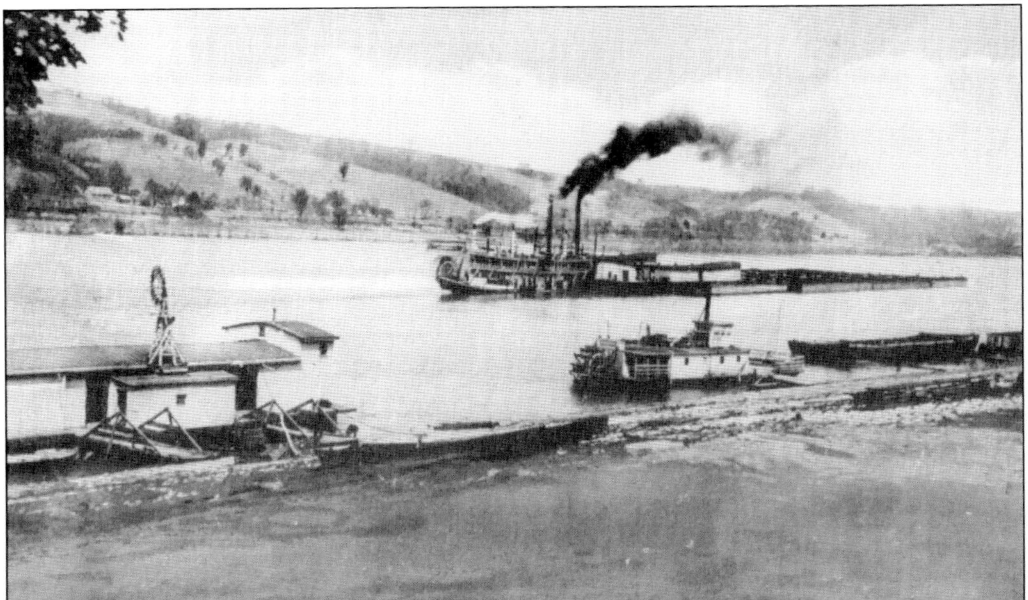

Augusta Wharf Provided Ships Access. Pictured above is the Augusta wharf with one cargo boat moored next to its landing. On the river, a larger tug steams upstream with a heavy load. In June 1930, the wharf boat was destroyed by fire. Wharf master James Wayson and his adopted son, Hobart, age 14, perished in the blaze. (Courtesy of Bob Adams.)

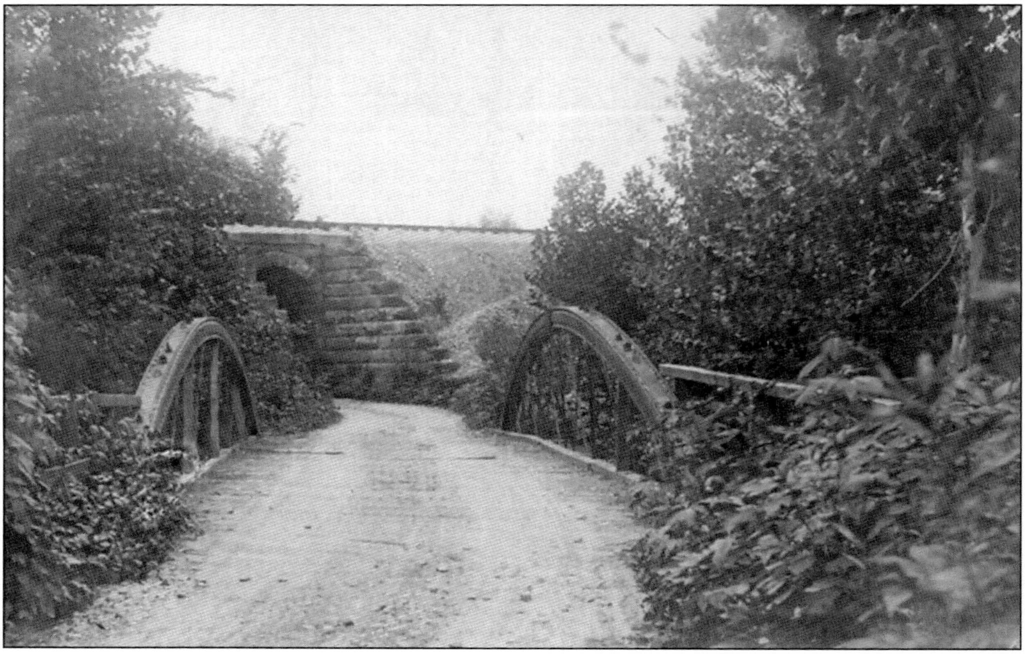

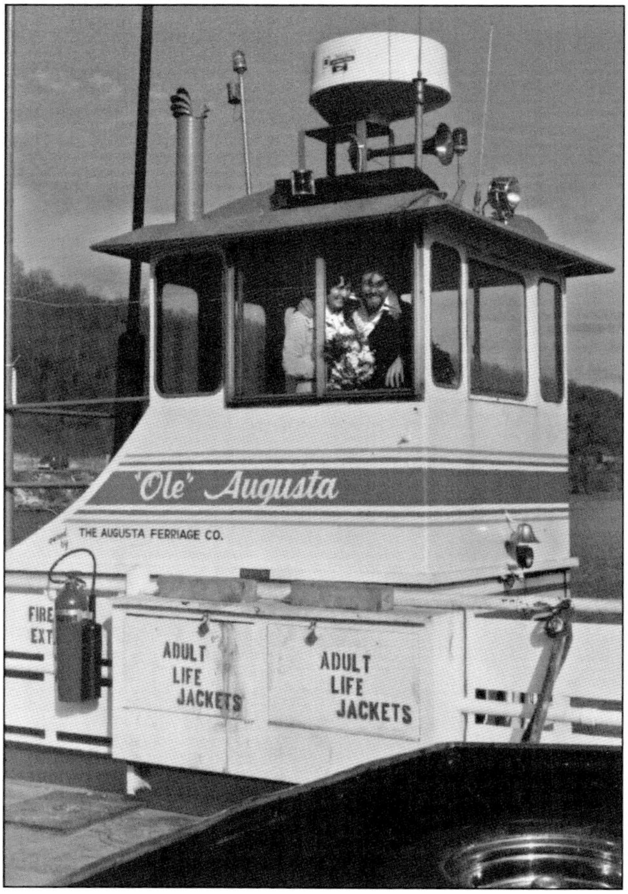

RAILROADS AND FERRIES. Seen above, the long stretch railroad arch west of Augusta was a frequent place for spooning but later became defaced with graffiti. This backwater was the location of an unsolved murder, known as the "Bloody Mary" ghost story. Ferries have been in operation in Augusta since 1798. Kline O'Neill was the owner and operator of the longest running business, crossing to Boude's Landing in Ohio. In 1932, O'Neill purchased *Relief*, formerly used as a ferry in Maysville, to begin his business. Pictured at left are newlyweds who took their vows on the *Ole Augusta* ferry in the 1970s. Currently the *Jenny Ann* operates daily as the ferry. (Above, courtesy of Bernard Spencer; left, courtesy of *Bracken County News*.)

CAPT. ANTHONY MELDAHL DAM. Meldahl was regarded as a beloved captain of the river fraternity. In 1916, he became master and pilot of U.S. Army engineer steamer *Cayuga*, and he remained in this capacity until his death. The lock and dam on the Ohio River near Foster were named in Meldahl's honor. The cost of the dam was estimated at $73 million, and it took three years to complete. The dedication ceremony took place in Chilo, Ohio, on May 22, 1965. Another project is developing at the Meldahl Dam—a hydroelectric power station owned by the City of Hamilton in Butler County, Ohio. (Both, courtesy of Carol Wallin Boney.)

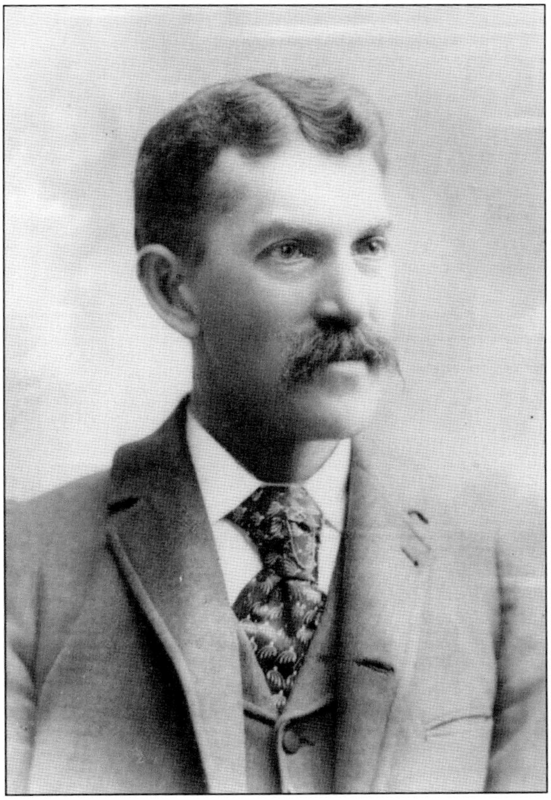

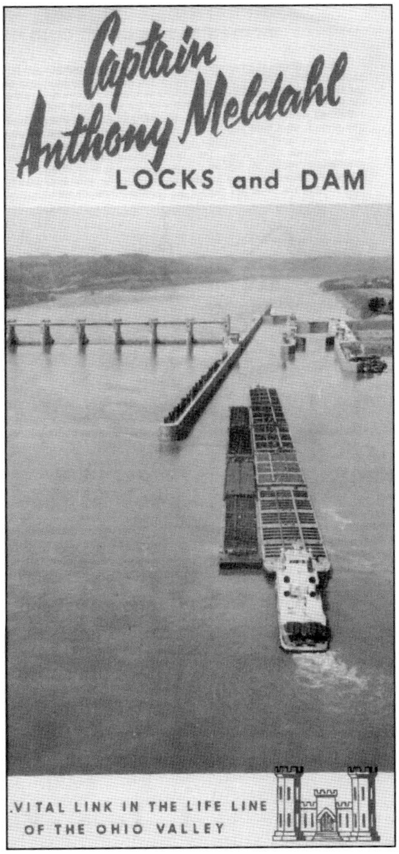

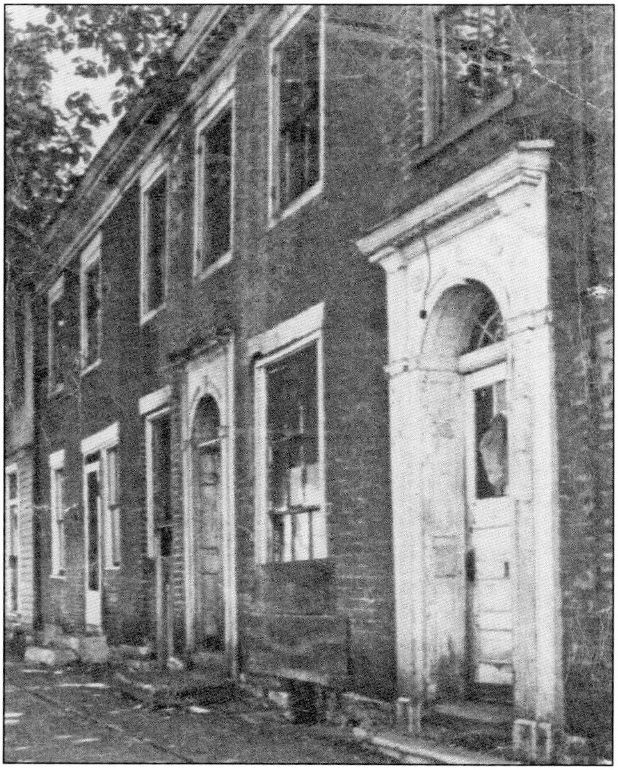

Battle of Augusta. Dr. Joshua T. Bradford was the local commander of the Home Guards, protectors of the city against invasion by Union or Confederate troops. On September 27, 1862, Augusta was invaded by seven companies of Confederate Morgan's Raiders led by Basil Duke. When Bradford flew the white flag of surrender from this Piedmont door on Front Street, the other soldiers were unaware and kept fighting. Duke ordered 33 homes and businesses set on fire. Pictured in his later years is Civil War veteran Zed Craycraft (1822–1890), a member of the Union army's 24th Kentucky Infantry, Company D. His descendants include great-grandchildren Tom Jefferson, Norma Sizemore, Eugene Tull, Lynda Huesing, and great-great-granddaughter Judith Cooper. (Left, courtesy of Donald A. Clark; below, courtesy of Judith Cooper.)

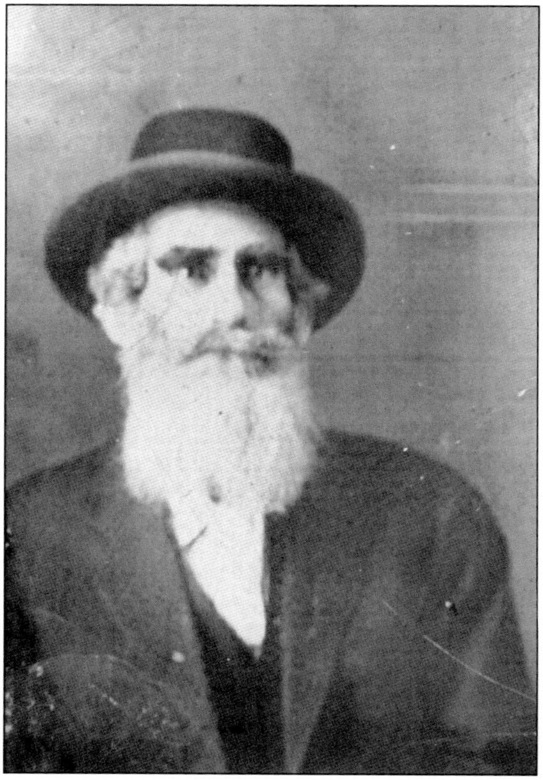

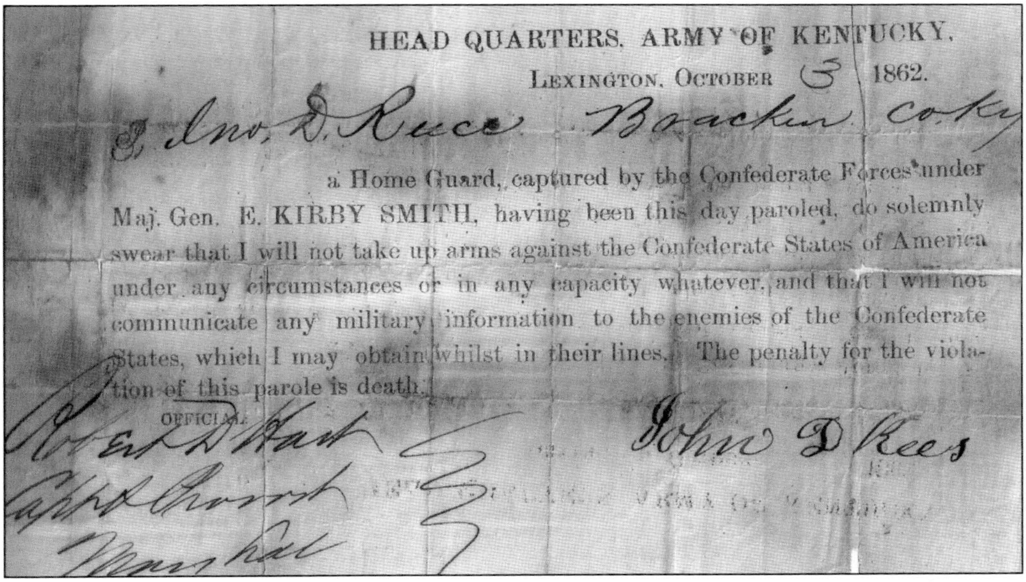

HEAD QUARTERS, ARMY OF KENTUCKY,

LEXINGTON, OCTOBER 3 1862.

I, Jno. D. Reece Bracken Co. Ky

a Home Guard, captured by the Confederate Forces under Maj. Gen. E. KIRBY SMITH, having been this day paroled, do solemnly swear that I will not take up arms against the Confederate States of America under any circumstances or in any capacity whatever, and that I will not communicate any military information to the enemies of the Confederate States, which I may obtain whilst in their lines. The penalty for the violation of this parole is death.

OFFICIAL:

Robert D. Hart
Capt & Provost
Marshal

John D Rees

PARDONS ISSUED TO HOME GUARDS. Pictured above is a pardon issued to John D. Reece of Augusta by Maj. Gen. Kirby Smith's officers. Reece had been held by Confederates since the Battle of Augusta on September 27, 1862. According to historian Walter Rankins, three Augusta men were camped with Duke at Cynthiana, and they persuaded the commanders not to place the Augusta prisoners in slave pens. (Courtesy of Earl Phanstiel.)

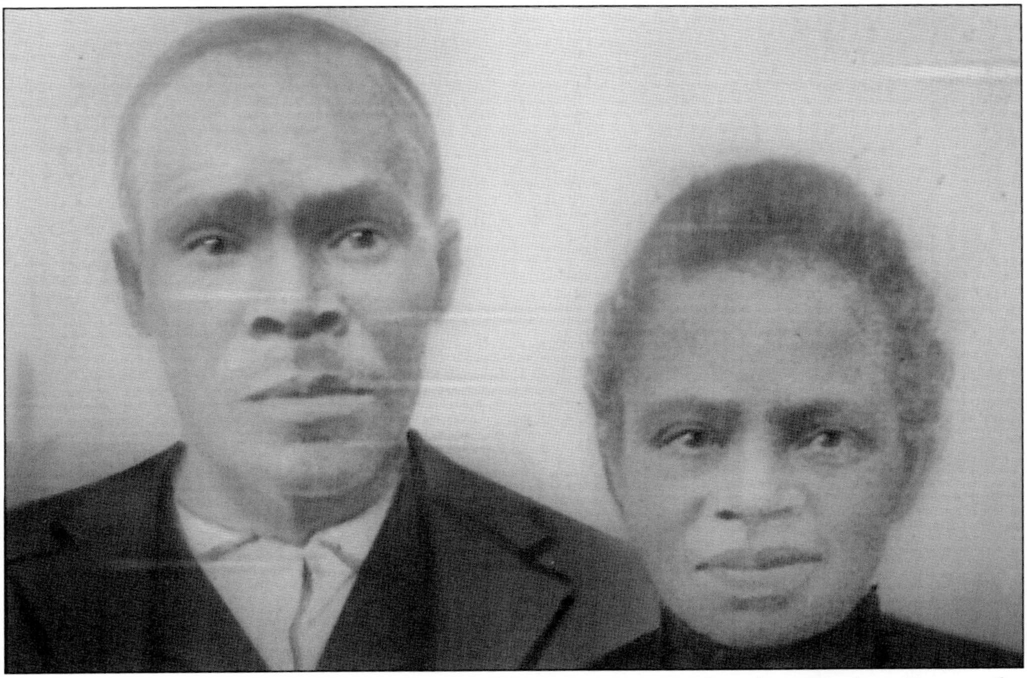

ELIJAH BASS AND NANCY SPENCER. Bass and Spencer were enslaved in Bracken County for nearly 25 years until freed by the 13th Amendment. After they married, they chose to live in Germantown, build a church, and strive for public education for African Americans. Spencer served as the midwife to several women as well as the area nurse during the deadly Spanish influenza pandemic of 1918. (Courtesy of Caroline Miller.)

by the white congregation until it was able to carry on without support. Some of the churches continued the old practice until the Negroes of their own volition decided to withdraw. However, this separation required years to complete.

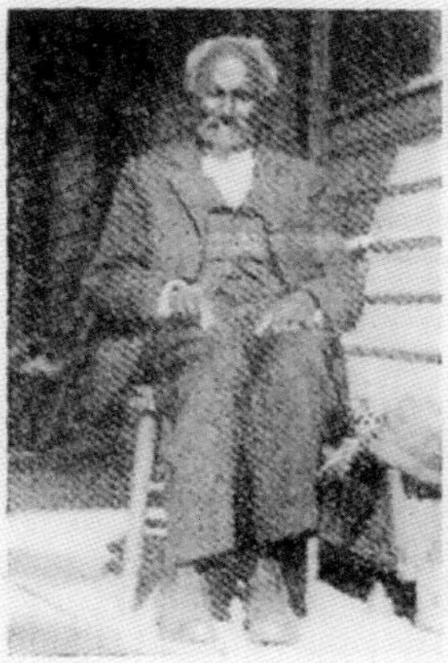

ARNOLD GRAGSON

Who was a member of the inter-racial congregation and moved as a charter member into the Colored Church at Germantown, Ky.

R. H. Peoples says, "The separation of the two into distinct churches was a gradual process. In some it came soon. It came soon after they were organ-

NORTHERN KENTUCKY'S GREATEST CONDUCTOR. Pictured sitting in the porch chair is one of Kentucky's leading conductors of slaves, Arnold Gragston. As a young adult, he was asked to forward a female slave to Rev. John Rankin in Ripley, Ohio. After this attempt, Gragston noted to a Federal Writer's Project interviewer that he rowed over 300 slaves to freedom in Ohio. (Courtesy of Rev. William Johnson.)

KU KLUX KLAN. In the early 1920s, approximately 150 northern Kentucky Klansmen met in Bracken County to donate money toward a church's mortgage. A local cobbler remarked he could recognize some of the men in the line, as he was familiar with their shoes. The Klan was responsible for at least three cross burnings—two above Augusta and one at French's High Hill. (Courtesy of Bracken County Historical Society.)

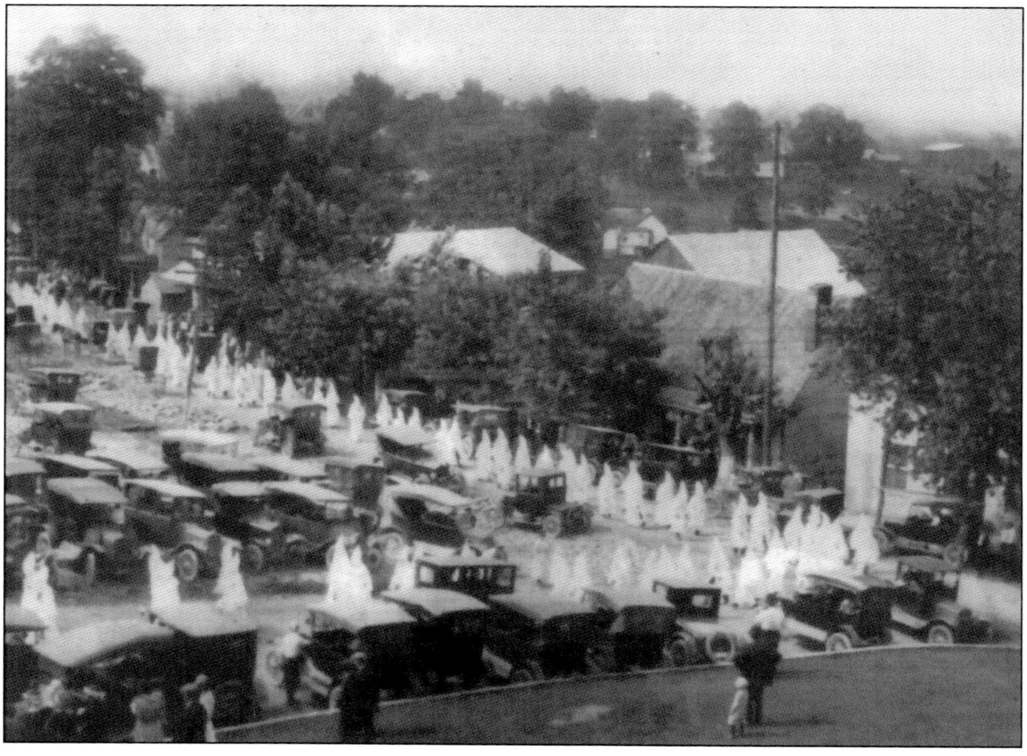

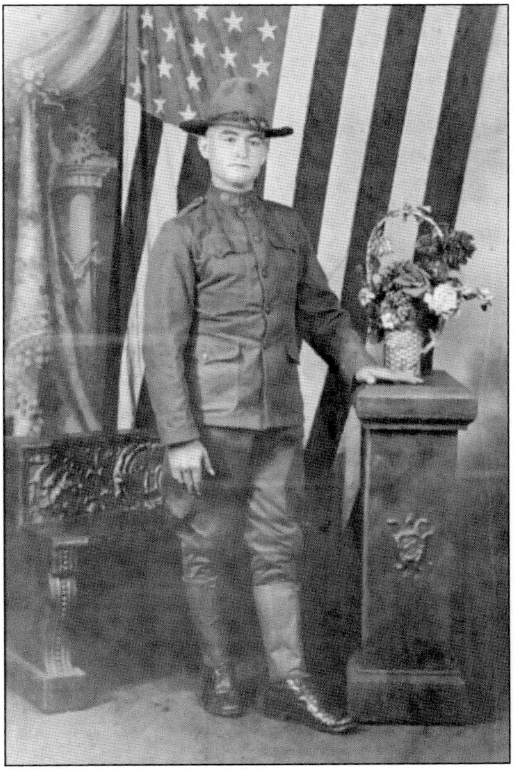

Men in World War I. Serving his county and nation proudly was Newton "Newt" Downard, posing at right with the American flag. The other soldier was Will Rankins of Augusta. Involvement of the United States in World War I lasted from 1917 to 1918 and was part of the conflict of the great nations of Europe—the Allies and the Central Powers. The war took on several names after it began with the German, Austro-Hungarian, and Russian attacks in Europe, such as World War I, the Great War, the World War, and the War to End All Wars. (Both, courtesy of Bracken County Historical Society.)

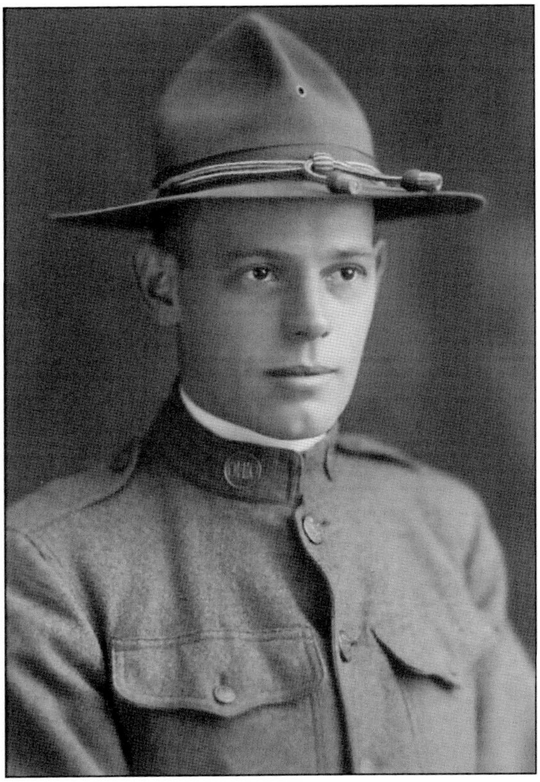

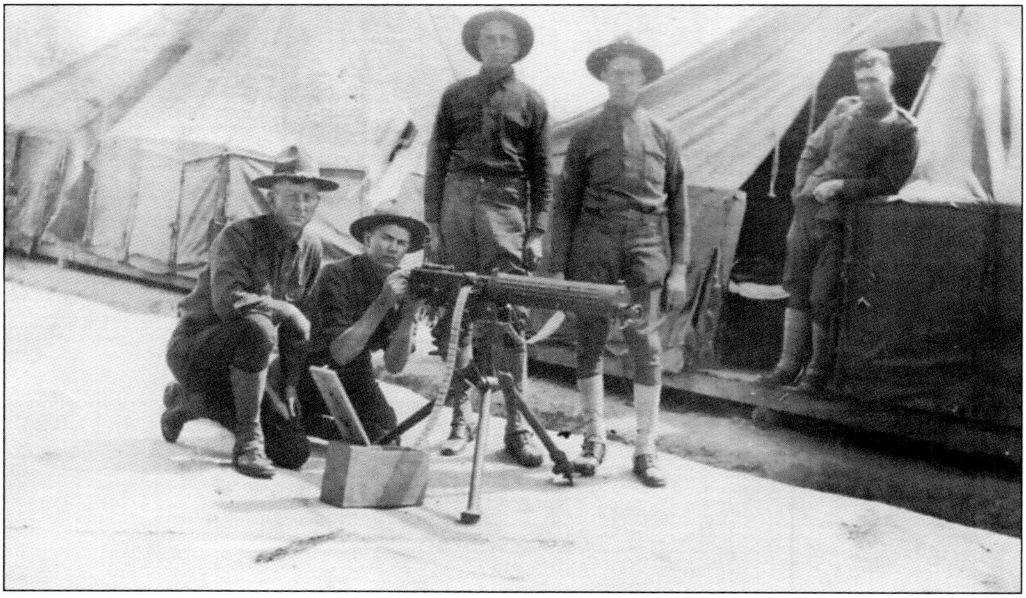

DOUGHBOYS IN WORLD WAR I. Everett Earl Phanstiel was in an army camp in France when the photograph above was taken. Phanstiel is the soldier sighting along the machine gun. While in France, he worked as an interpreter. Phanstiel was a tall, thin, unmarried 23-year-old teacher at Brooksville High School when he registered for the military. Pictured below is a large group of county men who had served in World War I and later gathered in the late 1920s. Note the varying and unusual hats they wore, which might have denoted the military rank or branch in which they had served. (Both, courtesy of Earl Phanstiel.)

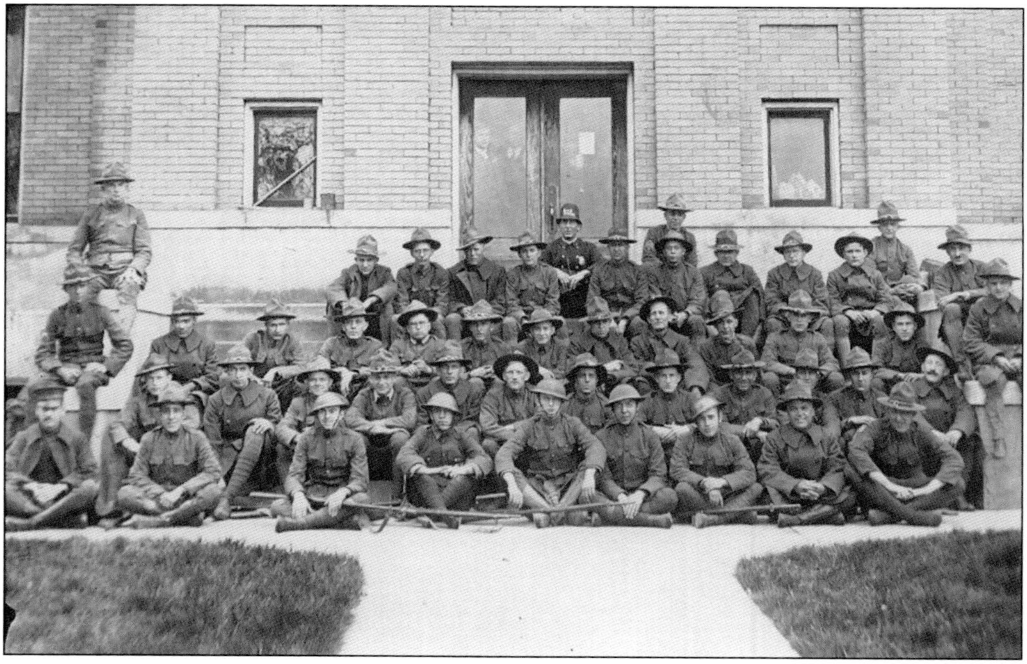

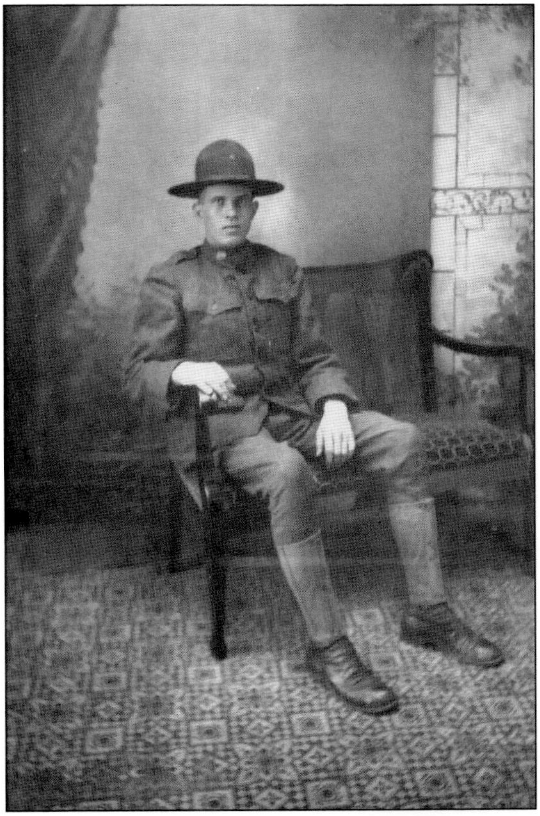

World War I Soldier. Ray Courts was a young man living near Bradford when he enlisted and joined his fellow Bracken County residents to serve on foreign soil in Europe. Courts sat proudly for this photograph, and his family was much relieved for his safe return. (Courtesy of Jenny Lou Courts McGee.)

War Stabilization Board. The men in this photograph served after World War I. They are, from left to right, (first row) ? Clarke, ? Pinckard, L. McGill, H. D. Galbraith, and unidentified; (second row) William Miller, Andrew Meyer, William DeLisle, E. King, H. C. Griffith, H. F. Moneyhon, Roy Cummins, and John Dunn; (third row) C. A. Fox, Jesse Magee, R. J. Lundregan, Virgil C. Hester, John Tolle, Disher McDowell, and John Meyers. (Courtesy of William Miller.)

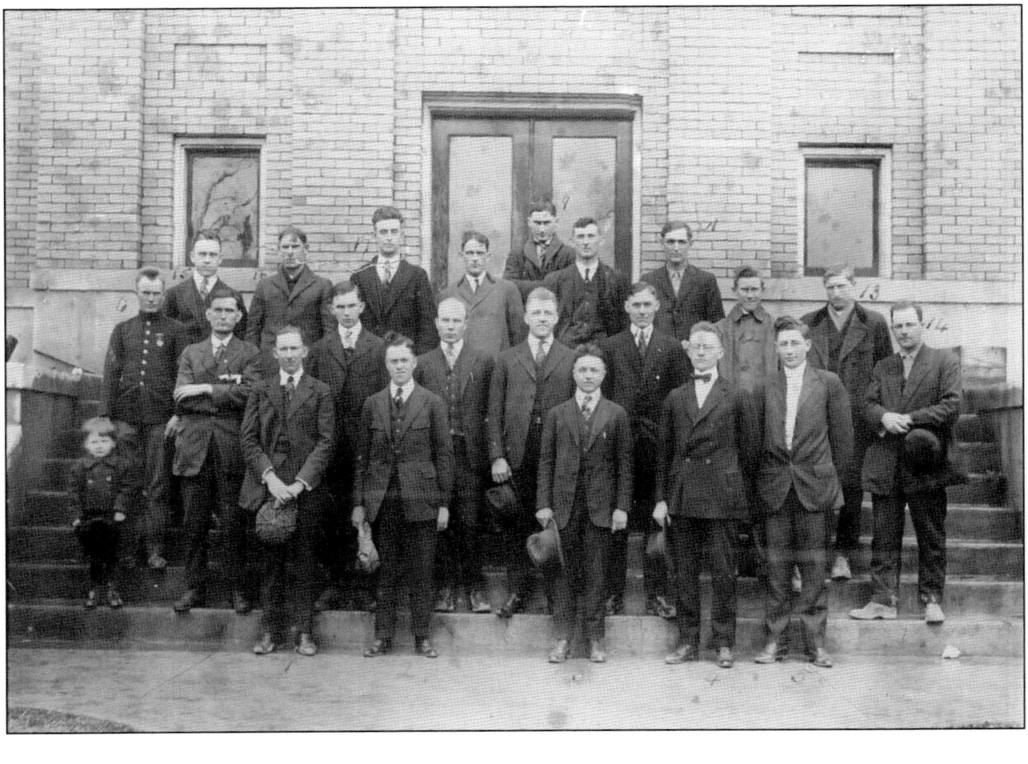

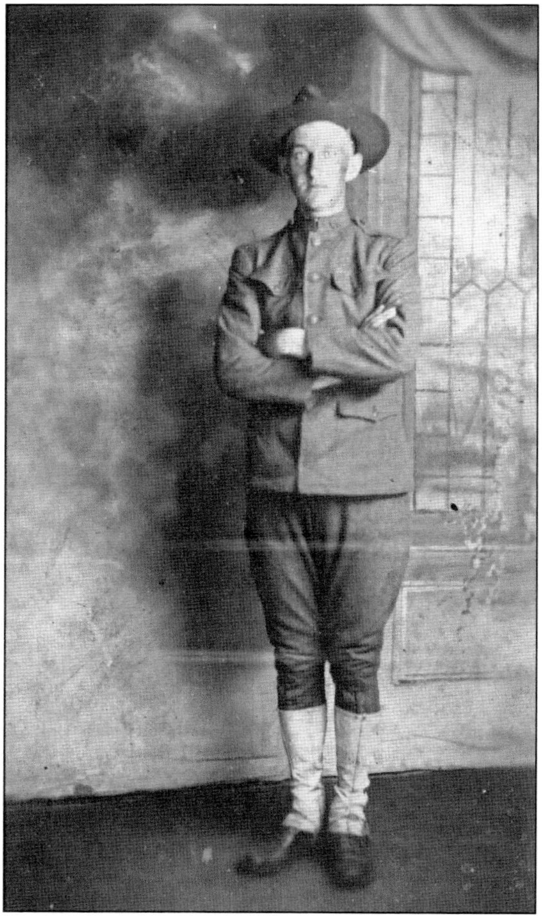

OTTIE CASE. Ottie Case, shown kneeling in the center of this group on a firing range in Europe, was killed in action on November 1, 1918, in France and posthumously awarded the Belgian Croix de Guerre. A letter to his mother written the week he died included these words: "This is a dark and gloomy day . . . shells are flying over my head. We were in shell fire when we were in the big drive. It was just luck for me to escape. I guess it was the prayers of our dear mothers which saved us from those whistling shells. We were on the line for seven days going through the machine gun fire and shrapnel of the big guns of the Fritz." (Both, courtesy of Roberta Shepherd.)

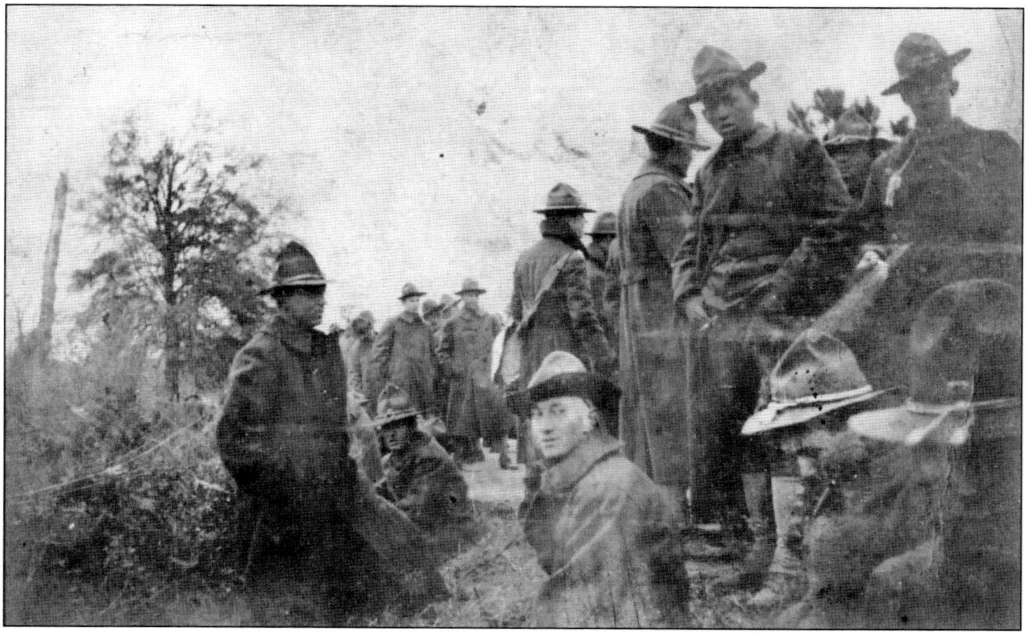

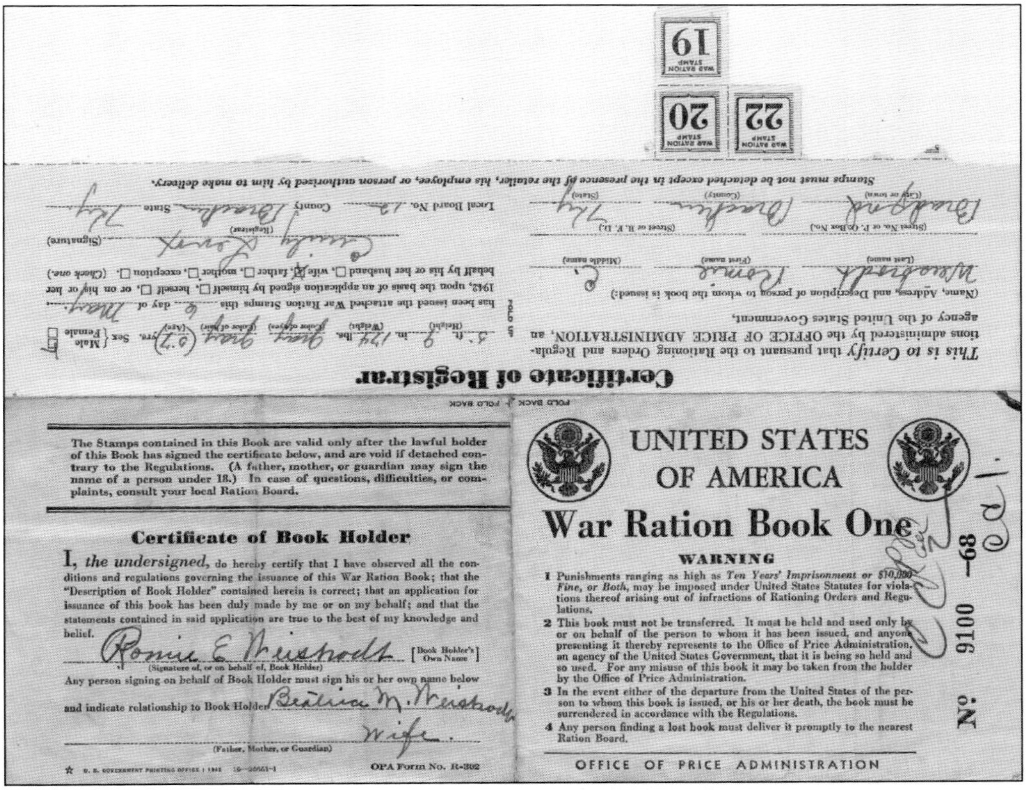

WAR RATION STAMP 19

WAR RATION STAMP 20

WAR RATION STAMP 22

Stamps must not be detached except in the presence of the retailer, his employe, or person authorized by him to make delivery.

Certificate of Registrar

This is to Certify that pursuant to the Rationing Orders and Regulations administered by the OFFICE OF PRICE ADMINISTRATION, an agency of the United States Government,

FOLD BACK

The Stamps contained in this Book are valid only after the lawful holder of this Book has signed the certificate below, and are void if detached contrary to the Regulations. (A father, mother, or guardian may sign the name of a person under 18.) In case of questions, difficulties, or complaints, consult your local Ration Board.

Certificate of Book Holder

I, *the undersigned,* do hereby certify that I have observed all the conditions and regulations governing the issuance of this War Ration Book; that the "Description of Book Holder" contained herein is correct; that an application for issuance of this book has been duly made by me or on my behalf; and that the statements contained in said application are true to the best of my knowledge and belief.

Romie E. Weisbrodt [Book Holder's Own Name]
(Signature of, or on behalf of, Book Holder)

Any person signing on behalf of Book Holder must sign his or her own name below and indicate relationship to Book Holder Beatrice M. Weisbrodt
Wife.
(Father, Mother, or Guardian)

☆ U. S. GOVERNMENT PRINTING OFFICE : 1942 16—26561-1 OPA Form No. R-302

UNITED STATES OF AMERICA

War Ration Book One

WARNING

1 Punishments ranging as high as *Ten Years' Imprisonment or $10,000 Fine, or Both,* may be imposed under United States Statutes for violations thereof arising out of infractions of Rationing Orders and Regulations.

2 This book must not be transferred. It must be held and used only by or on behalf of the person to whom it has been issued, and anyone presenting it thereby represents to the Office of Price Administration, an agency of the United States Government, that it is being so held and so used. For any misuse of this book it may be taken from the holder by the Office of Price Administration.

3 In the event either of the departure from the United States of the person to whom this book is issued, or his or her death, the book must be surrendered in accordance with the Regulations.

4 Any person finding a lost book must deliver it promptly to the nearest Ration Board.

OFFICE OF PRICE ADMINISTRATION

No. 9100 —68

WORLD WAR II RATION BOOK. Booklets of stamps for sugar, shoes, butter, and other basic supplies were issued in to Americans in World War II, as these products in short supply and rationing was ordered. Romie Weisbrodt was given this booklet on May 6, 1942, and stamps could only be removed in the presence of a retailer. (Courtesy of John Lenox.)

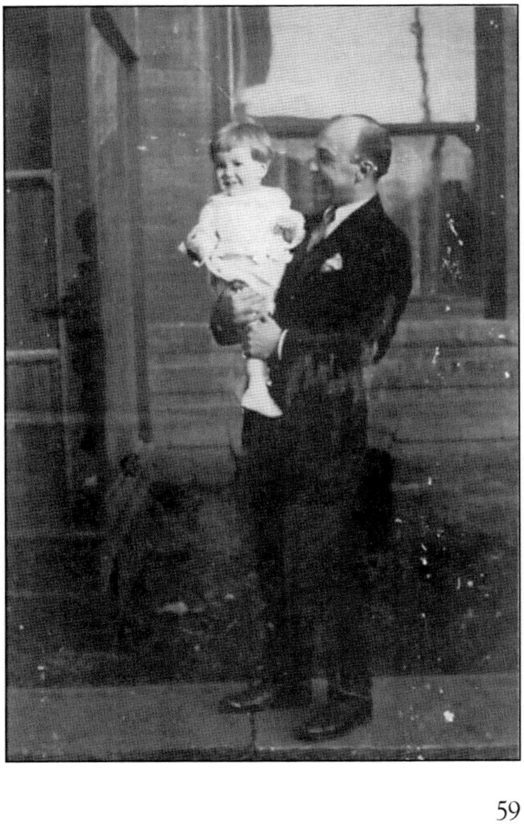

AT&T MARKETED PRINCESS TELEPHONE. Bartlett Miller of Johnsville spent his childhood in an orphanage before graduating from Brooksville High School. In the early 1900s, he ventured into telephone communications in the west and later redesigned the standard black box telephone for AT&T. The newly designed telephone was marketed as the "Princess." Miller, shown with his son Bart, was vice president of marketing the novel invention. (Courtesy of William Miller.)

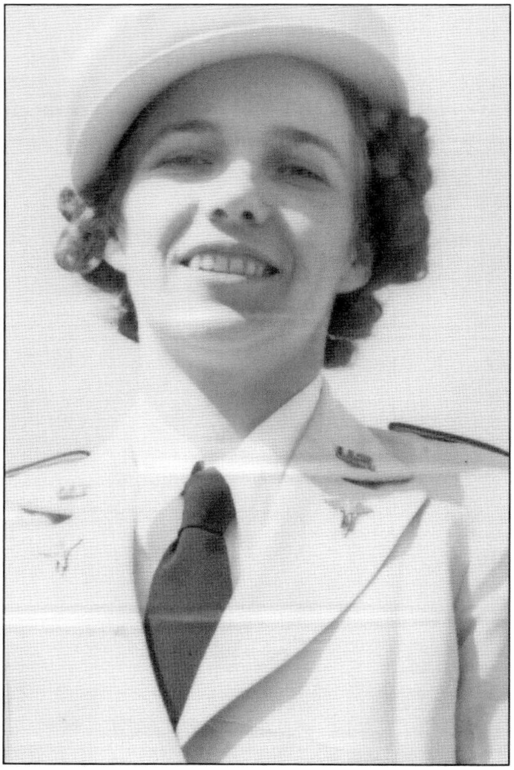

STRANDED IN ALBANIA. In 1943, Wilma Dale Lytle volunteered for duty as an air evacuation nurse. Her military plane crashed in Albania, and the nurses aboard were hidden from the Nazi army for two months until rescued. However, three, including Lytle, were secluded for four months until being led to safety across the Adriatic Sea in Italy. (Courtesy of Carolyn Lonaker.)

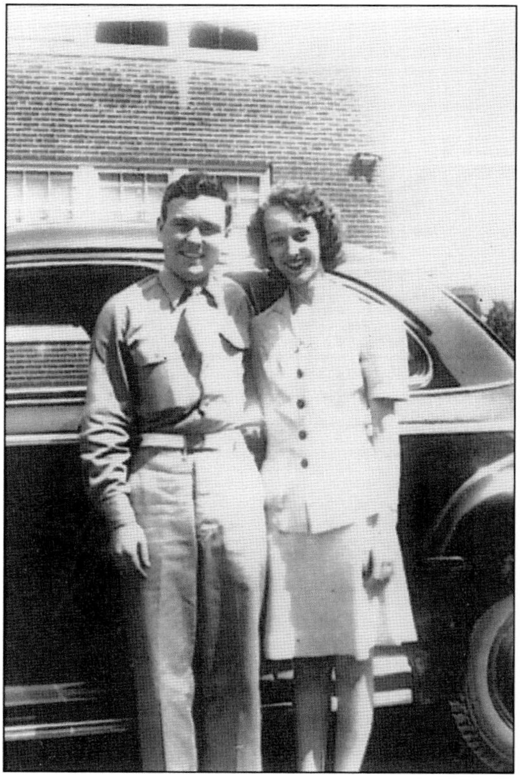

LAMONDAS SEPARATED BY WAR. Louis and Ruby McKibben LaMonda had just married when they posed for this picture. Ruby would cherish this image, as Louis reported for World War II duty the next day. Louis spent his overseas tour in Europe in an engineer's division, although his responsibility was to transport a commander on rounds. Nevertheless, this duty did not lessen Ruby's worries until his return to Bracken County. (Courtesy of Ruby LaMonda.)

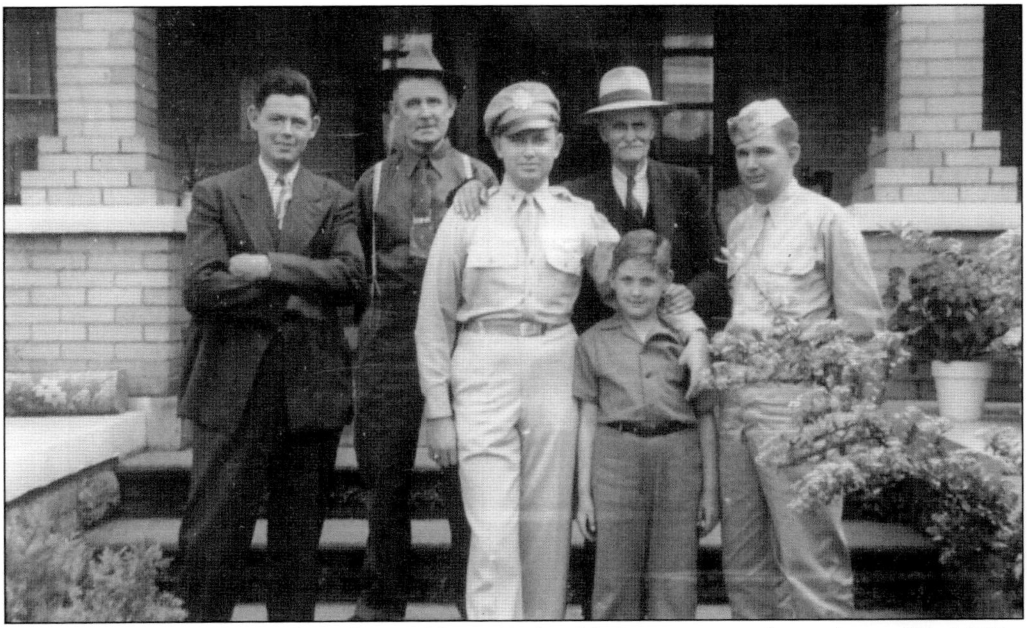

Home on Leave. When Bill Wallin and Louis Parker Mathews were on leave during World War II, they posed for this family photograph at the Wallin home on Locust Street in Brooksville. Standing proudly on the bottom steps are, from left to right, Wallin, cousin Jack Brooks, and Mathews, and in the back row are Asbury Books, John Brooks, and William Wallin. (Courtesy of Carol Wallin Boney.)

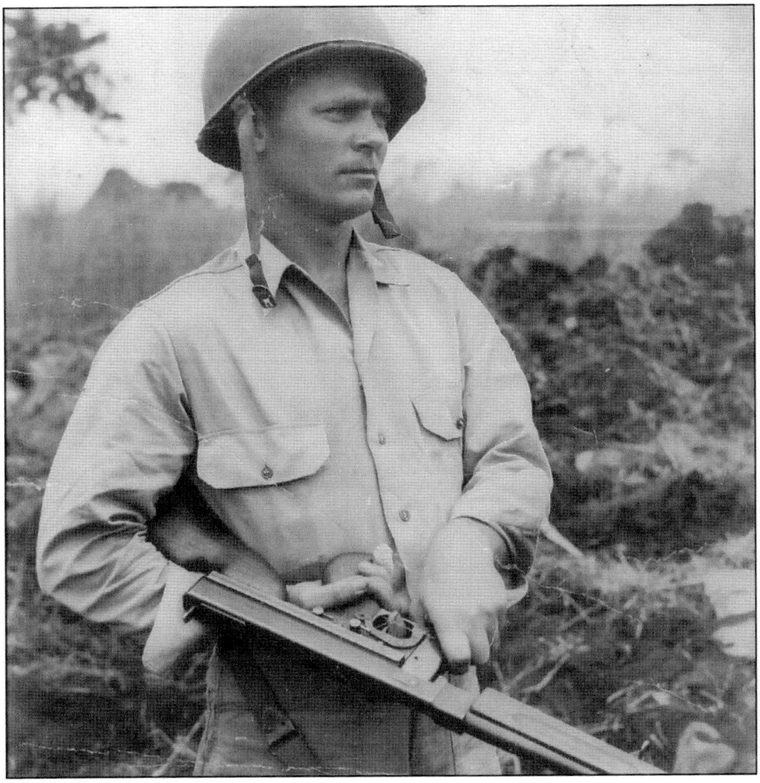

Capito Awarded Silver Star. Marine John E. Capito of Bradford was awarded the Silver Star for bravery during World War II while operating a bulldozer under fire at Cape Gloucester, New Britain, in the Southwest Pacific campaign. Capito also received the Presidential Citation Ribbon with Star and a Purple Heart for action at Guadalcanal. He spent four years of the war overseas. (Courtesy of Charles and John Capito.)

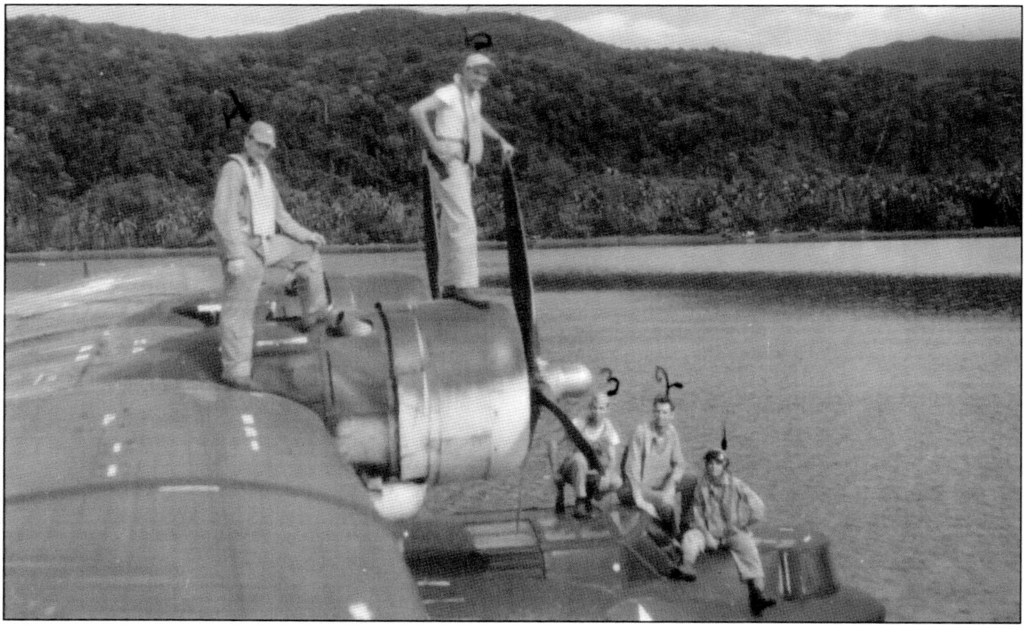

World War II Aircraft. Wallin's South Pacific missions required transporting wounded soldiers and sailors. Bill Wallin is pictured standing on his PBY air sea rescue plane at Port Real. Major Wallin later labeled this picture: 1. Sergeant Cannon; 2. Pilot Lieutenant Griffith; 3. Sergeant Lessure; 4. Captain Leviten; and 5. Pilot Bill Wallin. Twenty years later, Major Wallin hung up his wings and retired. (Courtesy of Carol Wallin Boney.)

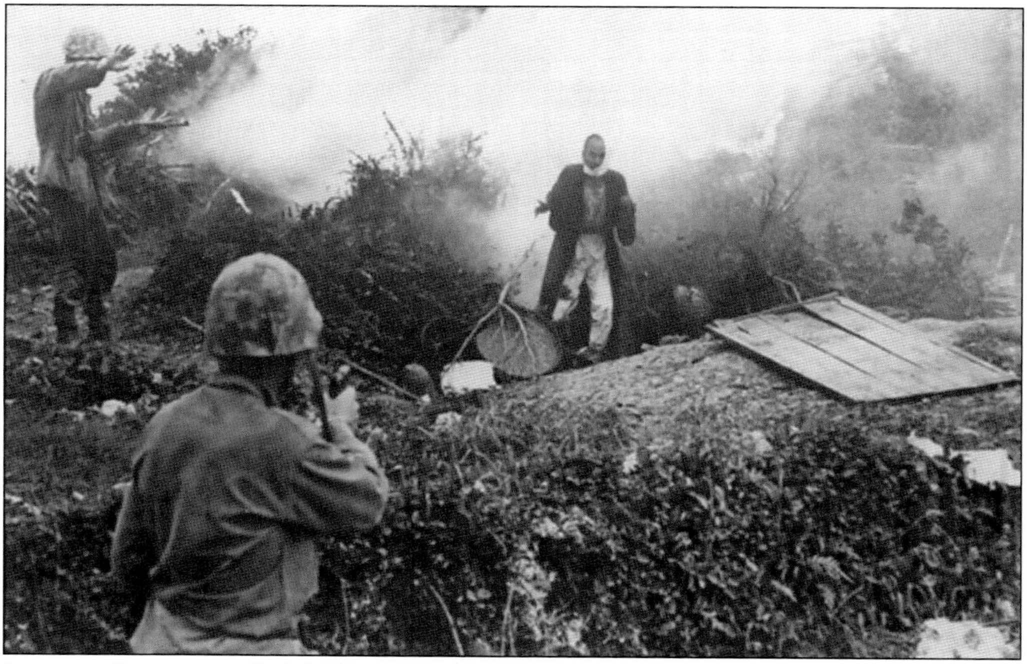

Japanese Surrender. Jack Miller of Bradford was with fellow army soldiers in 1945 when he snapped this photograph of a Japanese pilot from a downed plane on Okinawa. Miller was managing the base post office and maintained an album of images from Okinawa during the last months of World War II. (Courtesy of William Miller.)

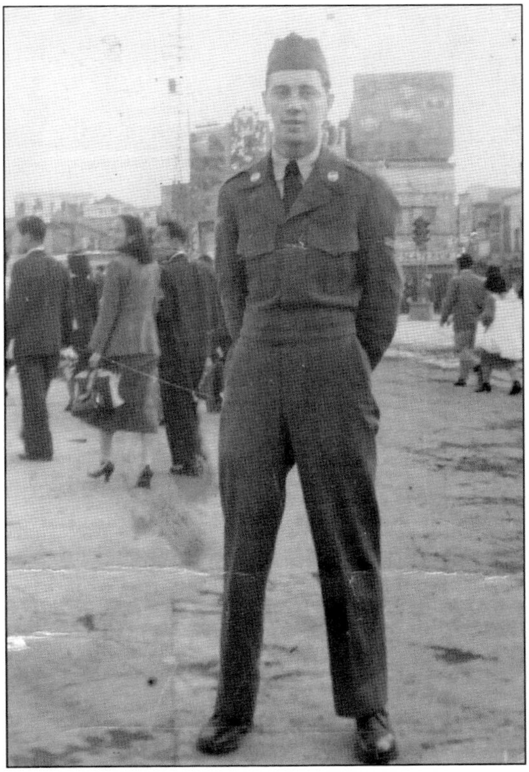

Sherman Shepherd. Brooksville resident "Buddy" Shepherd was a young Air Force serviceman during the Korean War in 1951. Although Shepherd was stationed 10 miles from the demilitarized zone in Korea, he was enjoying some rest and relaxation in Japan at the time the photograph was taken. (Courtesy of Roberta Shepherd.)

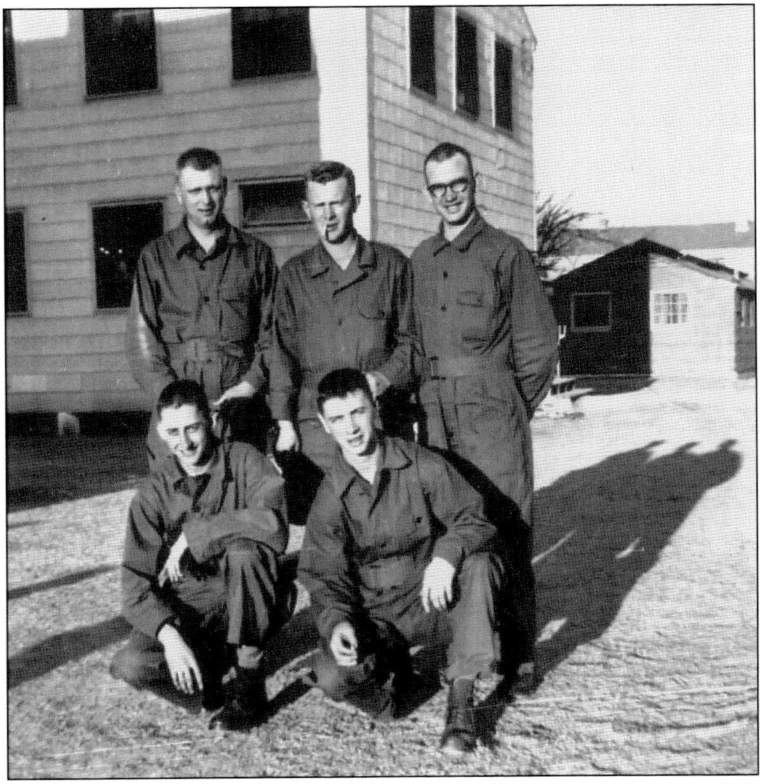

Air Force Volunteers. Five men from Bracken County accompanied each other to enlist in the Air Force during the Korean War in 1951. They are, from left to right, (kneeling) Gerald Ross and Sherman "Buddy" Shepherd; (standing) Victor "Butch" Hamilton, John Bonfield, and William "Bill Bob" Hause. (Courtesy of Roberta Shepherd.)

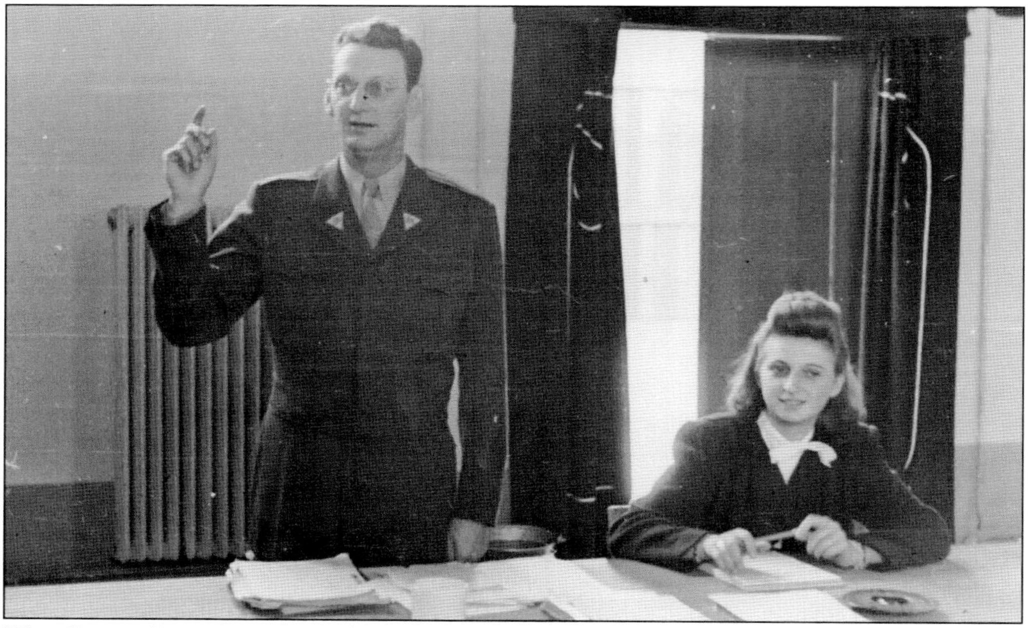

WAR CRIMES PROSECUTIONS. After World War II, William O. Miller (1914–1986) of Johnsville and Bradford was appointed to serve as an investigator at the Nuremberg war crime trials. Weeks later, he was assigned to act as one of 50 multinational lawyers at the Dachau trials in Germany. Miller was prosecuting attorney in several cases and obtained a high rate of death sentences. (Courtesy of William E. Miller.)

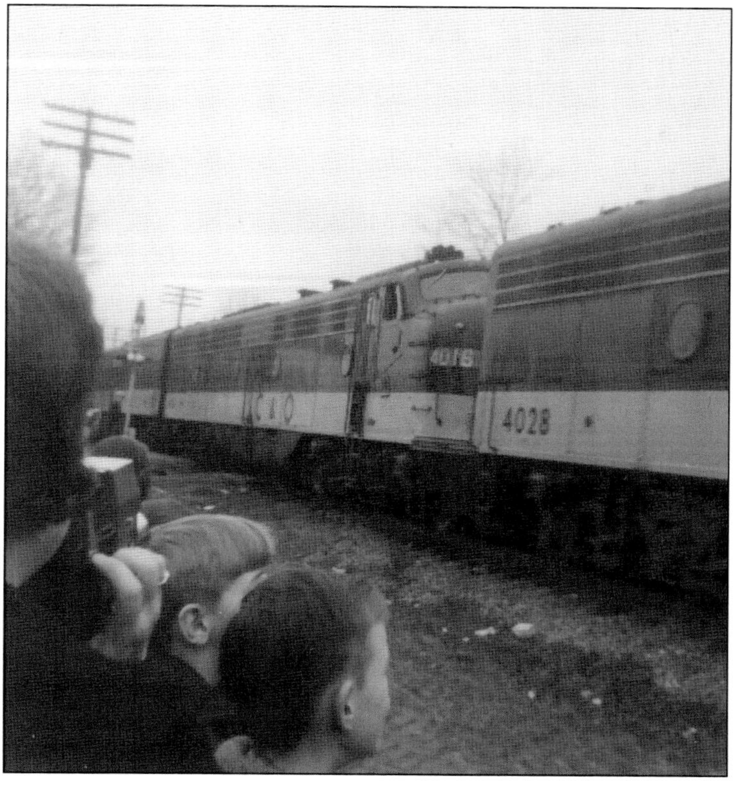

EISENHOWER'S FUNERAL TRAIN. On a chilly April day in 1969, hundreds of Bracken County residents assembled on Third Street in Augusta to pay respect to a former general of World War II, Pres. Dwight D. Eisenhower. His body was aboard this train traveling to Abilene, Kansas, in a flag-draped coffin. (Courtesy of Roberta Shepherd.)

Four

Farms and Industries Identified Residents

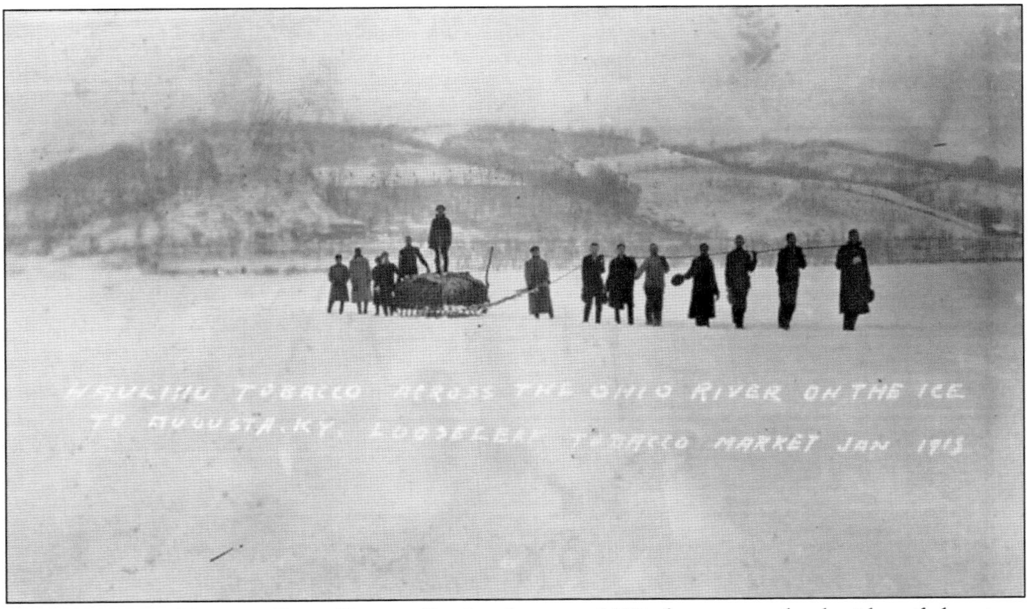

Men Crossing Frozen Ohio River. During January 1918, farmers on both sides of the river took advantage of the frozen ice. This postcard shows several men hauling tobacco loaded on a sled crossing the river. They were taking the loose-leaf tobacco to one of the markets in Augusta for sale. There are several similar pictures taken of the frozen river in 1918. Perhaps this could be attributed to local professional photographers having offices in Augusta. Certainly the Ohio River froze over several times each decade, but the numerous postcard images taken that year must have pointed to an extreme depth of the ice—to the extent that several thousand pounds of livestock were able to be driven over the river. (Courtesy of Pat Feagan.)

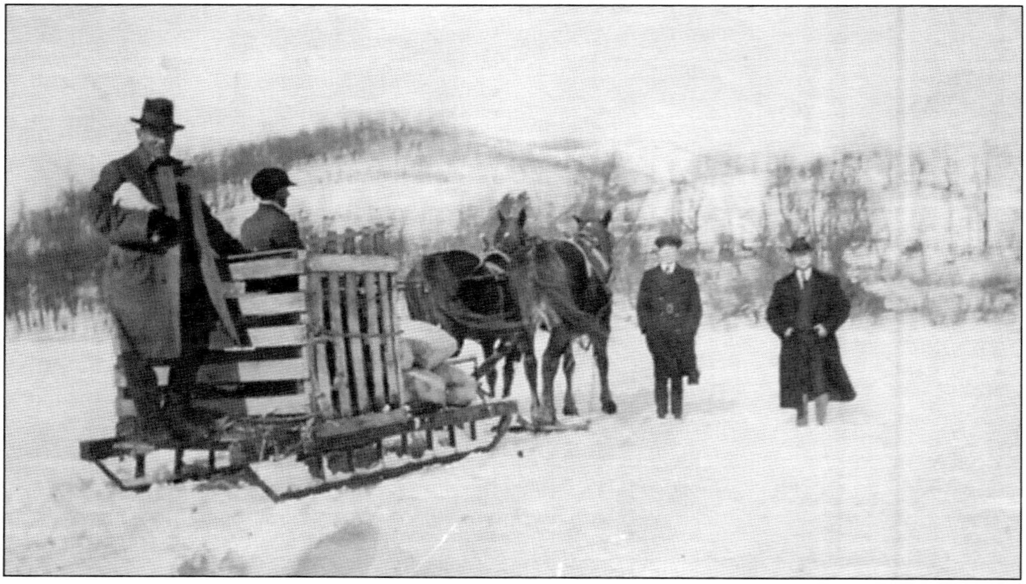

LIVESTOCK HERDED ACROSS ICE. These scenes on the frozen Ohio River at Augusta were captured in January 1918. The Ohio River has only frozen across once during modern history in this area. The men on the sled with produce are unknown, but the two men on the ice are, from left to right, Gaylord Morris and Lewis Wolfe. The photograph below illustrates the dangerous but necessary mission of delivering livestock on frozen water. The men were using staffs or tobacco sticks to herd hogs toward the bank for market or another farm. (Above, courtesy of Bernie Spencer; below, courtesy of Bob Adams.)

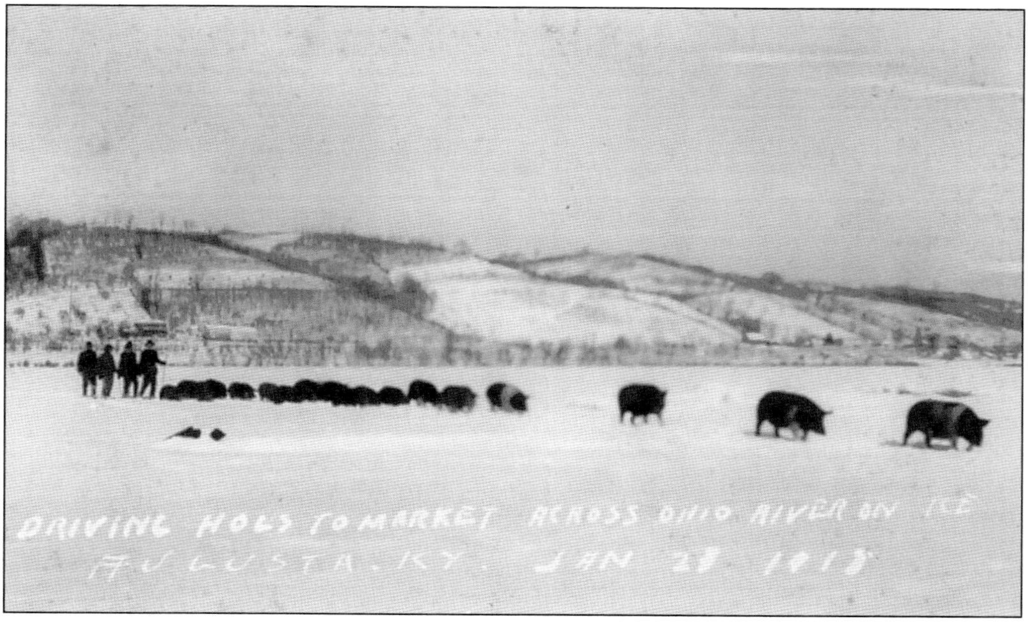

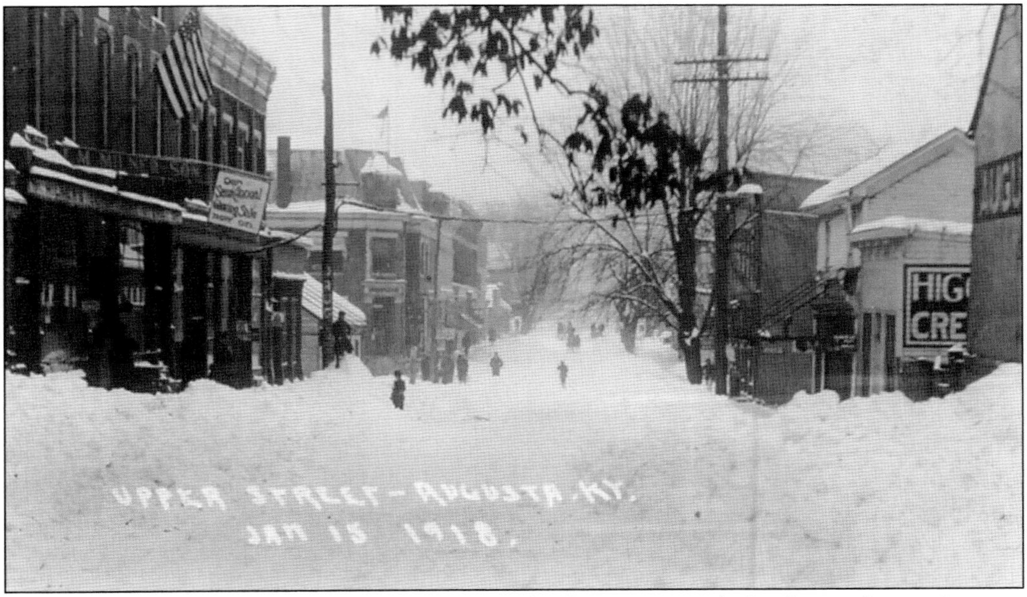

Record Snow Fall in Augusta. This photograph of a winter wonderland was taken on January 15, 1918, in what must have been a record snowfall. Upper Street of Augusta is covered in several feet of snow, making travel nearly impossible. Other record snows did not occur in the county until 1950, then again in January and February 1979. (Courtesy of Marilyn Bryant.)

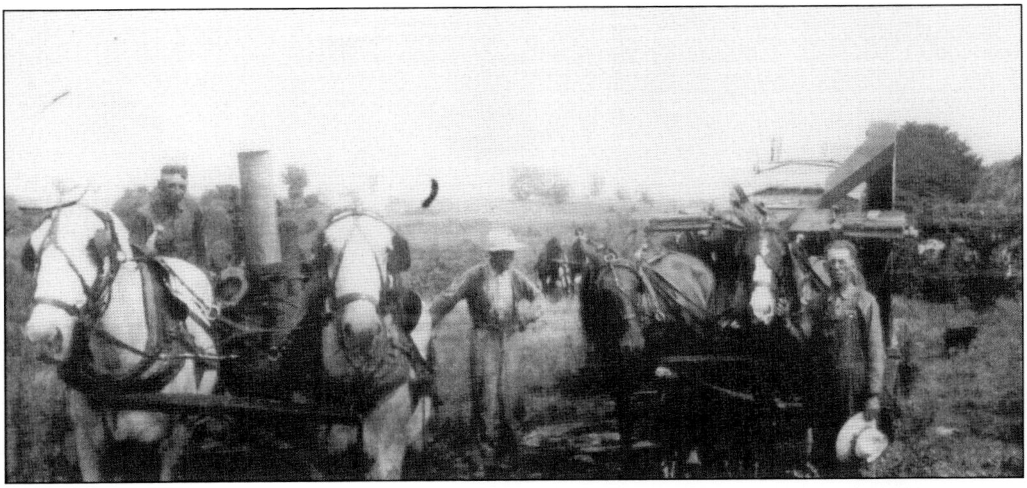

Horsepower. Three teams of horses were being used to draw wheat harvesters in the Germantown area. The unidentified farmer in the center seems to be giving directions to the driver of the horses. It took hours, if not days, to clear the fields and take the grain to the local mill. (Courtesy of John H. Henderson.)

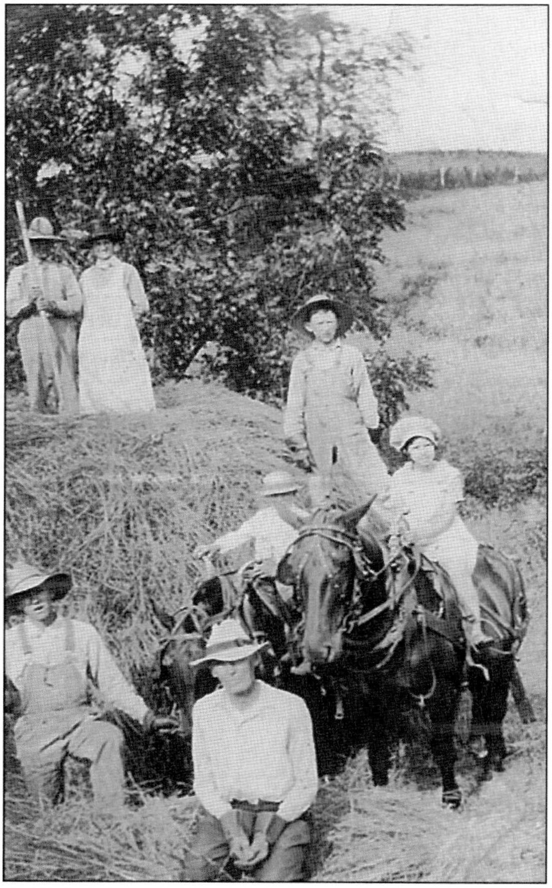

Wilson Family Harvests Crops. Several of the Wilson and Reese families were involved with stacking hay on Hook and Gillespie Lanes east of Chatham. Young brothers Charles and Steve Wilson are leading two horses in the early 1940s picture below. With Charles holding the reins, the wagonload of tobacco was carefully driven to the barn to be unloaded and hung on wooden tier rails. The wagons moved on wooden wheels, which made for a bumpy ride over tobacco stalks and ruts. Utmost control over the horses had to be maintained so that the load did not slip onto the dusty ground. Tobacco was "cash in the bank," as proceeds from the crop paid farm mortgages, college loans, and household bills for the majority of Bracken County farmers. The entire economy of the county was dependent upon the sale of tobacco or its related industries. (Both, courtesy of Charles Wilson.)

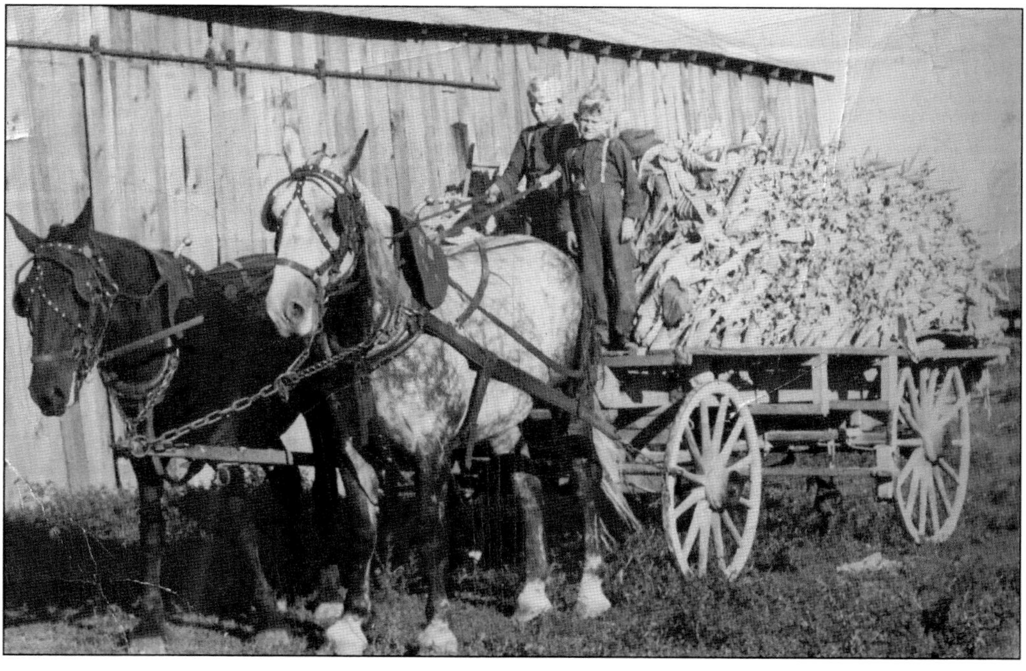

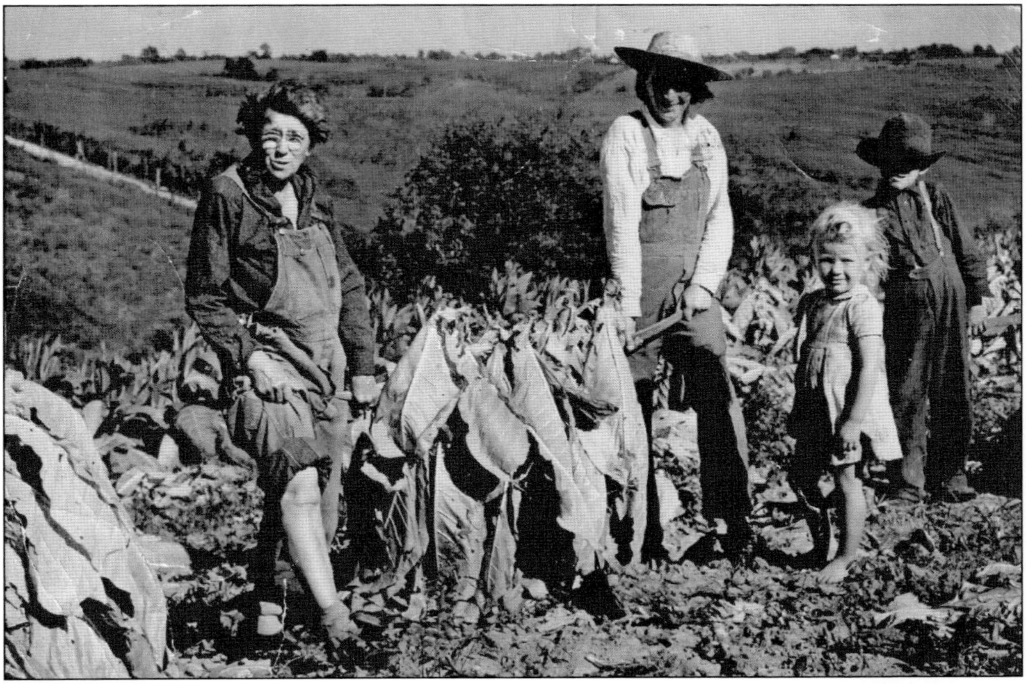

Tobacco, the County's Major Crop. All family members usually reported to the fields to help in some small way. The children pictured here are Steve and Norma Wilson, who were playing in loose dirt, perhaps picking up some leaf remnants, which were not to be wasted. To the right is their mother, Dorothy Wilson, and on the left is Leona Reese. (Courtesy of Charles and Alberta Wilson.)

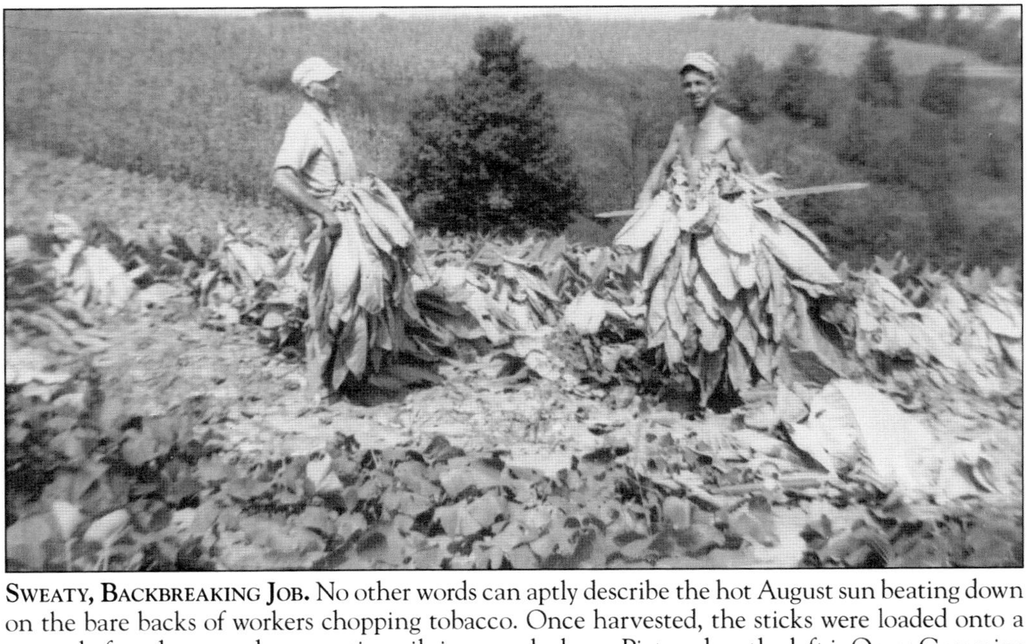

Sweaty, Backbreaking Job. No other words can aptly describe the hot August sun beating down on the bare backs of workers chopping tobacco. Once harvested, the sticks were loaded onto a wagon before they were hung on tier rails in a nearby barn. Pictured on the left is Omar Cummins at his farm in Gertrude during 1950. The tobacco cutter on the right is Omar's son-in-law, John Ivan Hutchison. (Courtesy of Greg Cummins.)

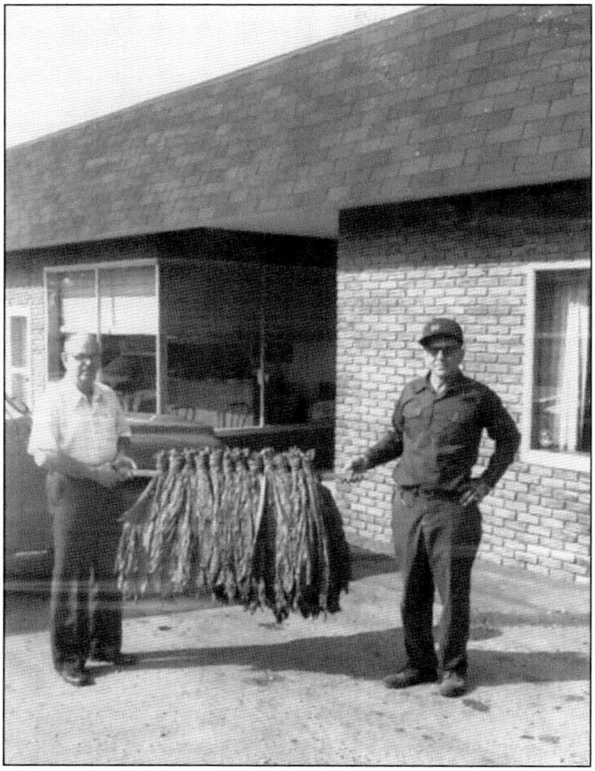

Display of Tobacco Hands. Standing next to the *Bracken County News* office are two Brooksville men holding a tobacco stick filled with hands of cured tobacco. Once tobacco leaves were stripped from the stalks, they were held gathered together until a "hand" could be filled. The hand was tied by a moist leaf, which would hold the leaves together while on the stick. (Courtesy of *Bracken County News.*)

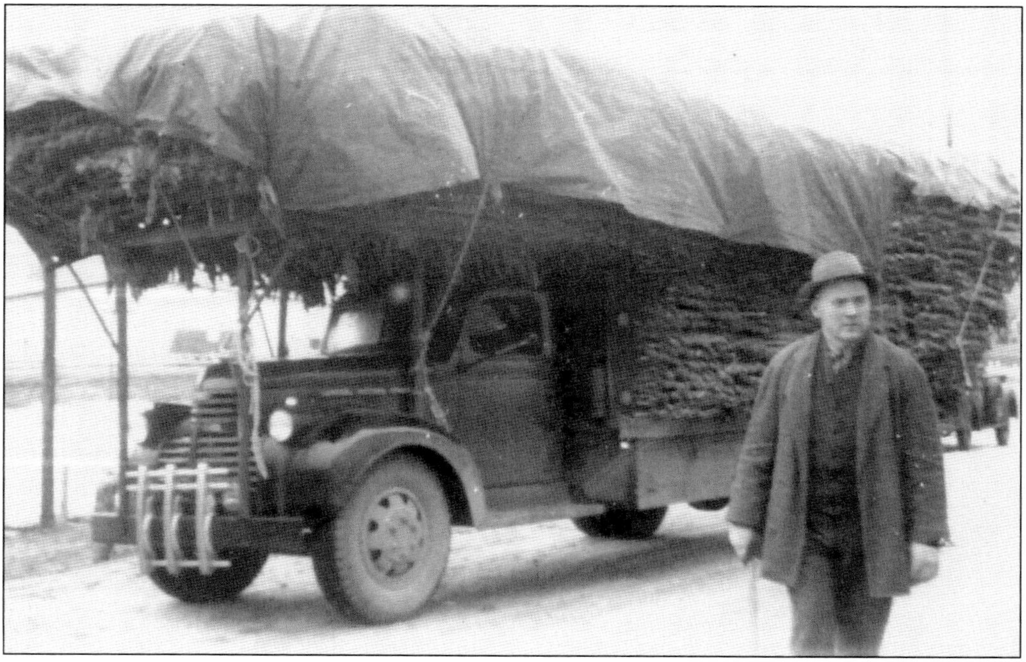

Tobacco Truck. John Flanigan is pictured next to his heavily loaded truck, hauling 16,000 pounds of hands of tobacco that had been pressed to shrink the size but not the weight. Farmers were paid for their tobacco based on the number of pounds and grade of the leaves. (Courtesy of Carol Wallin Boney.)

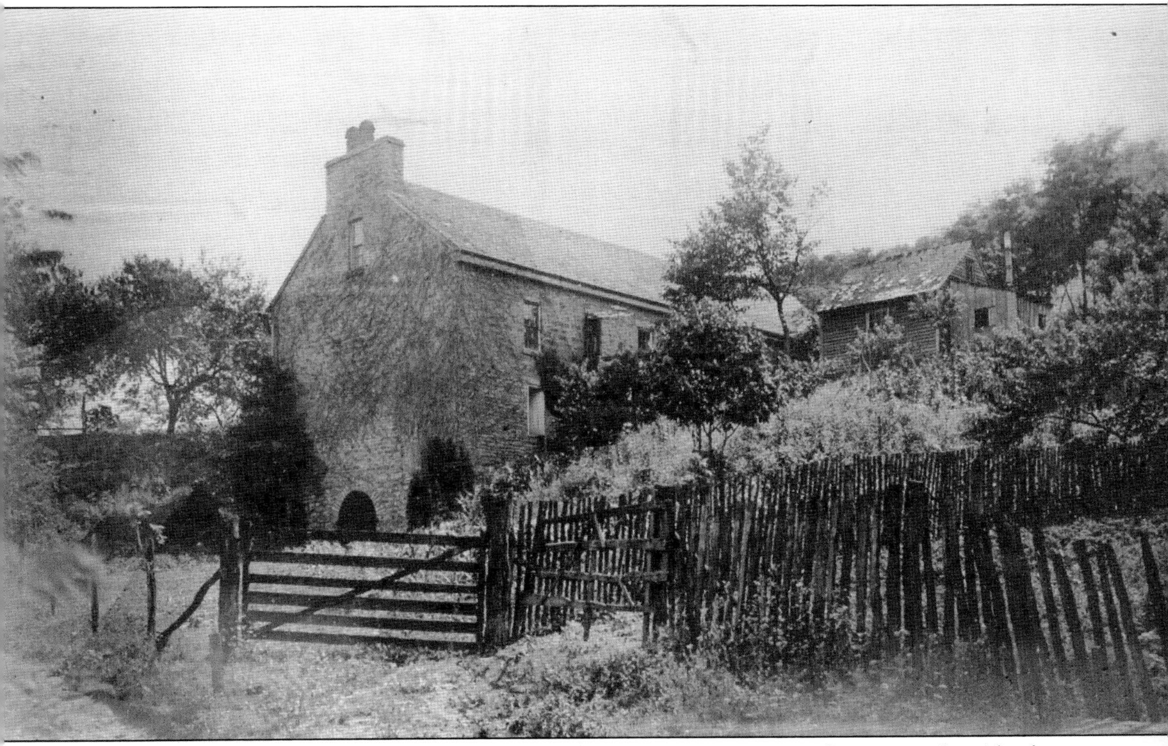

BAKER, BRADFORD, AND BANDEL WINERIES. In the 1850s, construction began on the Abraham Baker wine cellar near the intersection of Kentucky Routes 19 and 8 on Augusta's eastern edge. Previously, Baker had set out grapevines on the hills above Augusta with the help of several Germans who immigrated to Bracken County to engage in vine dressing. These vinedressers, Constantine, Schweitzer, Federer, Weitlauf, and Steifvater, also supervised the crew as they cut the massive stones to erect the 26-foot-tall by 104-foot-long cellar. The reported cost of the cellar was $22,000, which would have been higher except that slave labor was used in the construction. Other wine cellars in or near Augusta were owned by Laban Bradford and August Bandel. These businesses were quite profitable in the 1870s, and Bracken County became the leading wine-producing county in the United States. Around 1880, Blight infected the vines and soil, making the vines useless for the next century. Recently, Dinah Bird-Westerfield purchased the Abraham Baker cellar to begin the preservation and restoration of this unique winery. (Courtesy of Bernie Spencer.)

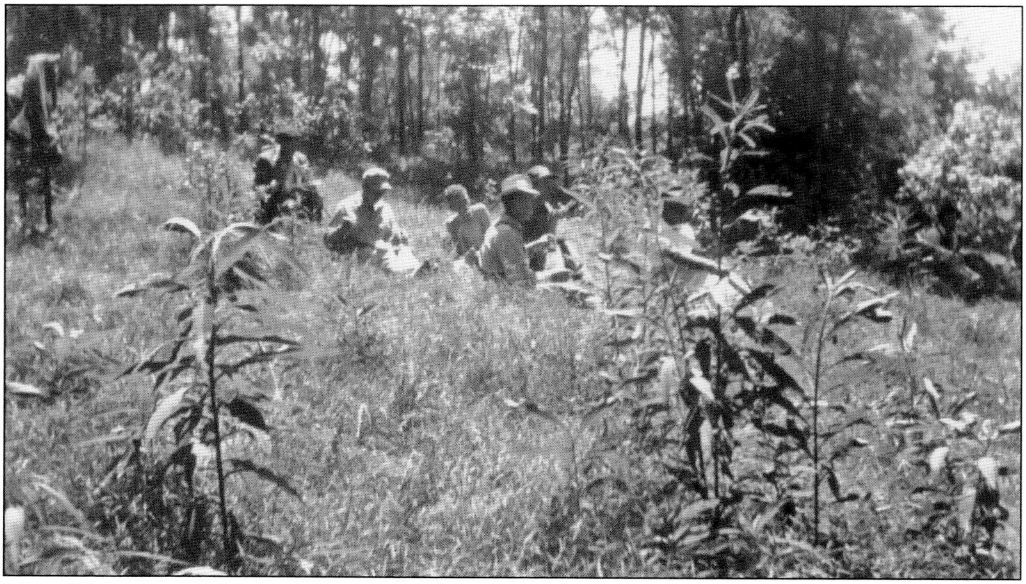

Men Working in Hemp Field. Growing hemp as a cash crop was quite common in Bracken County and surrounding areas until the late 1940s. Hemp was harvested and sent to market, perhaps in nearby Maysville, where it would be stored until shipment. The government was in the market for hemp seeds, which the men appear to be gathering in their sacks above. (Courtesy of Carol Wallin Boney.)

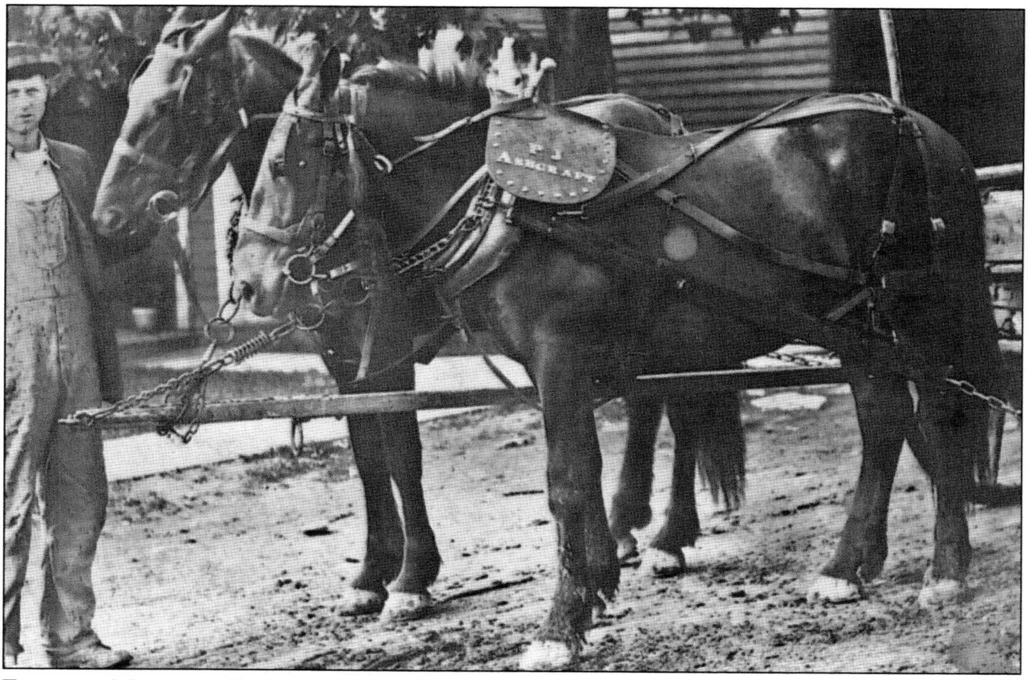

Farming Methods Changed with Technology. Jett Ashcraft and his mules (one named Beck) are delivering a heavy load of farm supplies in the only manner that Ashcraft had access to in the early 1900s. Farm implements were usually made of wood with few metal parts, causing quick deterioration. Mules, horses, and oxen were well maintained, as they were considered quite valuable on the farm. (Courtesy of Pat Feagan.)

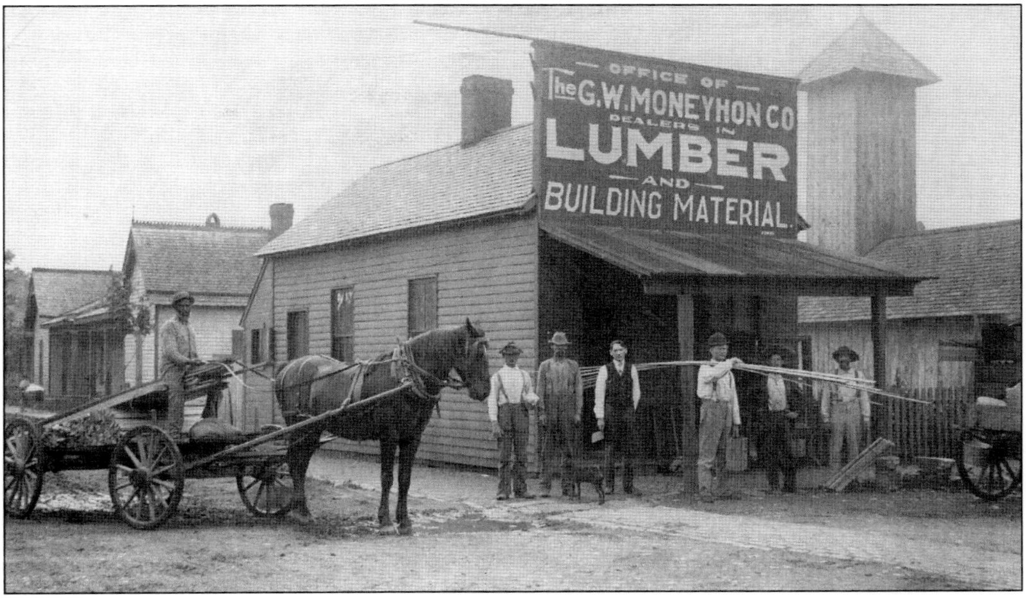

G. W. Moneyhon, Lumber Dealer. Moneyhon constructed this office building when he founded a lumber business around 1862. According to writing on the picture, they men are, from left to right, Sam Berry (guiding the horse, Frank), Frank Fields, ? Kiskaden, Frank Moneyhon, William Nash, Jeffrey White, and John Owens. This photograph holds the honor of appearing as the front cover on the 100th-anniversary edition of the *Kentucky Building Materials Association* journal. (Courtesy of William E. Miller.)

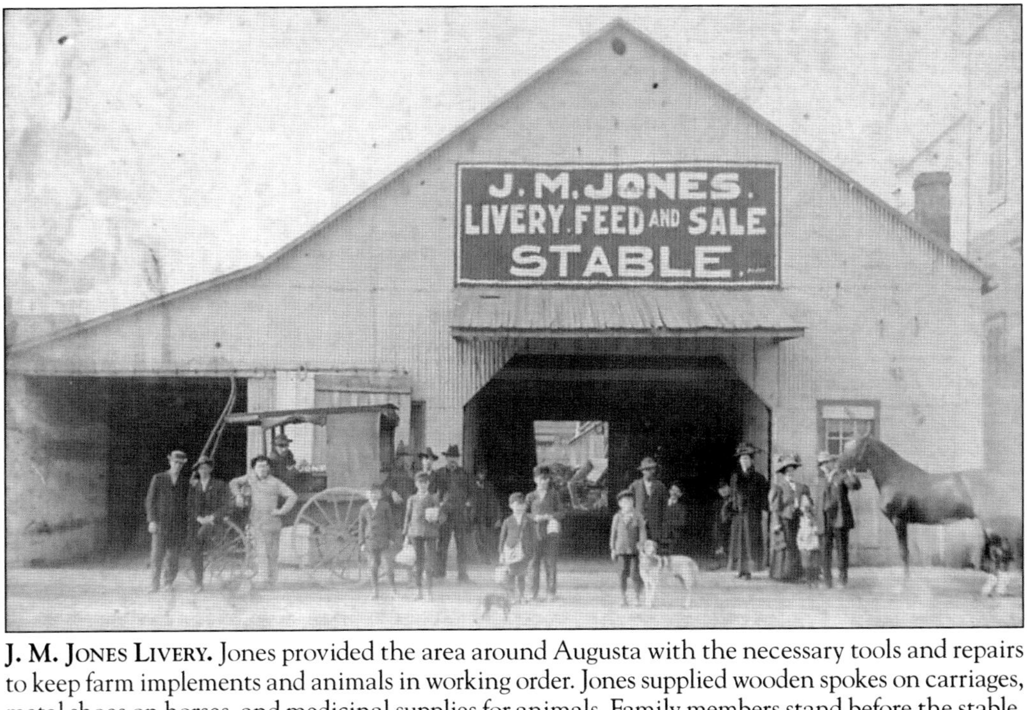

J. M. Jones Livery. Jones provided the area around Augusta with the necessary tools and repairs to keep farm implements and animals in working order. Jones supplied wooden spokes on carriages, metal shoes on horses, and medicinal supplies for animals. Family members stand before the stable, perhaps for a special occasion or simply to pose for this early-1900s family portrait. (Courtesy of Greg Cummins.)

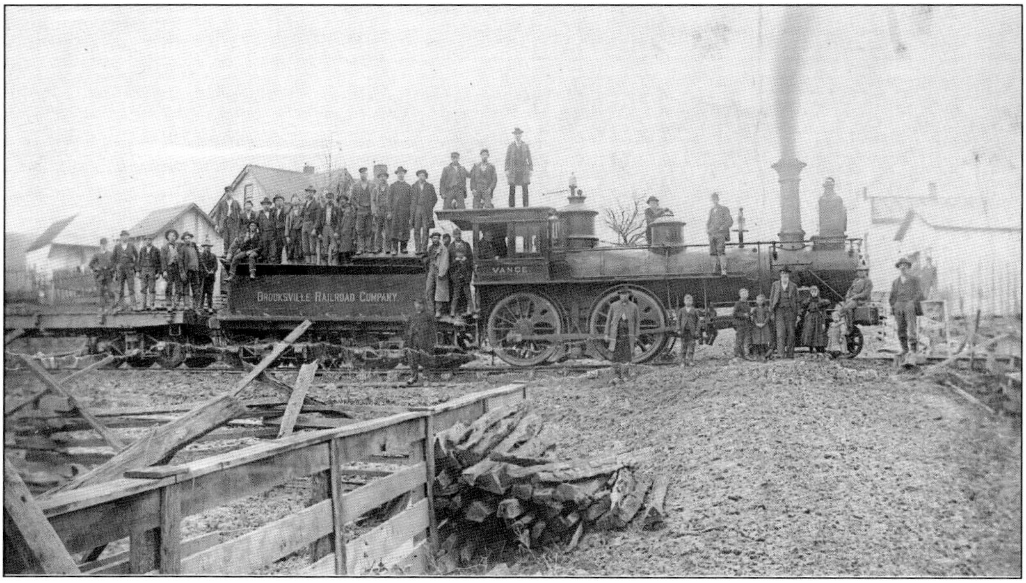

THE SOUNDS OF "BIG WINDY." For several decades, farmers between Wellsburg and Brooksville could hear shrill sounds echoing from the large brass whistle of Big Windy. The train was put into operation in June 1897 and incorporated as Cincinnati and Licking River Railroad Company. The depot was located below Brooksville High School near the old Brooksville Lumber. (Courtesy of John H. Henderson.)

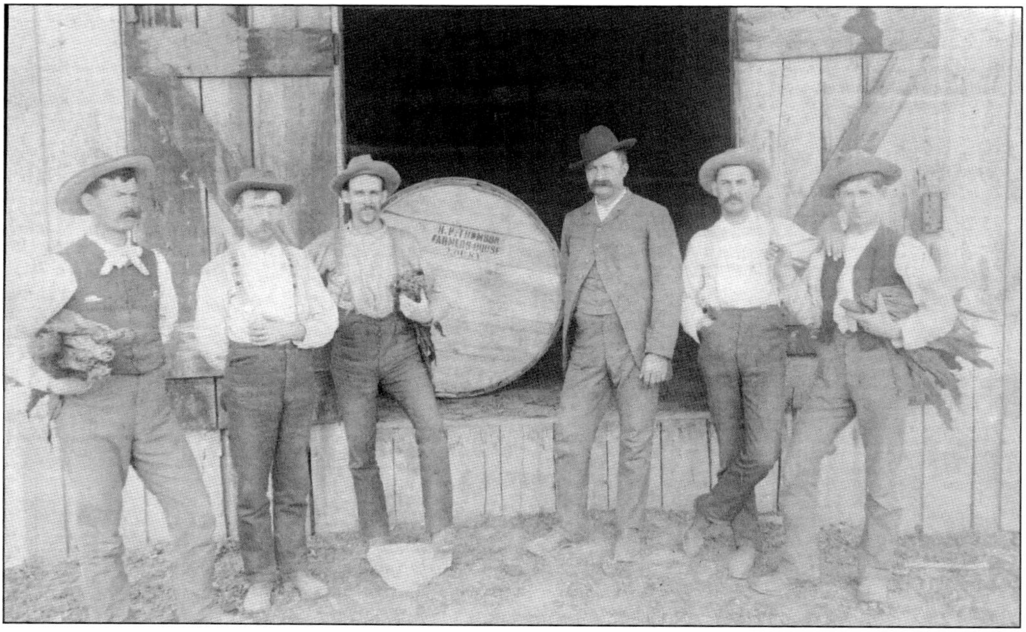

MILFORD TOBACCO WAREHOUSE. The large tobacco warehouse at Milford and unidentified tobacco farmers are seen in this early photograph from the 1900s The hands of tobacco being held under the arms of a worker reflect the appearance of tobacco before it was pressed. Once the baskets filled with leaves of reds, brights, lugs, trash, flyings, and tips were delivered, the tobacco was priced according to weight and grade. (Courtesy of Ruby LaMonda.)

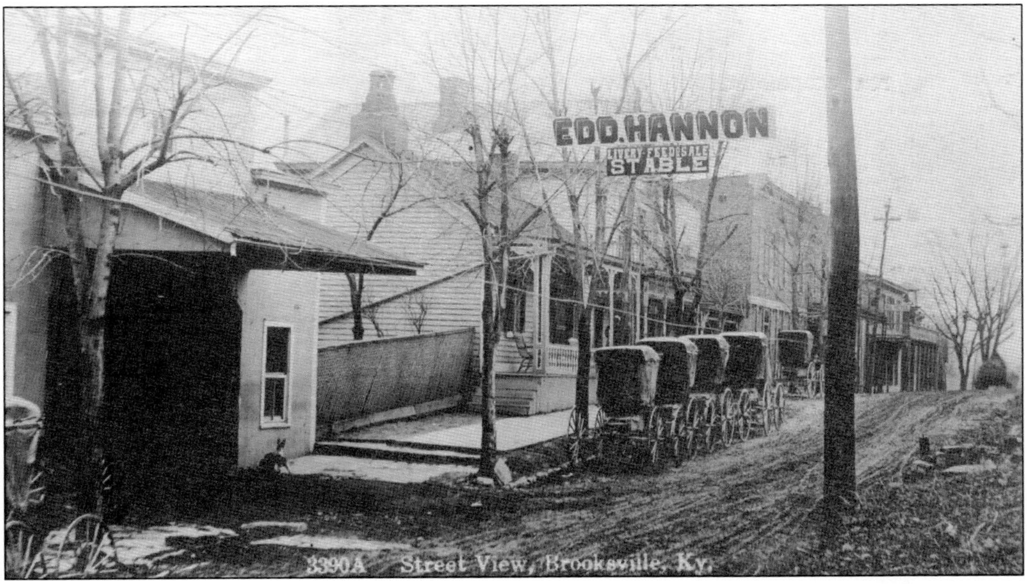

Edd Hannon's Livery Stable. In this photograph from the early 1900s, buggies line Miami Street in Brooksville. Shown on the north side of the street was Edd Hannon's Stable, where the carriage horses were shoed or feed. Hannon also sold tinctures and balms for horses that might be lame. (Courtesy of John H. Henderson.)

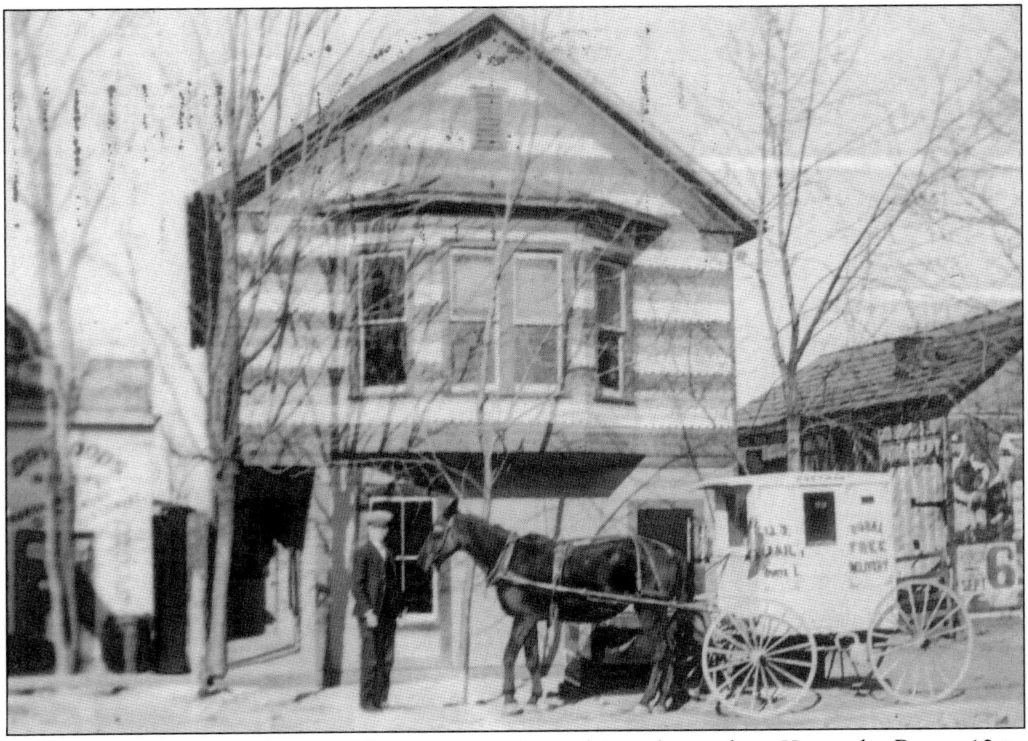

Germantown's Post Office. This two-story log cabin is located on Kentucky Route 10 in Germantown; however, it is covered with siding. The cabin served for many years as the post office for the town and area farmers. In front of the cabin is a stagecoach, which may have just delivered the mail. The log cabin has been converted into a residence. (Courtesy of John H. Henderson.)

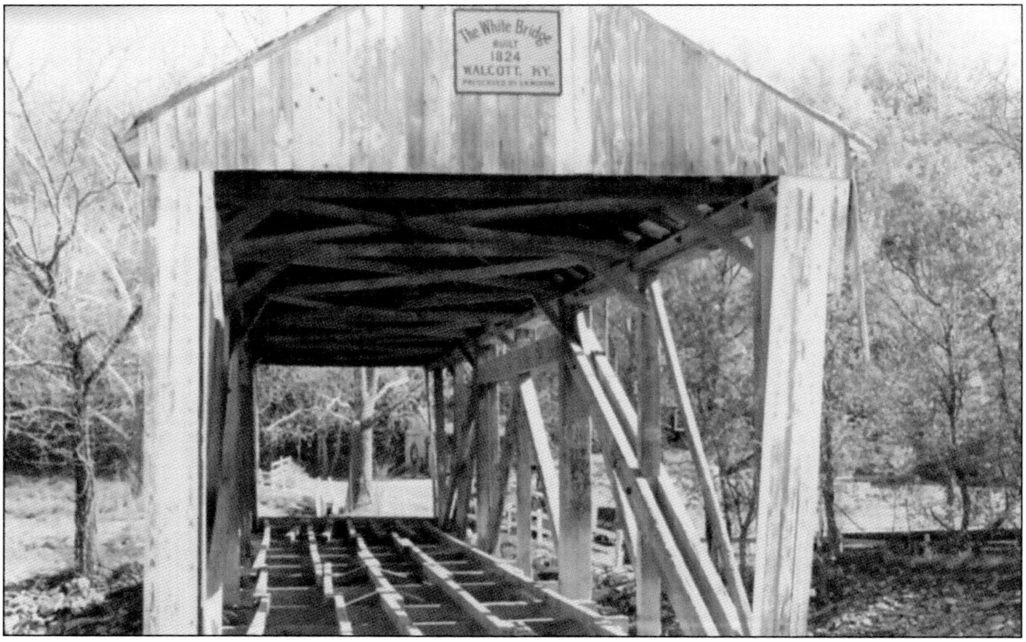

Walcott Covered Bridge. This bridge, situated over Locust Creek, is one a few remaining in Kentucky. This original portion of the bridge was constructed in 1824 at Walcott and maintained by the Murray family. Shown above is a late 1990s photograph of the bridge as it was being dismantled, revealing the king and queen post–style trusses spanning 74 feet across Locust Creek. (Courtesy of Bracken County Historical Society.)

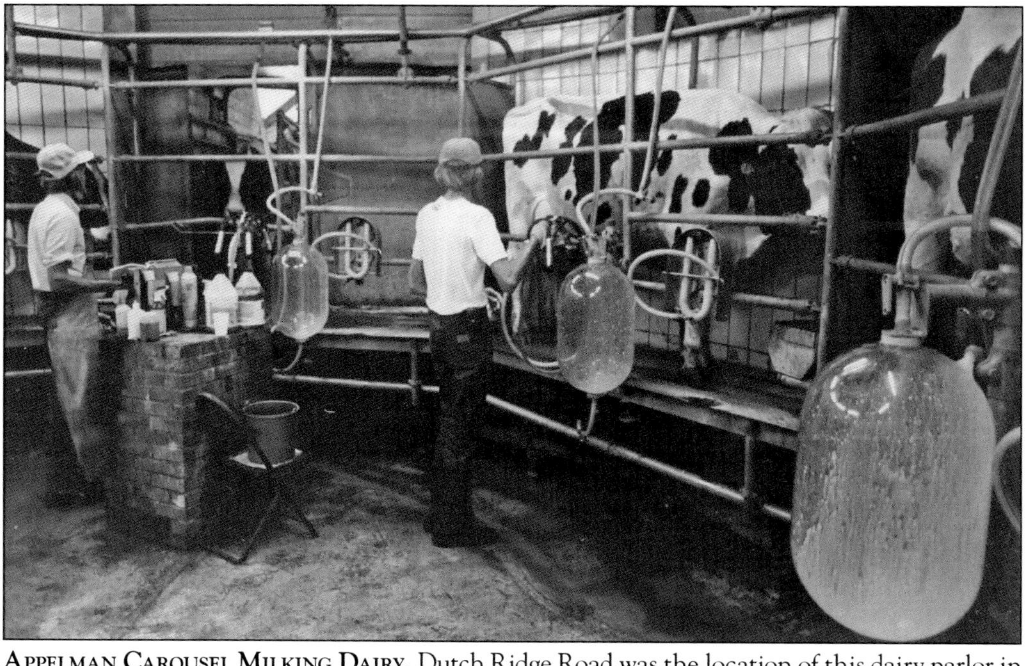

Appelman Carousel Milking Dairy. Dutch Ridge Road was the location of this dairy parlor in 1973. Shown operating the carousel equipment are brothers Bob and Ted Appelman. Although no longer in the dairy business, the Appelman family continues to raise tobacco and explore other products that benefit the farm industry. (Courtesy of Bob and Jane Appelman.)

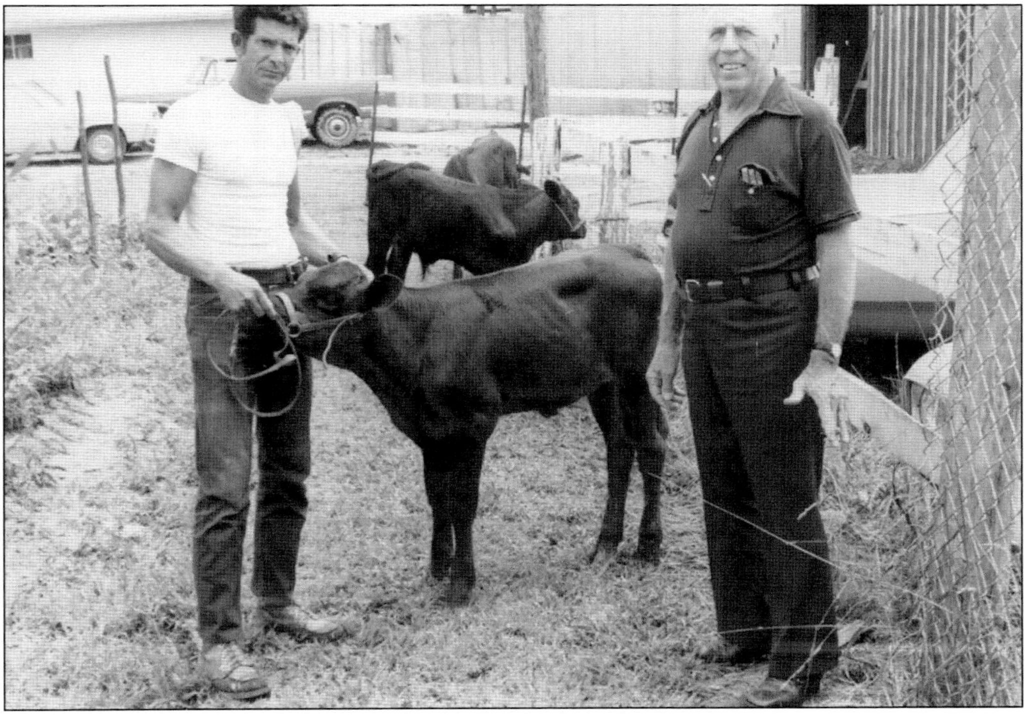

Heifers and Herefords. Tom Cline holds the halter of a young heifer as Lytle Maloney examines his young cows for possible sale. In the 1960s, Maloney owned hundreds of acres along the Ohio River, along with the family farm, Fantasia, on Asbury Road near Germantown. Cline was a young farmer who was responsible for the large herd. Pictured below is the Brook Dale Farm, where Adam Kalb and his son Robert ran a dairy and, later, a fruit stand. The Kalbs were quite proud of their Hereford cows and delivered the milk and cream to several towns in the county. (Above, courtesy of *Bracken County News*; below, courtesy of Jeannine Appleman.)

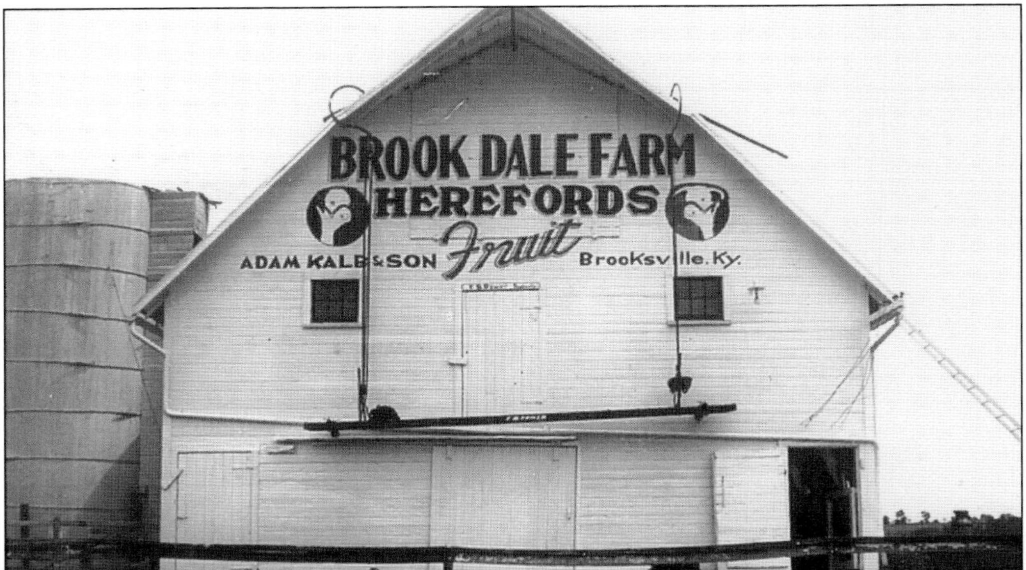

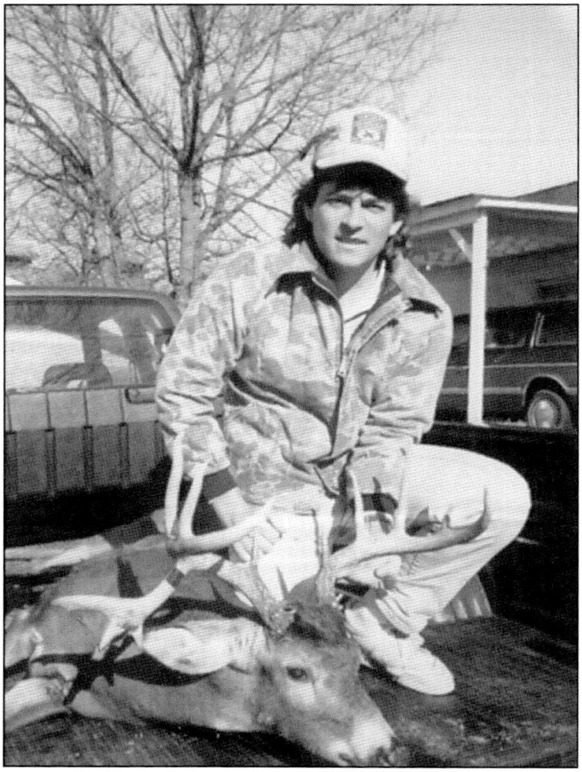

Undomesticated Animals and Predators Cohabit. Mark Litzinger shot this unique whitetail buck in the late 1970s. The number of deer in Kentucky has increased dramatically in the last few decades, and predators have been reintroduced into the county. Below, Richard Norris (left) and David Workman are holding the body of a coyote, taken from a local farm. Coyotes roam the hollows near wooden areas, feeding on small game and rodents. However, they are quite aggressive when hungry or traveling in packs. (Both, courtesy of *Bracken County News.*)

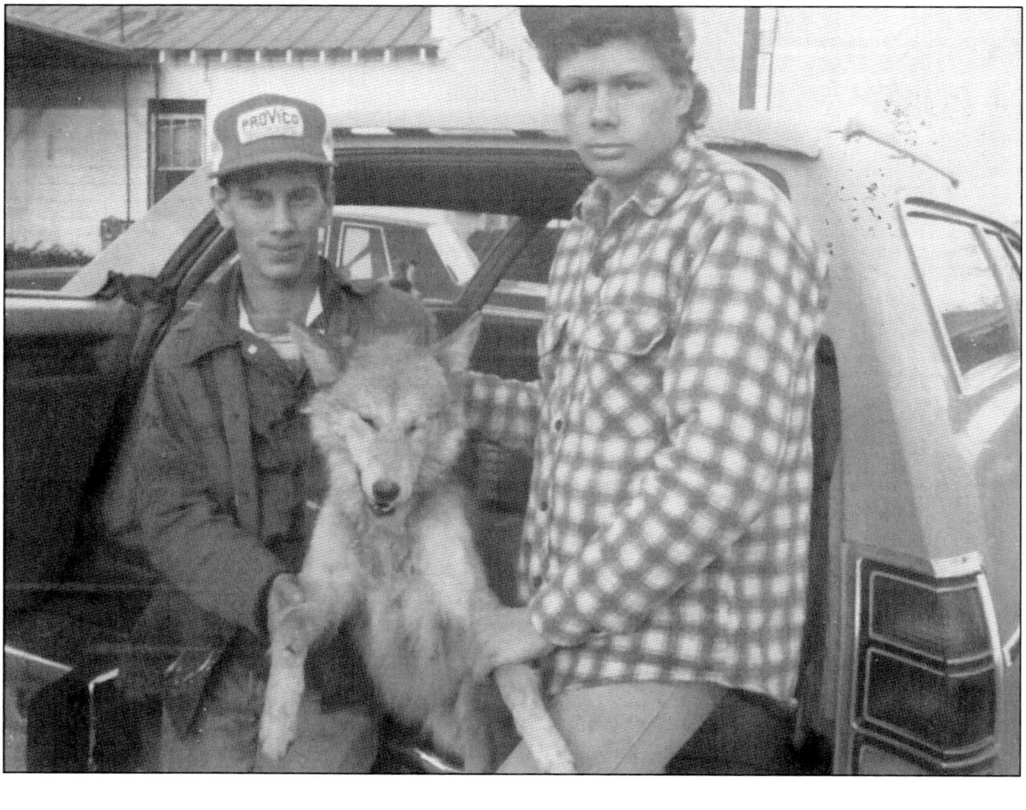

FFA Sponsored Outstanding Young Farmer. This photograph of Donald Bowles (standing on the left) was taken during a national American Farmer convention. In the early 1970s, Bowles accepted a national award and represented the Bracken County Chapter of Future Farmers of America. (Courtesy of *Bracken County News.*)

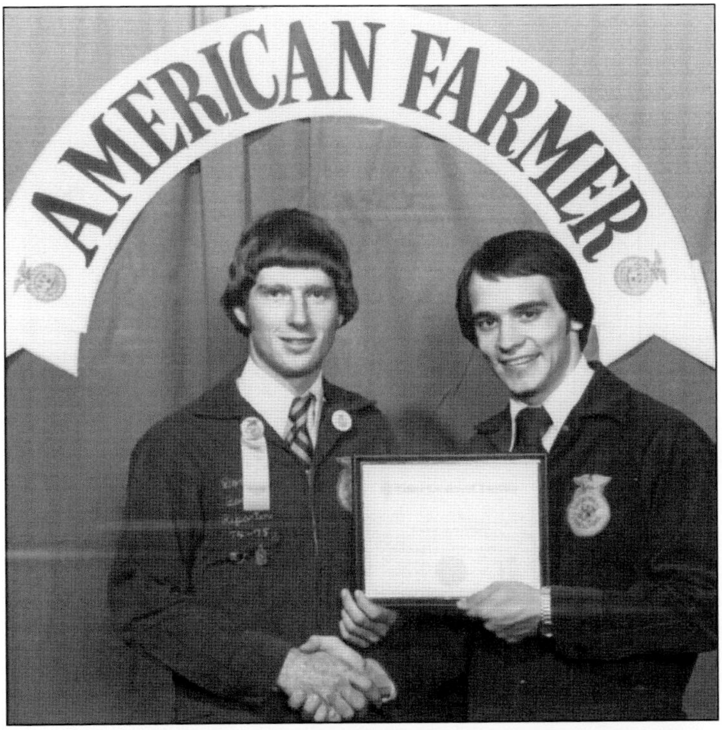

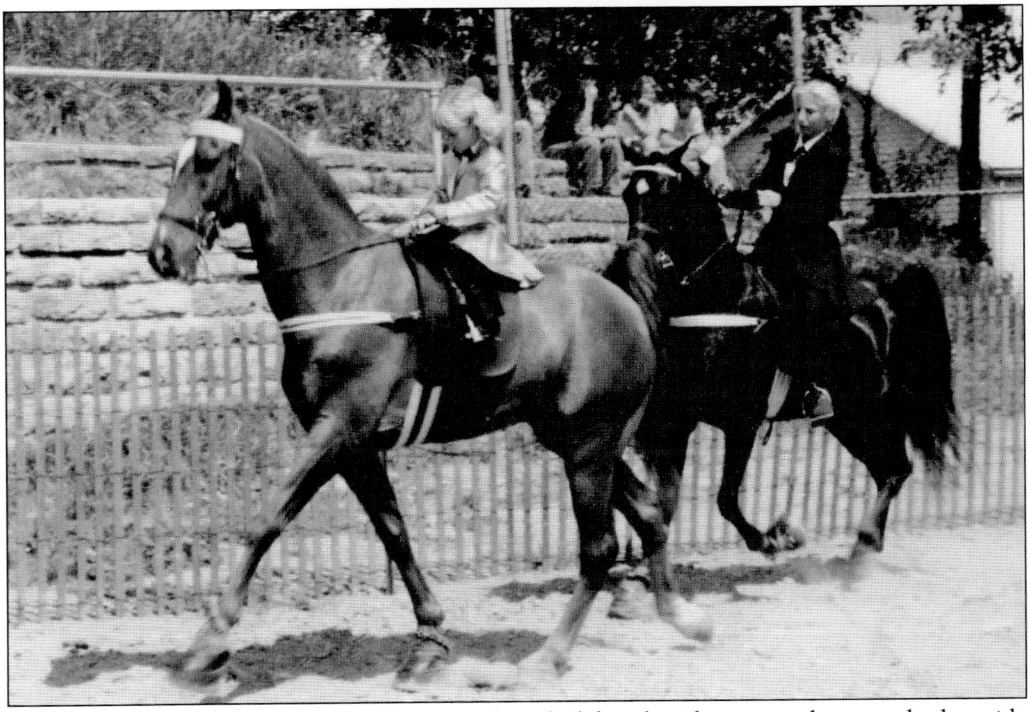

Gaited Horses Stepping High. These unidentified female riders were photographed astride their show horses at the old Brooksville ballpark. The girl appears to be in control of her horse, as the woman behind reins her horse in so not to startle the young rider. (Courtesy of *Bracken County News.*)

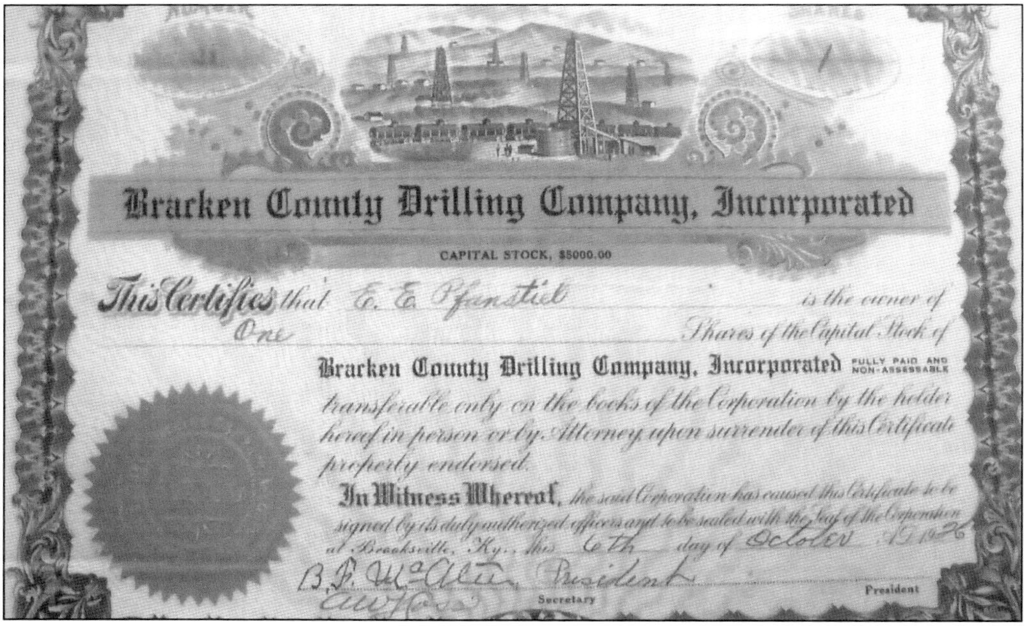

BRACKEN COUNTY DRILLING COMPANY. Everett E. Phanstiel was the owner of this stock certificate revealing that he held one share of capital stock in the Bracken County Drilling Company. According to newspaper records, at least one hole was drilled for natural gas near Chatham. However, the amount measured was not sufficient to warrant further drilling. (Courtesy of Earl Phanstiel.)

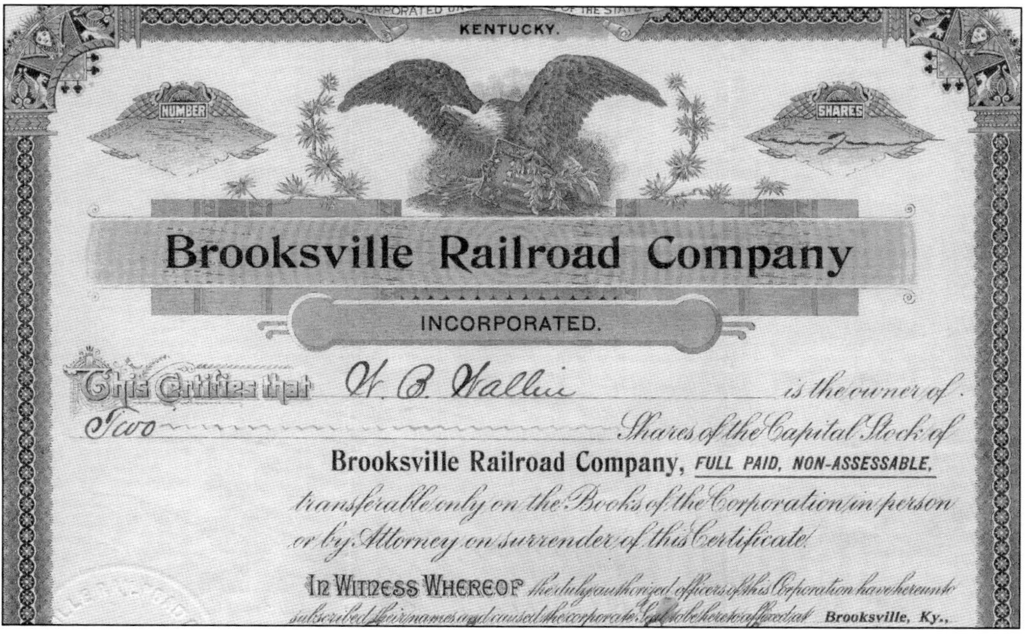

BROOKSVILLE RAILROAD COMPANY STOCK. This share of stock, issued in December 1895, was owned by W. B. Wallin. The Brooksville Railroad Company, known as "Big Windy," ran from Wellsburg on the Ohio River, through the valley to Cumminsville, and up the hill to Brooksville. The old depot was at the bottom of the hill behind Brooksville High School. (Courtesy of John H. Henderson.)

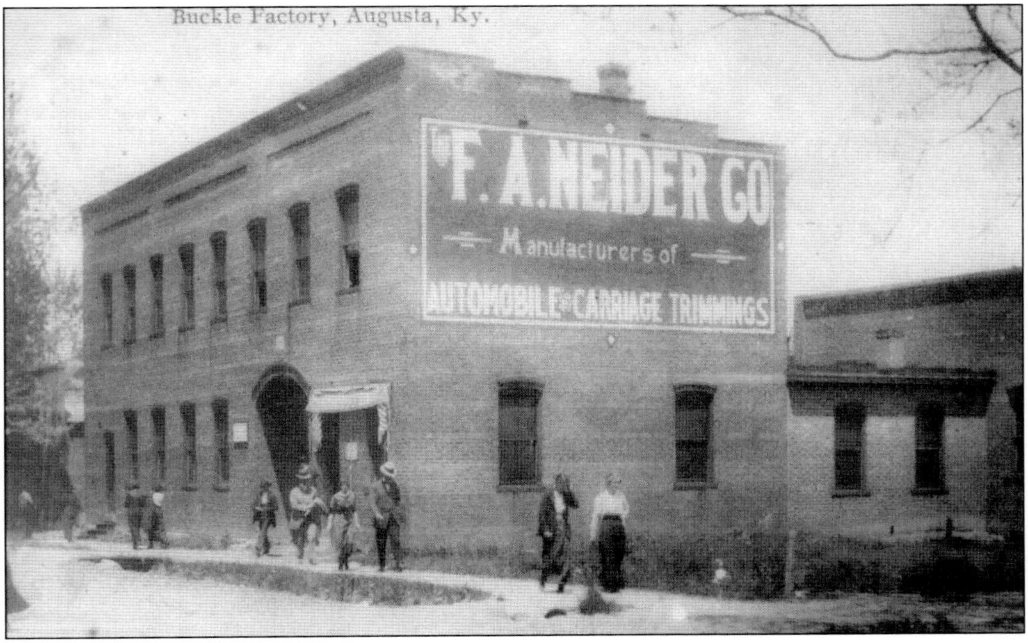

AUGUSTA'S EXCELSIOR HANDLE COMPANY. In 1883, the oldest manufacturing firm in Augusta was established on Seminary Avenue as the Excelsior Handle Company. Within five years, the company was renamed F. A. Neider Auto-Fastener Group. Most of the original items manufactured were related to hardware and trimmings for fine horse-drawn carriages. The company remained under this name for a century, marketing itself in several countries, until AUVECO (Auto Vehicle Company) purchased the building and operations. AUVECO continued to manufacture add-ons for the automotive aftermarket and boat industries. Pictured below in the early 1900s are approximately 36 employees (some appear quite young) and F. A. Neider, seen in the center of the back row near the open door. (Both, courtesy of John White.)

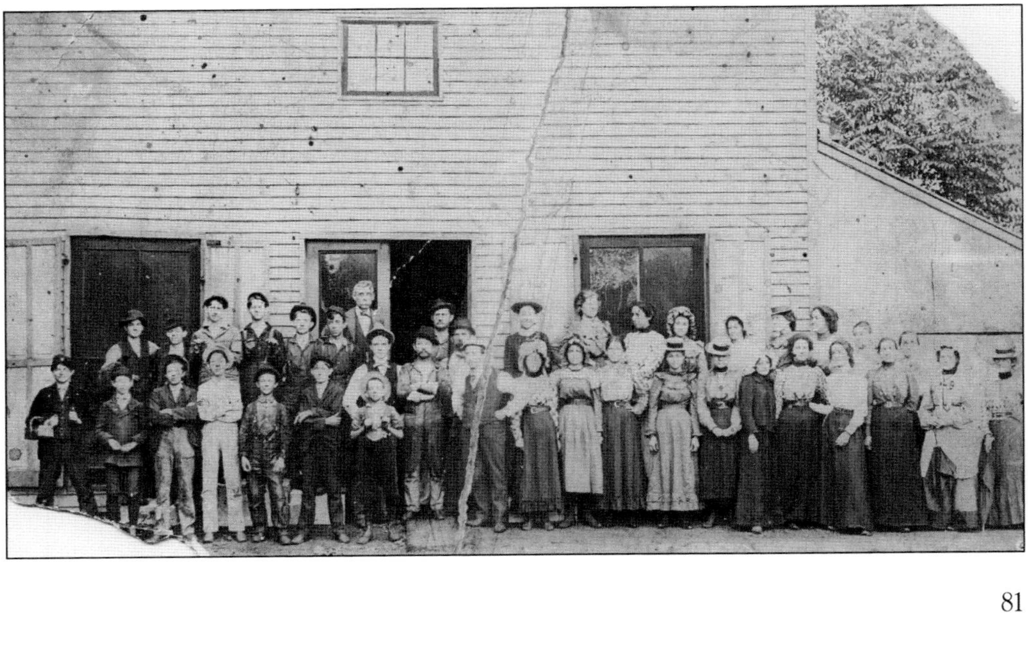

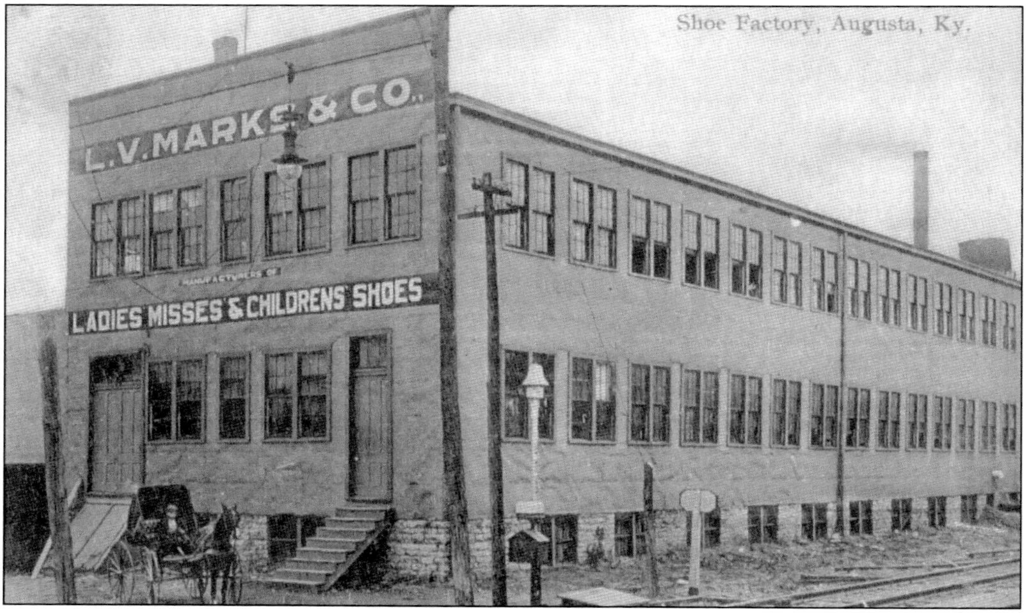

L. V. Marks Manufactured Shoes. L. V. Marks and Company, a manufacturer for several decades in Augusta, was located on Hamilton Avenue and supplied ladies' and children's shoes. C. K. Brown was manager, employing 153 persons who could make 1,000 pairs of shoes daily. On December 22, 1939, a dedication was held for the new addition on East Fourth Street. In 1955, Clopay Plastic Products, now a division of Griffon Industries, purchased the property and opened a plastic product manufacturing company. Below, the Augusta depot, which served the C&O Railroad and presently serves the CSX Railroad, was located at the intersection of North Seminary Avenue and South Third Street. Manufacturing companies in Augusta shipped their goods or obtained raw materials on railcars from throughout the 20th century. As early as 1900, travelers could purchase tickets at this depot and ride the rails across the nation. (Above, courtesy of John White; below, courtesy of Bob Adams.)

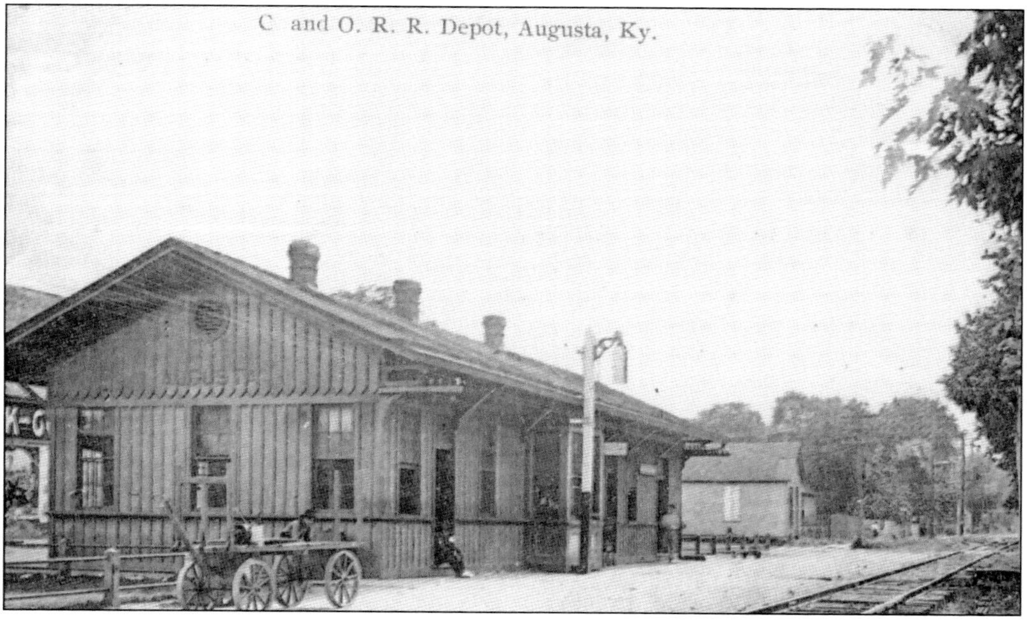

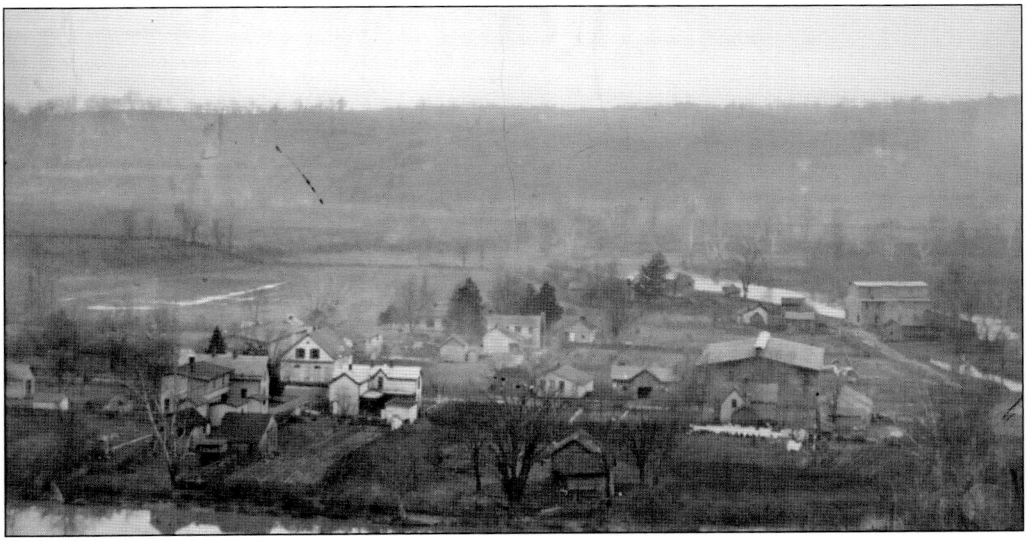

Milford and Sante Fe's Mills. The large mills located in these photographs used waterpower from the nearby North Fork of the Licking River. John Ogdon founded the larger Milford mill in 1831. Corn and wheat were ground to manufacture flour and meal for use in bread making. The product was sifted into cloth grain sacks and sold in stores throughout several counties. The mill in nearby Sante Fe is seen below, revealing the numerous houses and seminary that were once located on the bank of the river. Floods were difficult to contain, practically destroying once-thriving communities. The town of Sante Fe no longer exists. (Both, courtesy of Ruby LaMonda.)

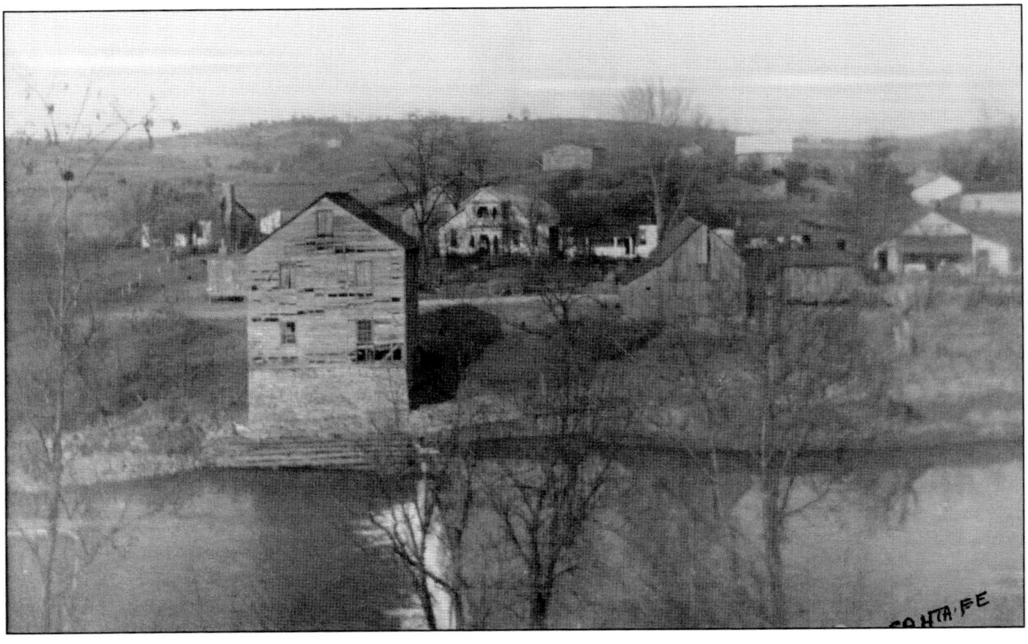

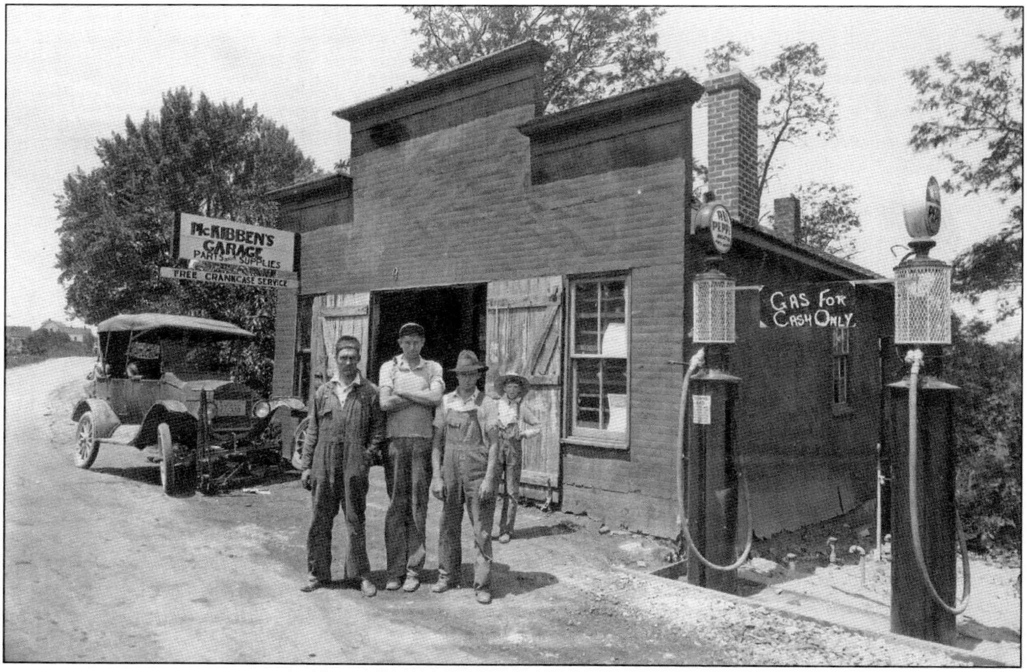

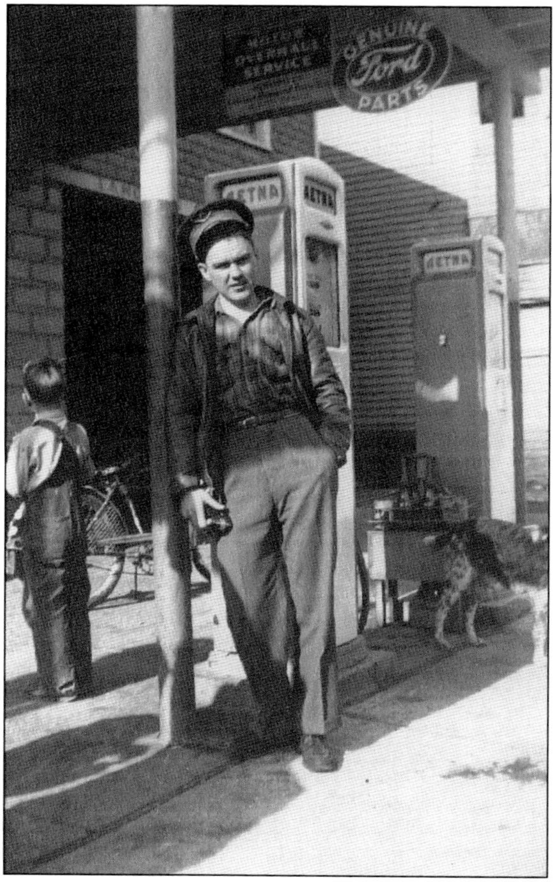

MILFORD'S MCKIBBEN GARAGE. Local men relied on McKibben's Garage for repairs or gas to keep their car running. The writing on the sidewall, "Gas for Cash Only," may have been added to this photograph later, since cash was the usual method of payment. Tom Ogdon, often called "The Great T-Cat-O," is standing in front of his store in the 1950s. (Courtesy of Ruby LaMonda.)

LOUIS LAMONDA'S GARAGE. A drive through Milford reveals a town devastated by floods and fires. One business that thrived since the end of World War II was LaMonda's Garage. Louis LaMonda repaired cars, tractors, and bicycles for over 50 years for county residents. (Courtesy of Ruby LaMonda.)

Germantown Milling Company. A grain milling operation was started in Germantown in 1910, continuing for nearly a century. At one time, Stanley Hill left his father's store and joined the milling company. Within five years, the wooden building burned to the ground, but company owners rebuilt and expanded the company into the area's most recognized distributor of Gilt Edge and Maid o' the Wheat flour. (Courtesy of John H. Henderson.)

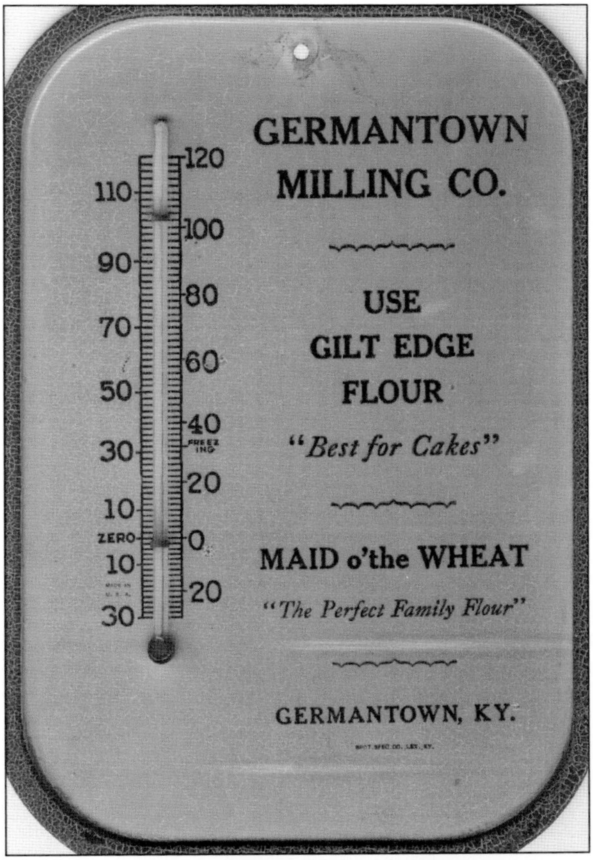

Moransburg School Bus. John M. Henderson Sr. constructed several buses and trucks during his blacksmith career in Germantown. Although his business was destroyed by fire in 1930, Henderson constructed a larger building for his business and White's General Store. This particular bus was purchased by Moransburg School, located near Maysville. These buses required many hours of physical labor. (Courtesy of John H. Henderson.)

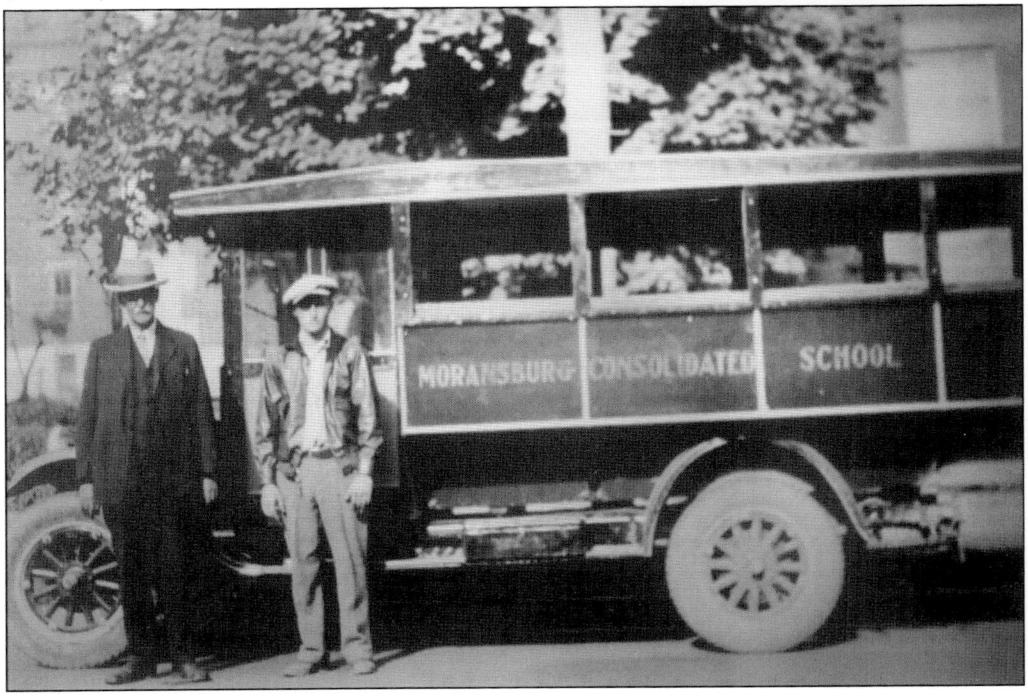

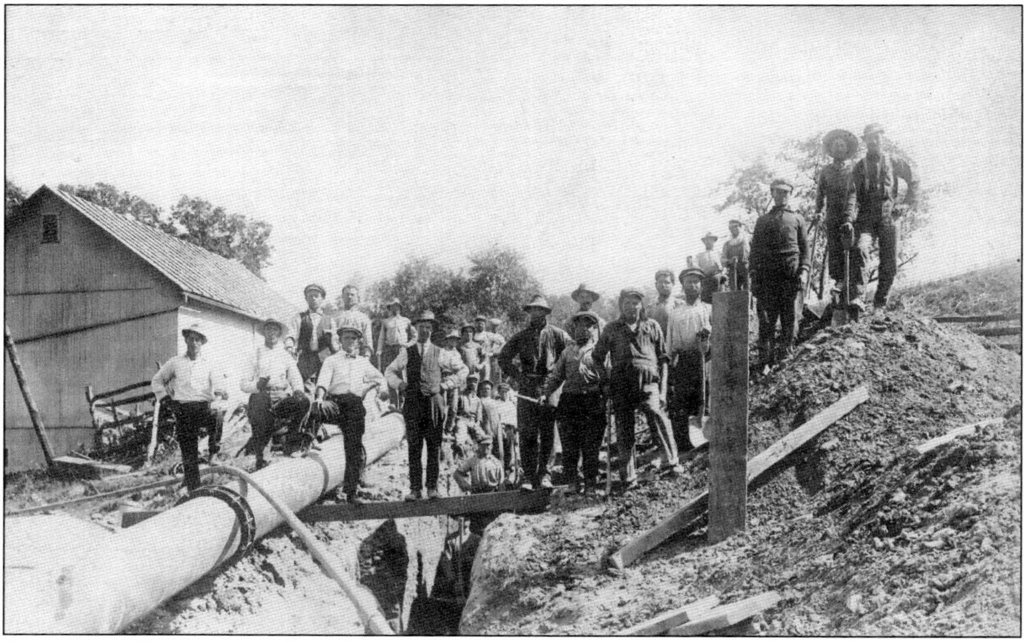

Johnsville Pipe Line. When the water line was being constructed through western Bracken County, a local photographer took this snapshot. There were several men either taking part in the labor or simply curious enough to stand for hours, watching the pipe being connected. (Courtesy of Delores McCane.)

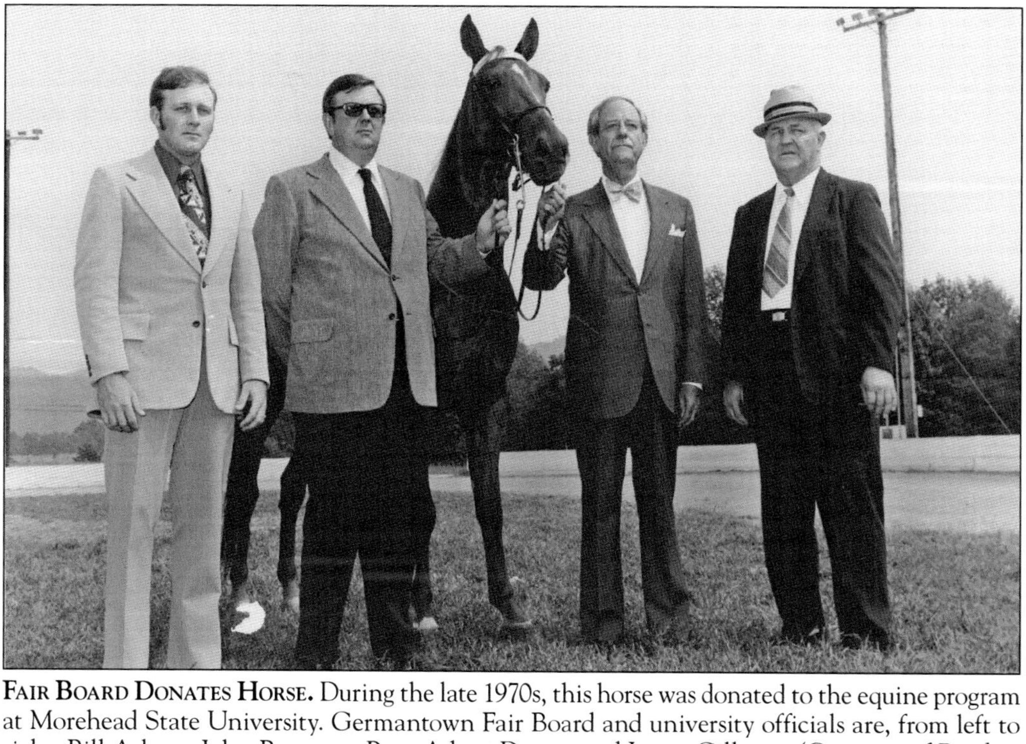

Fair Board Donates Horse. During the late 1970s, this horse was donated to the equine program at Morehead State University. Germantown Fair Board and university officials are, from left to right, Bill Asbury, John Brannen, Pres. Adron Doran, and James Gilligan. (Courtesy of *Bracken County News.*)

Five

Ingenuity Provided Activities

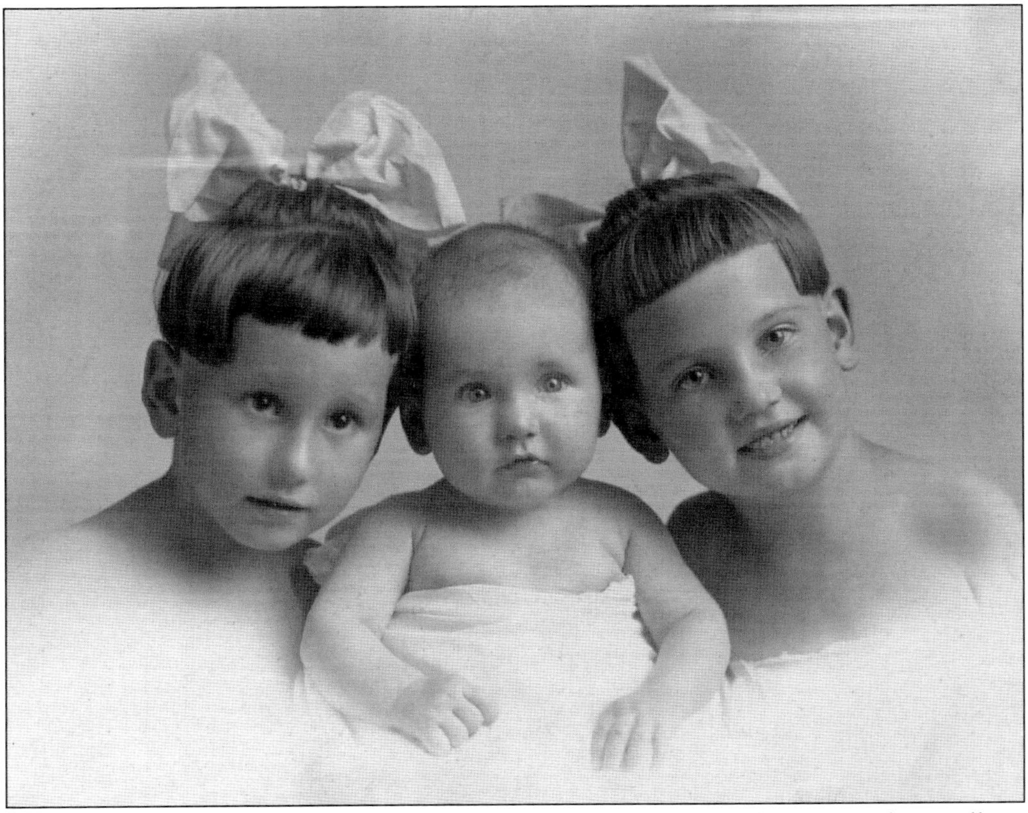

Milliner Styles Children's Hair. In the 1920s, Flossie Cline Weisbrodt was trained as a milliner in Augusta and would later use her skills to make bows for her daughters' hair. The fabric used in the bows was most likely lined with a stiff material or starched to retain its shape. Flossie's children are, from left to right, Louise, Paul, and Mabel Weisbrodt. (Courtesy of John Lenox.)

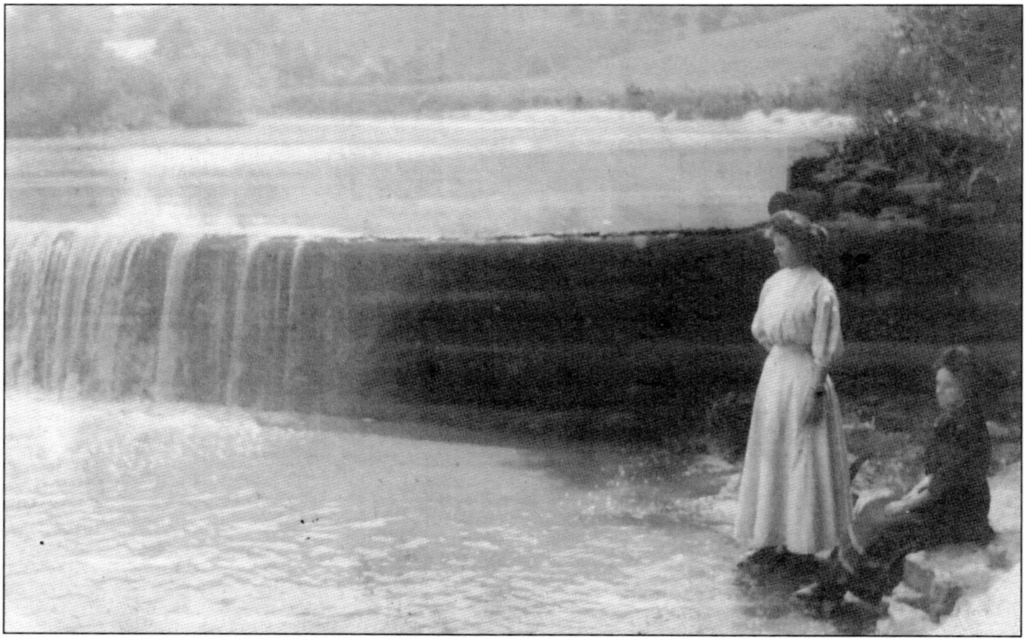

Pastoral Scene in Southern Bracken. According to relatives of these sisters, the North Fork of the Licking near Sante Fe may be the location where these ladies viewed the waterfall. Sitting on an outcropping are Nellie and Clara Pope from Sante Fe in the early 1900s. Nellie and Clara later married brothers Tom and Lewis Pope. (Courtesy of Ron and Diana French.)

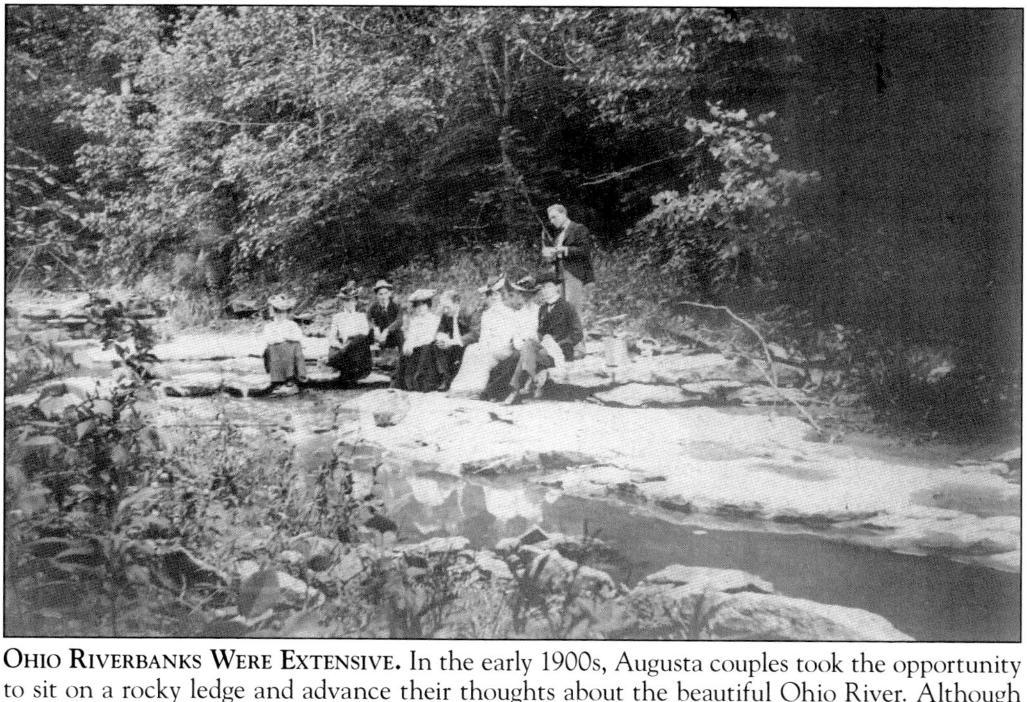

Ohio Riverbanks Were Extensive. In the early 1900s, Augusta couples took the opportunity to sit on a rocky ledge and advance their thoughts about the beautiful Ohio River. Although none are identified, the picture came from Chester Bryant's photograph albums. Sandy beaches were plentiful along Augusta, and swimming was a common occurrence until the system of locks raised the water level in the early 1960s. (Courtesy of Marilyn Bryant.)

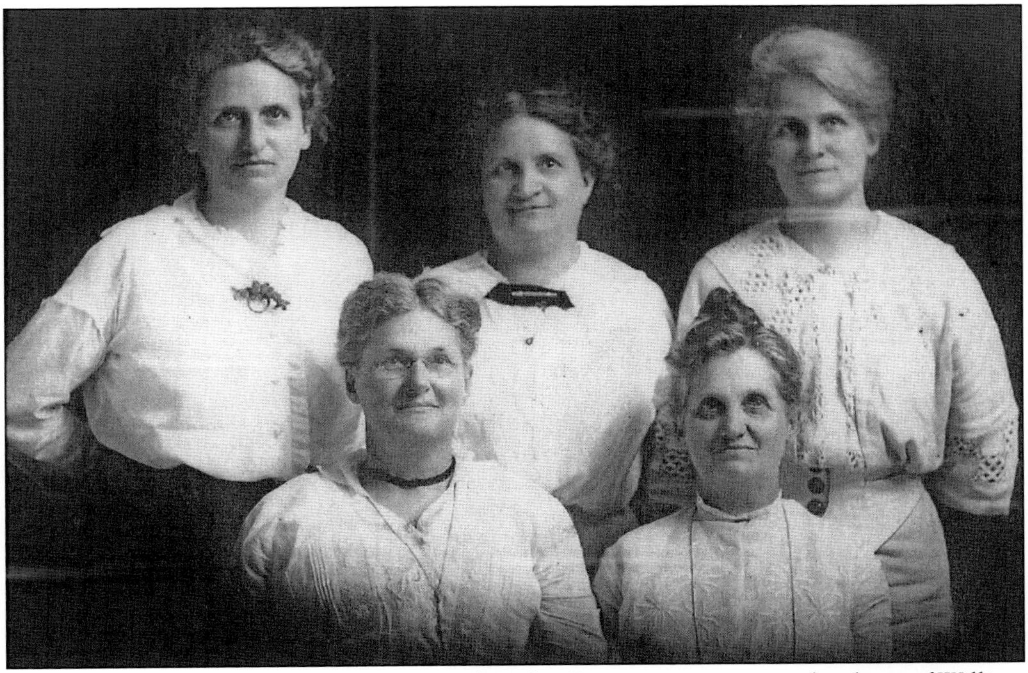

Family Photographs Retain Memories. These five Browning sisters were daughters of William T. and Elizabeth Anderson Browning. William (1833–1911) operated a general store and blacksmith shop in Browningsville. Pictured are, from left to right, (first row) Anna Showalter and Frederica Culberson; (second row) Elizabeth King, Nannie Cook, and Mollie Grimes. The photograph below of the Brooks sisters, Sue Mary and Helen, portrays the special moment when young couples were allowed to court without chaperones. Eventually, Sue Mary married Mr. Mathews, and Helen married W. B. Wallin. The identity of the young men in the picture is unknown. The Brooks home was located at the intersection of Kentucky Route 19 and Mount Zion Road near Chatham. (Above, courtesy of Ann Bettison and Mary Sue Edwards; below, courtesy of Carol Wallin Boney.)

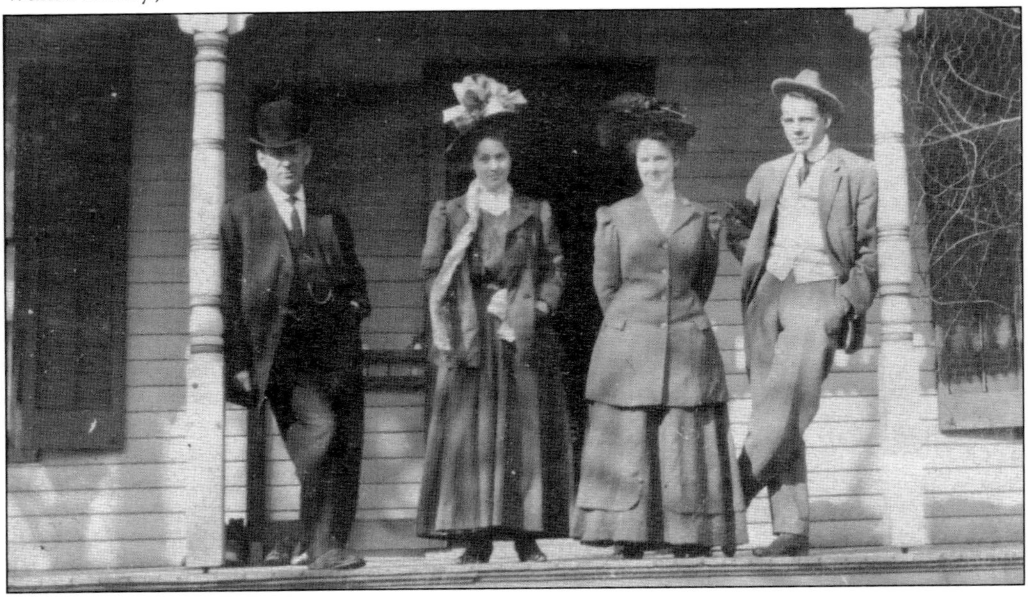

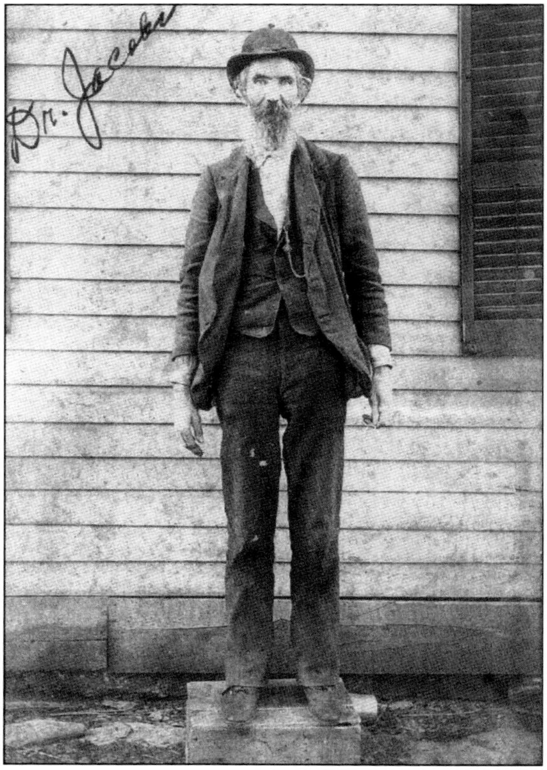

Dr. Jacobs Served. Dr. Jonathan W. Jacobs practiced from his office and operated a local drugstore of sorts at Mount Hor on Belmont Road. Around 1830, Jacobs and his parents came to Bracken County from Pennsylvania, where he studied medicine. Rudy LaMonda's family maintains that Jacobs kept his pills in his hollowed-out cane so they would not be stolen. (Courtesy of Ruby LaMonda.)

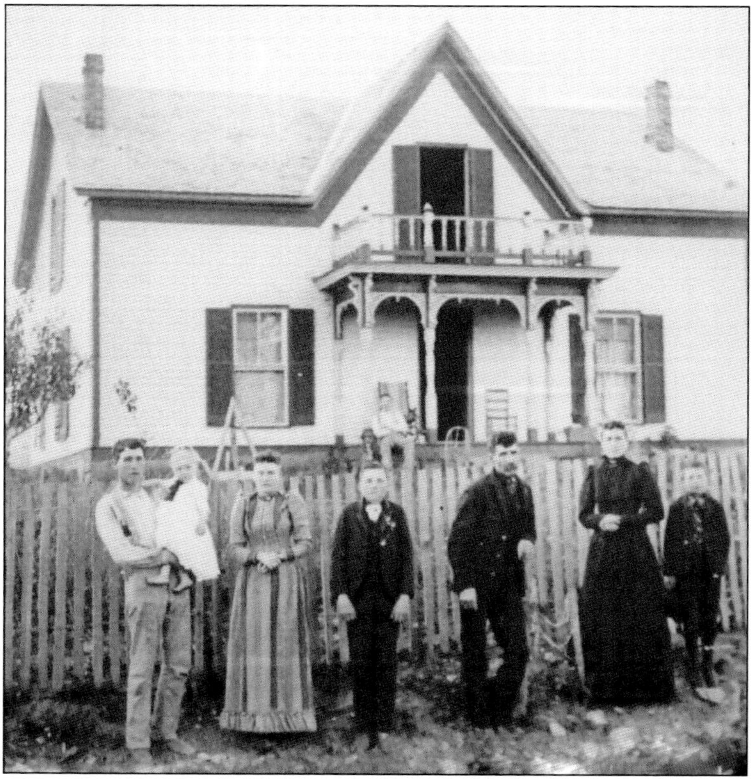

Kentucky Landmark Home. This home, built around 1880, was originally owned by William Henry Hanson. In 2000, the house, located on Garrison Road, was designated a Kentucky Landmark by the Kentucky Heritage Council. Standing before the high fence are, from left to right, Leslie Galbraith (holding Flora), Liza Galbraith Hamilton, Thomas Hamilton, William Henry Hanson, Martha Jett Hanson, and Jerry Hamilton. (Courtesy of Alice Fay Legge and Mary Seifert Kaiser.)

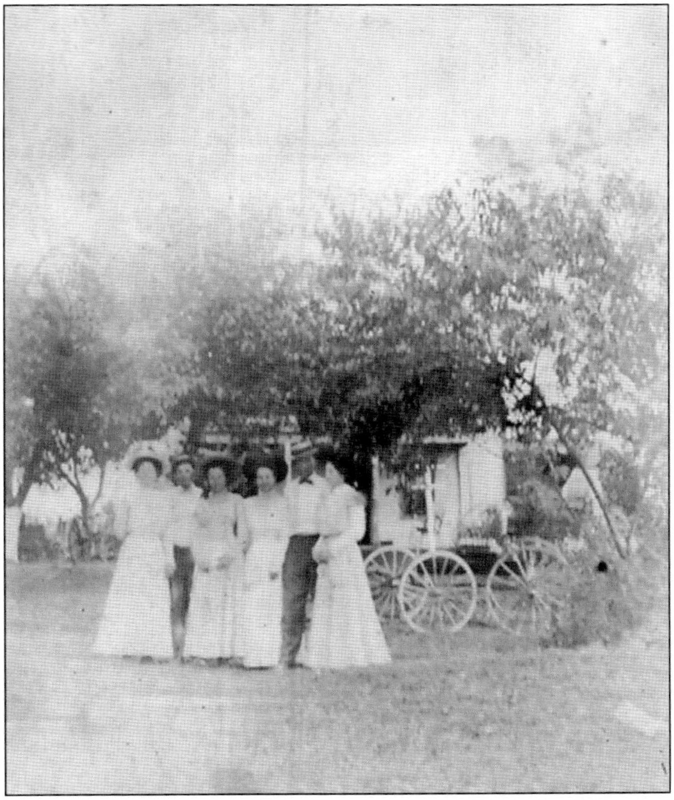

Germantown Fairgoers. Four ladies were accompanied to the Germantown Fair by gentlemen in a carriage, allowing them to keep their dresses free from dirt flying off the wooden wheels. This postcard provides an image of the women in their carefully chosen long dresses with tight waists and large bonnets. The Germantown Fair is the oldest fair in Kentucky, holding its first exhibition in 1854. (Courtesy of Bernie Spencer.)

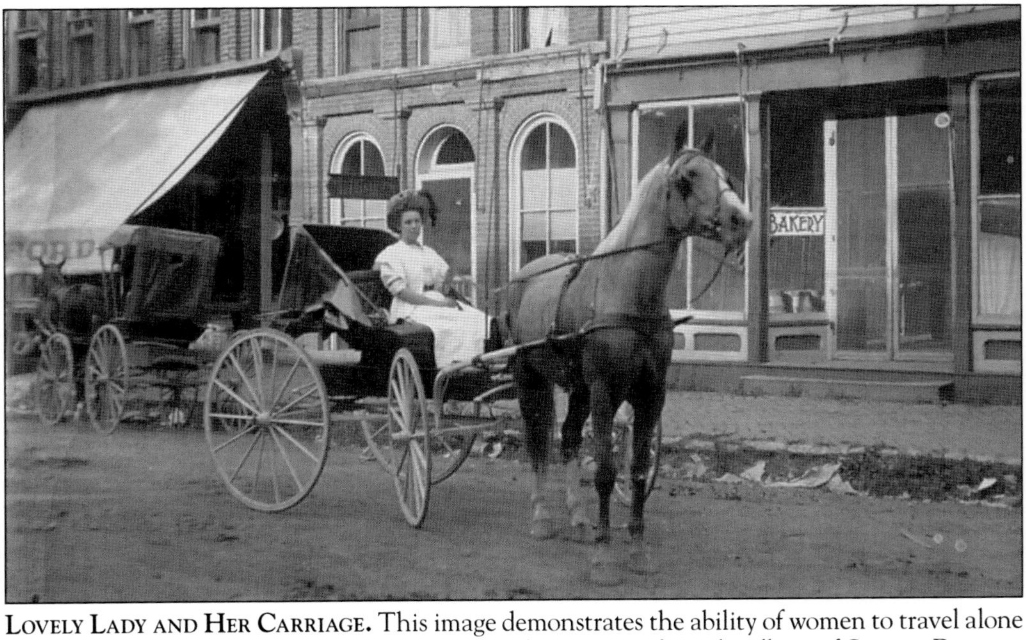

Lovely Lady and Her Carriage. This image demonstrates the ability of women to travel alone and manage a spirited horse pulling her carriage. The picture is from the album of Garnett Duncan, whose family was from Milford. Although the awning to the left has the partial word "FORD" shown, which could mean this picture was taken in Milford, researchers cannot determine if this is correct. (Courtesy of Bracken County Historical Society.)

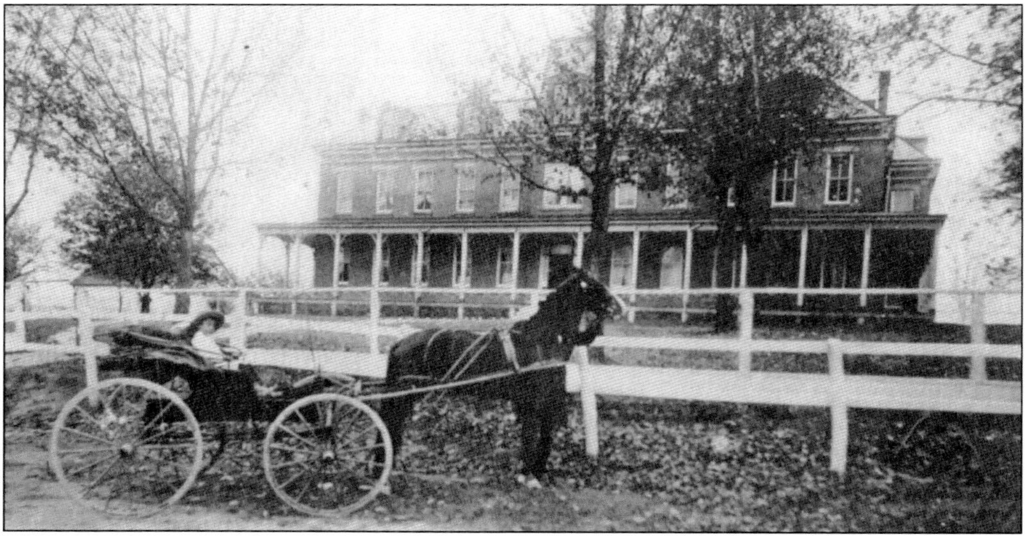

Bracken County Infirmary. The original poor house was located on Turtle Creek Road, but the county court ordered a larger one built in Chatham. This 1885 infirmary, pictured above in a 1910 postcard, was a much healthier place for the invalid and ill to recuperate or live out their remaining years. In the 1970s, the building was renovated and became the Heritage Heights Apartments; it was destroyed by fire in the 1980s. (Courtesy of Bob Adams.)

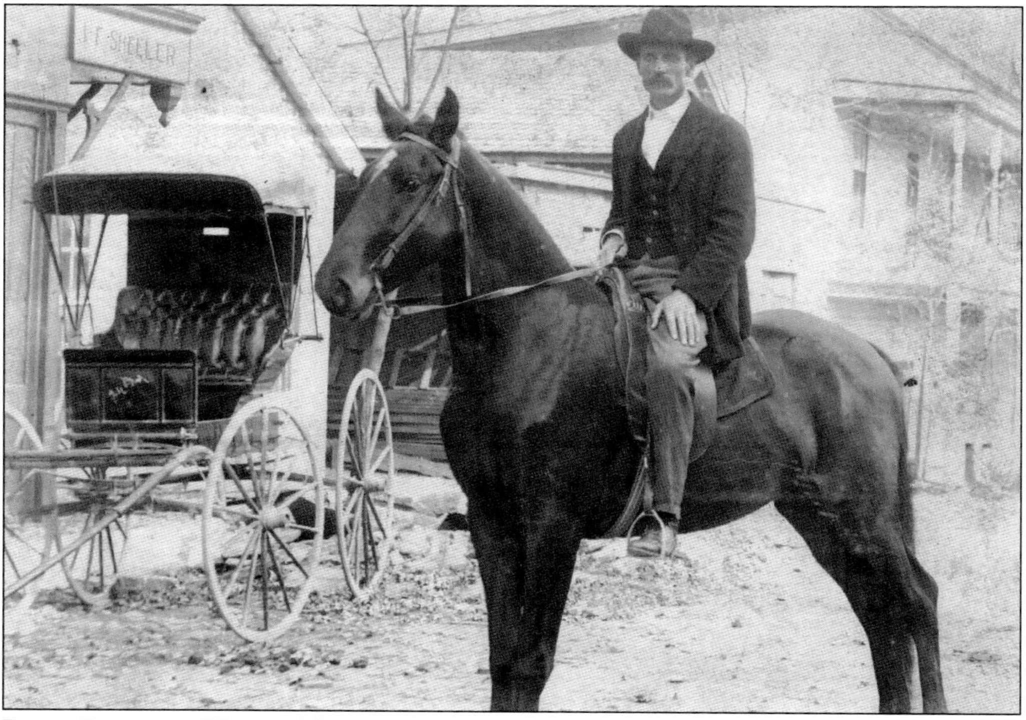

Proud Rider and Horse. A horse was a man's preferred method of travel before the automobile was a conventional means. This rider appears to be holding the horse's reins so that it would stretch out and raise its head to impress a nearby friend. Many horses in the county are descended from breeds brought over from Spain that flourished when introduced to Kentucky's bluegrass. (Courtesy of Ron French.)

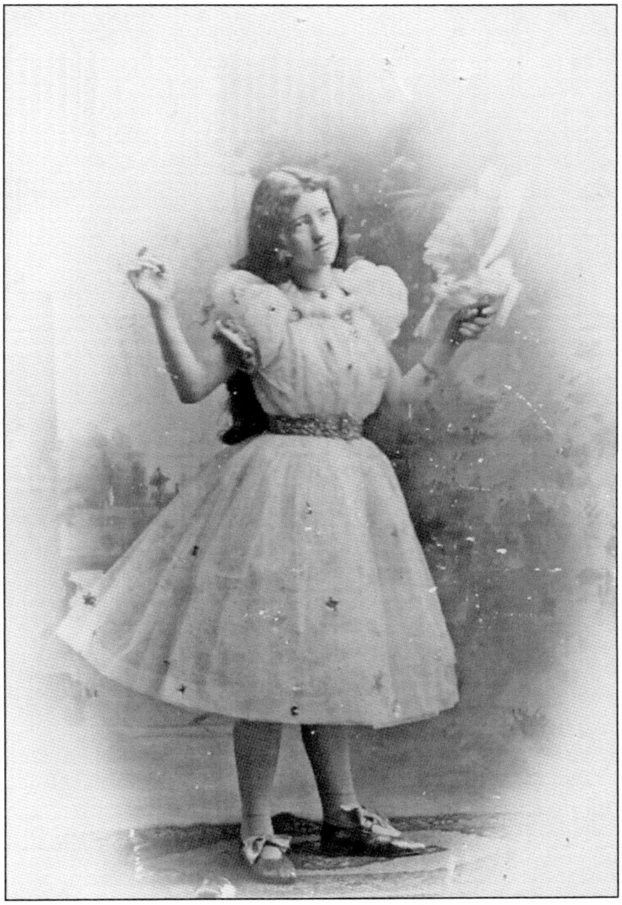

Frivolous Dresses for Social Events. These pictures portray more lighthearted times. Standing alone with an ostrich-feathered fan, posing as if she is in a Broadway musical, is a frolicsome Elizabeth (Rankins) Powers from Augusta. The Peak Sisters, also from Augusta, were being lead in a song by Emma Rankins, directing the music from her stand. Members of her group are, from left to right, Ida Taylor, Lizzie Ammer, Lizzie McKibben, Margurita Cowan, Birdie Blades, Jennie Stroube, Katie Keene, Lizzie Miller, and Jane Whitehead. Each young woman donned a pointed bonnet, which is obviously why the name "Peak Sisters" was selected. They carried bamboo heart-shaped fans to accent their song or simply for the overall effect of their performances. (Both, courtesy of Bracken County Historical Society.)

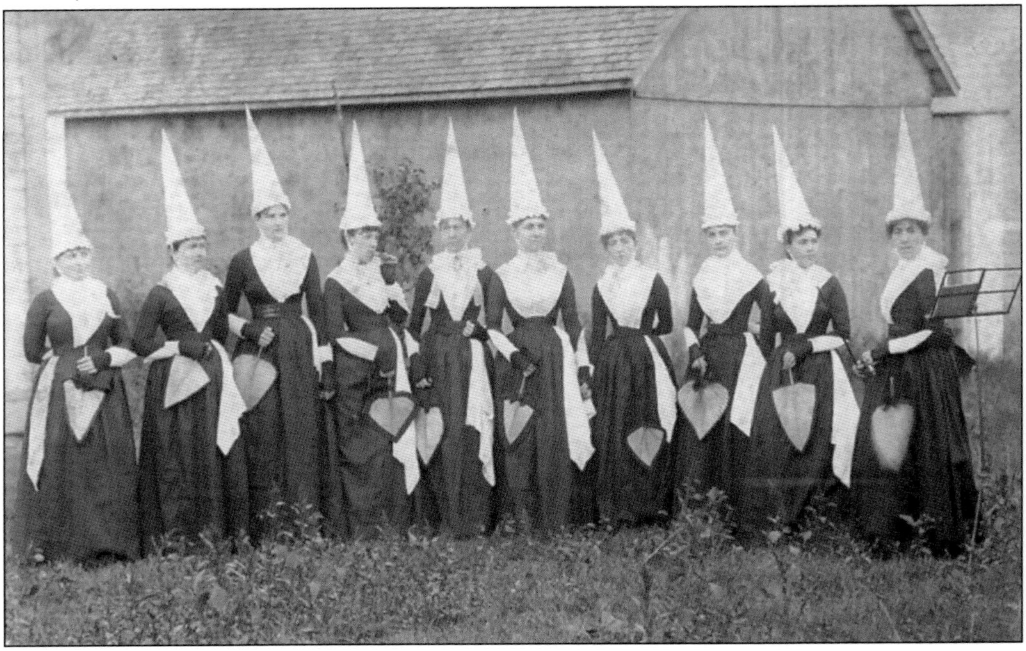

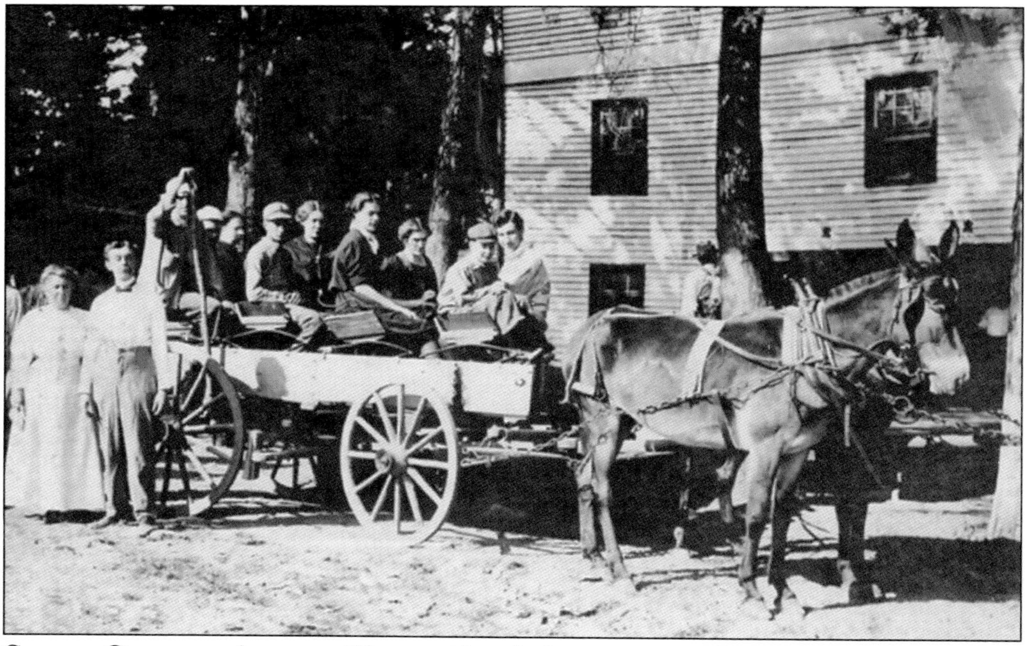

Couples Gather in Augusta. These unidentified young men and women were photographed in their strikingly different modes of transportation, enabling them to cruise Augusta. The larger group was sitting on buckboard seats placed in a large wagon pulled by what appears to be a team of donkeys. Someone had written on the back of the picture that the young men and women were students at Augusta College; however, this information cannot be confirmed. Thirty or forty years later, the preferred method of transportation was the open touring car, which allowed these four couples to travel much faster and more comfortably. (Both, courtesy of Bracken County Historical Society.)

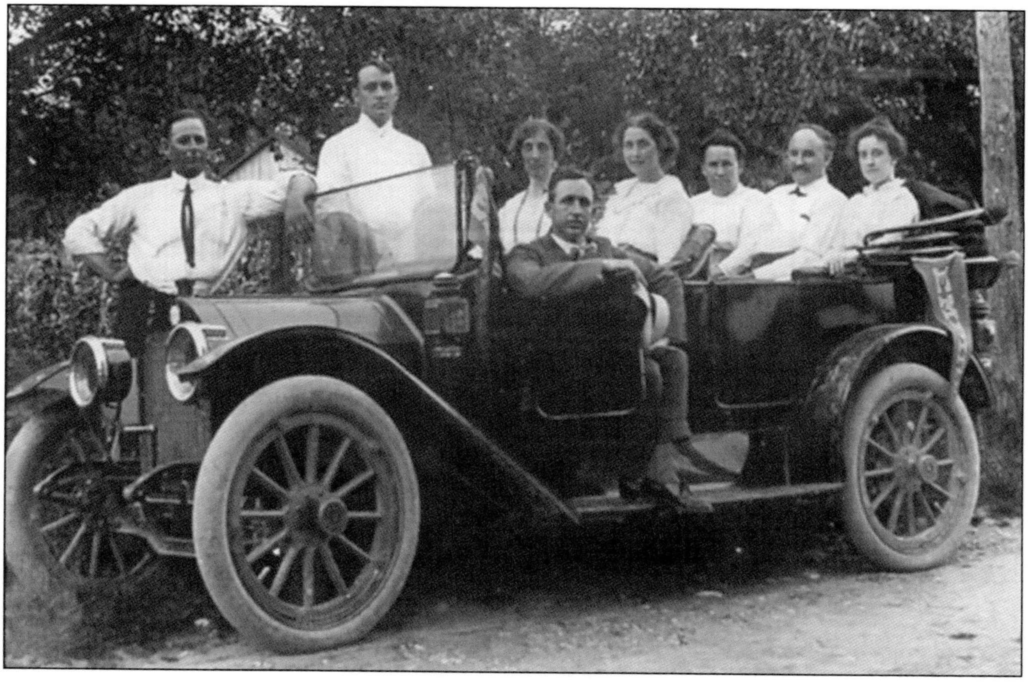

Tom Thumb Wedding. This local tradition certainly caused many spectators to roll in the aisles with laughter while looking at this miniature couple in their wedding attire. The fake marriage was also witnessed by the entire wedding party, dressed appropriately and standing in attendance. Photographed are Millard Byrne, the groom, and Jess (Poage) McClanahan, the bride. (Courtesy of Carol Wallin Boney.)

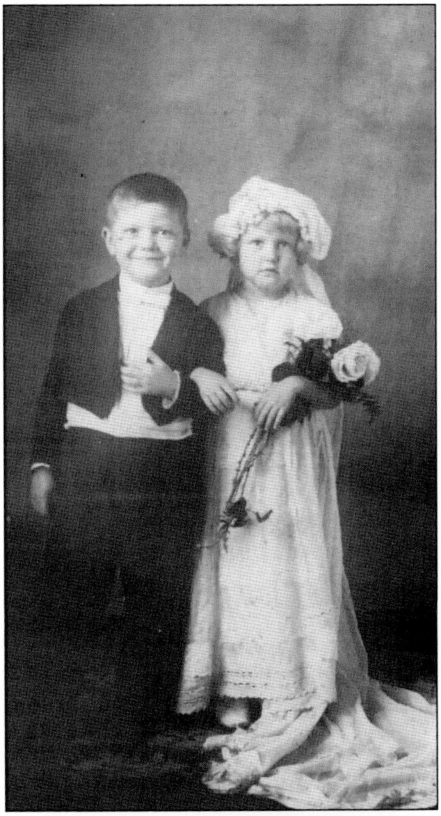

Milford Couples Gathered to Picnic. Several local couples enjoy a Sunday picnic near Milford. In the photograph are, from left to right, Paul Chaney, Hawley Askin, Lottie McKibben, Carl Moreland, Edna McKibben, Anna Moreland, Blanche McKibben, Dr. James Stevenson, William Ward, Cora Moreland, Nimrod Moreland, Gladys Boots, and Hughie McKibben. (Courtesy of Ruby LaMonda.)

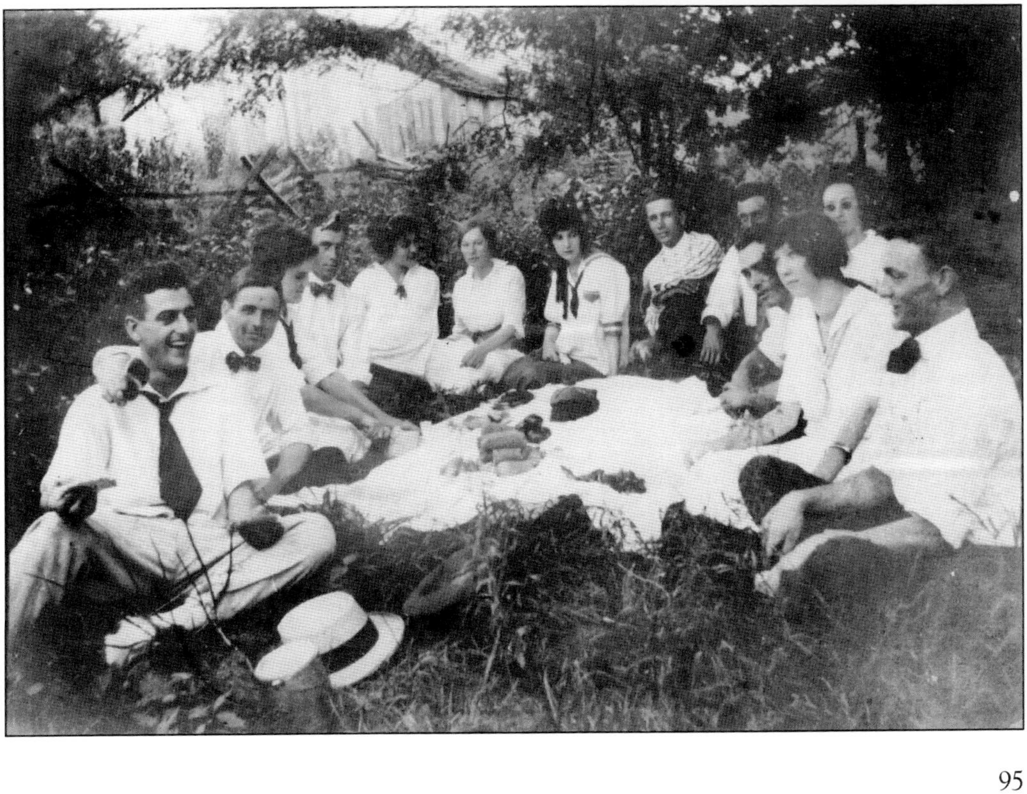

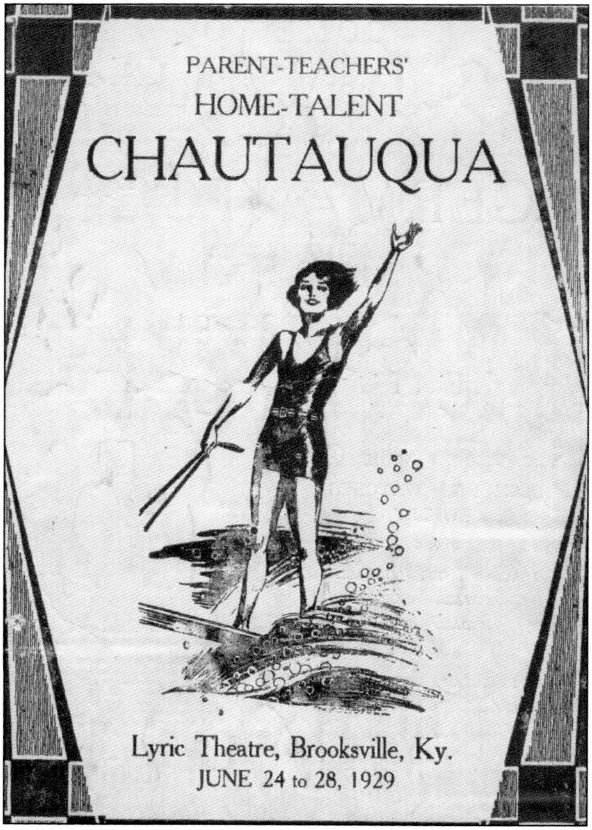

PRIVATE AND PUBLIC GATHERINGS. Shown is the program cover of a Chautauqua that ran for a week at the old Lyric Theatre in Brooksville. Some of the Chautauqua performances included singing duets, a minstrel, a lecture "In Ole Kaintuck," nymphs, elves, a short play, and instrumental solos. Local performers listed were Elizabeth Jett, John Hancock, Ann Asbury, Eugene McCracken, Naomi Kalb, Helen Poage, Bertha Poage, Esther Kalb, Clyde Moorhead, Tom Cummins, and Robert Jennet. Below, LaMonda couples pose in the 1910s. They are, from left to right (first row) Thomas LaMonda, Frank LaMonda, Jesse LaMonda, and William LaMonda; (second row) Lou LaMonda, Inez LaMonda, Nell LaMonda, Alta LaMonda, and Rachel LaMonda. (Left, courtesy of Carol Wallin Boney; below, courtesy of Ruby LaMonda.)

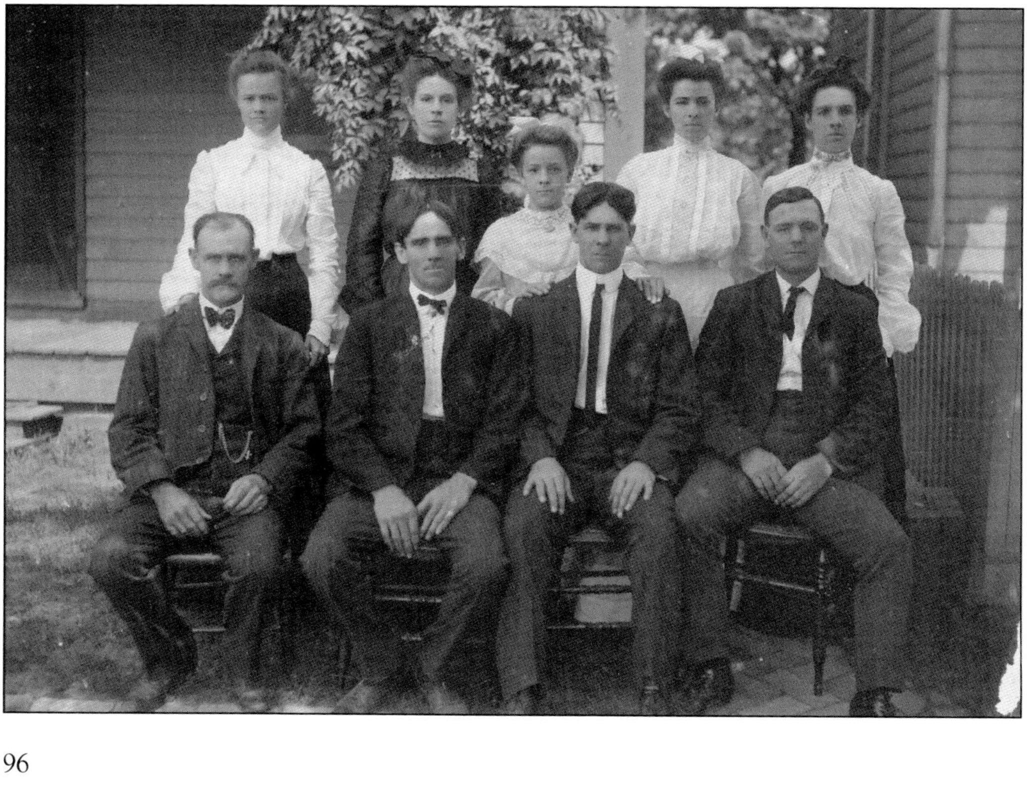

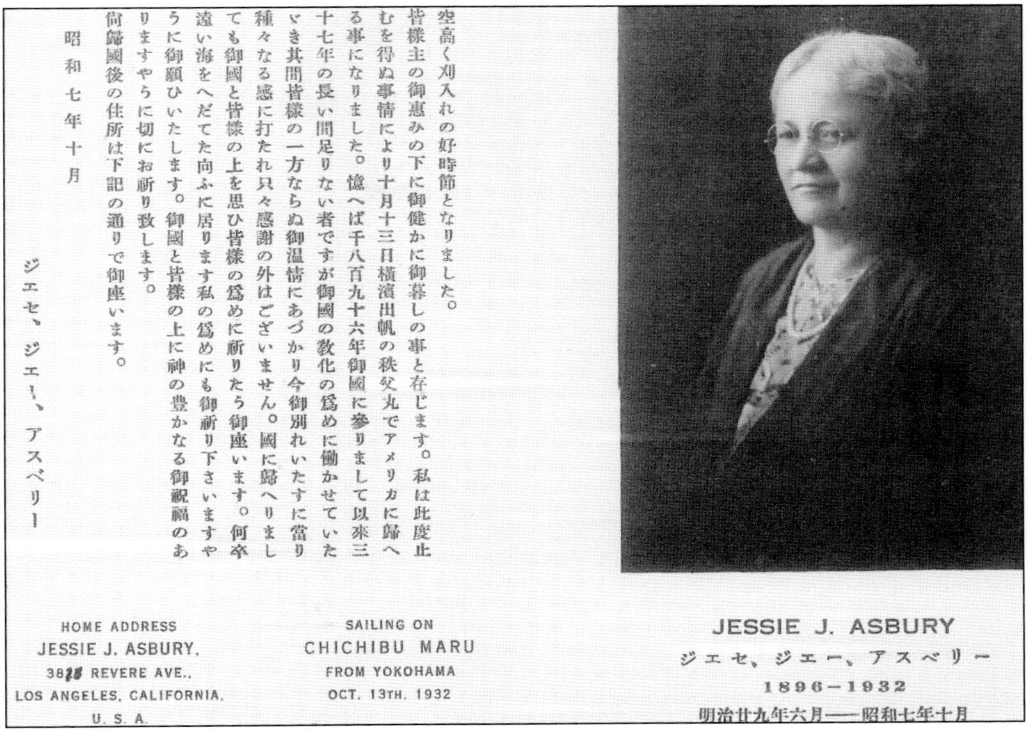

空高く刈入れの好時節となりました。
皆樣主の御惠みの下に御健かに御暮しの事と存じます。私は此度止
むを得ぬ事情により十月十三日横濱出帆の秩父丸でアメリカに歸へ
る事になりました。憶へば千八百九十六年御國に參りまして以來三
十七年の長い間足りない者ですが御國の教化の爲めに働かせていた
ゞき其間皆樣の一方ならぬ御温情にあづかり今御別れいたすに當り
種々なる感に打たれ只々感謝の外はございません。國に歸へりまし
ても御國と皆樣の上を思ひ皆樣の爲めに祈りたう御座います。何卒
遠い海をへだてた向ふに居ります私の爲めにも御祈り下さいますや
うに御願ひいたします。御國と皆樣の上に神の豊かなる御祝福のあ
りますやうに切にお祈り致します。
尚歸國後の住所は下記の通りで御座います。

昭和七年十月

ジエセ、ジエー、アスベリー

HOME ADDRESS
JESSIE J. ASBURY,
38[illegible] REVERE AVE.,
LOS ANGELES, CALIFORNIA,
U. S. A.

SAILING ON
CHICHIBU MARU
FROM YOKOHAMA
OCT. 13TH, 1932

JESSIE J. ASBURY
ジエセ、ジエー、アスベリー
1896—1932
明治廿九年六月——昭和七年十月

JESSIE ASBURY, MISSIONARY TO JAPAN. Augusta Christian Church supported missionary Jessie Asbury in Akita, Japan, where she traveled in 1896 with her sister Nina. Nina was the wife of Dr. E. S. Stevens, a homeopathic doctor. Asbury is shown in a 1911 picture taken for the *Missionary Intelligencer*. Asbury stated that she "chose to redeem and elevate women and girls of non-Christian countries." (Courtesy of Augusta Christian Church.)

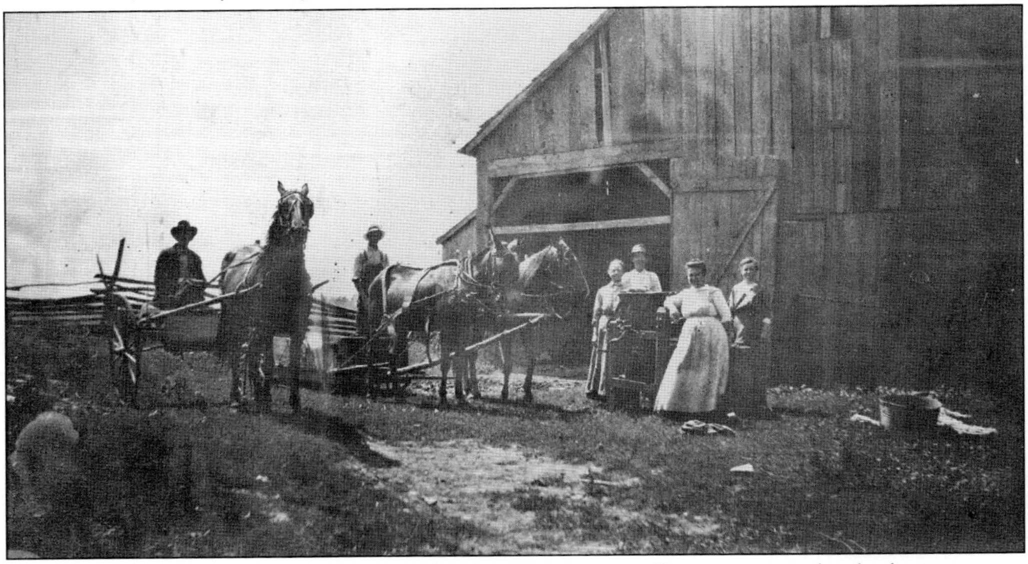

FARM SCENES DOTTED THE COUNTY. This barn scene near Germantown clearly depicts a way of life that families experienced in the early 1900s. Seen here are the typical tobacco barn, the stately horse and buggy, a close-knit family, and a barnyard of equipment used in completing the repetitive and exhausting farm chores. (Courtesy of Janice Monahon.)

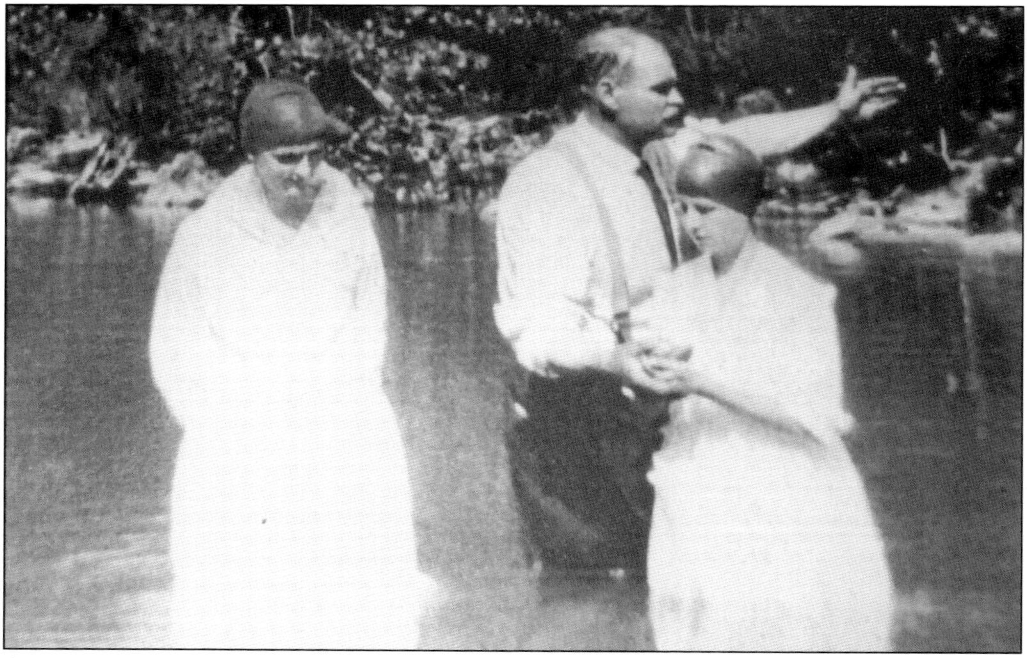

CREEK WATER BAPTISM. Rev. Everett Earl Phanstiel is standing knee-deep in creek water while baptizing two women. Phanstiel was a minister and teacher in Bracken County for several years after serving in World War I. This religious practice still occurs in the 21st century. The Ohio River used to be a frequent site of baptisms, but water conditions sometimes prevent its use. (Courtesy of Earl Phanstiel.)

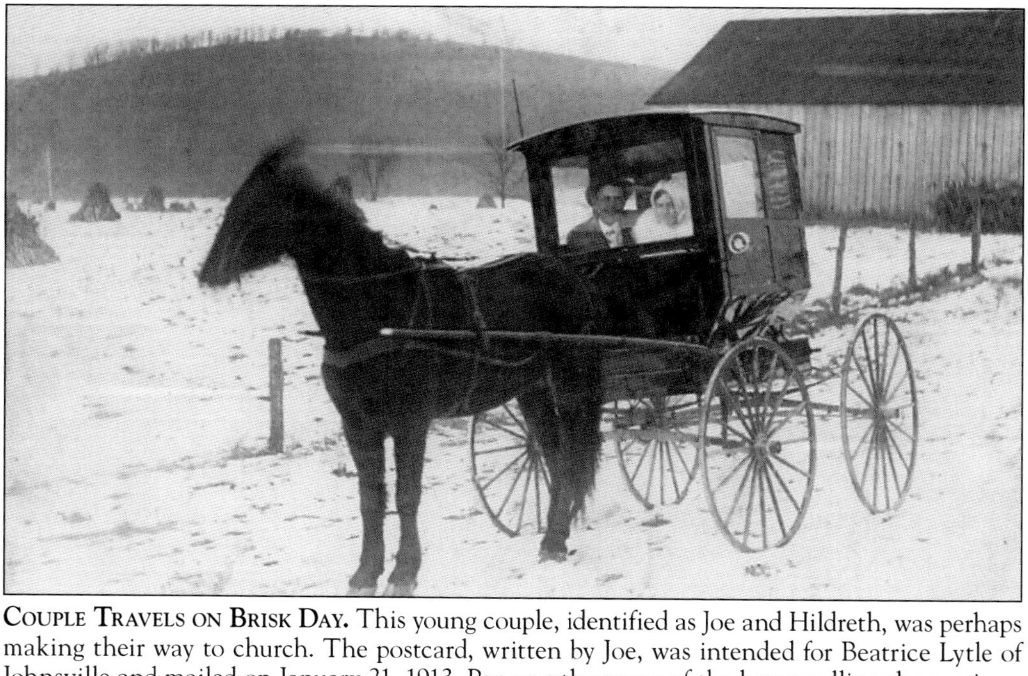

COUPLE TRAVELS ON BRISK DAY. This young couple, identified as Joe and Hildreth, was perhaps making their way to church. The postcard, written by Joe, was intended for Beatrice Lytle of Johnsville and mailed on January 21, 1913. Pan was the name of the horse pulling the carriage. Notice the hay or hemp mounds, which seem to form teepees in the background. (Courtesy of Caroline Miller.)

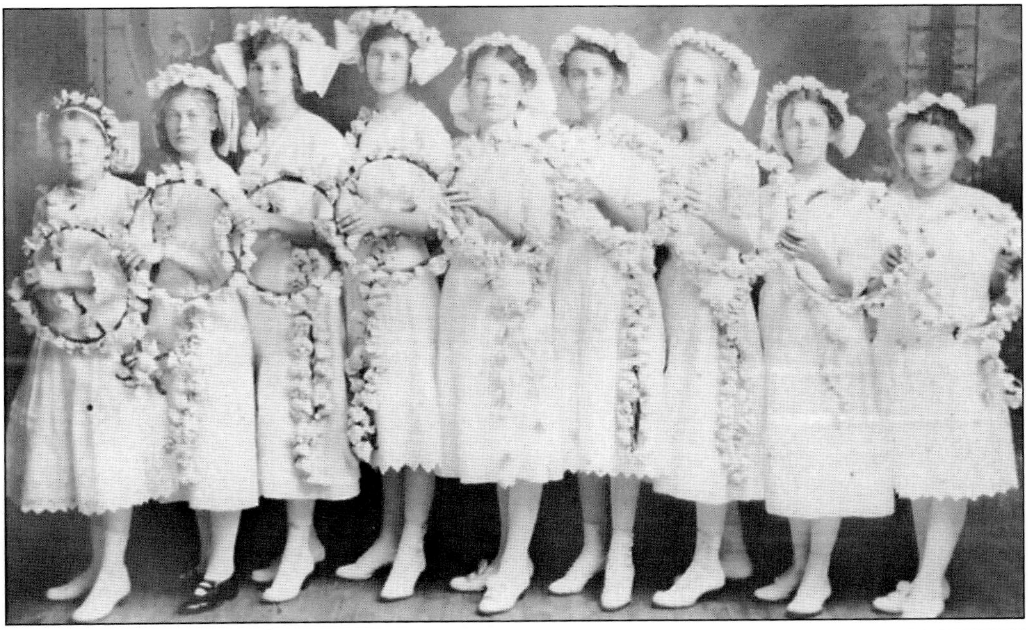

Flower Drill Girls. This early 1900s photograph shows nine young ladies dressed in clothing worn for some type of performance. The writing on the postcard refers to them as the "Flower Drill Girls." They had performed for an Augusta High School graduation exercise. The only person identified was "Ruth," standing in the middle of the group. (Courtesy of Caroline Miller.)

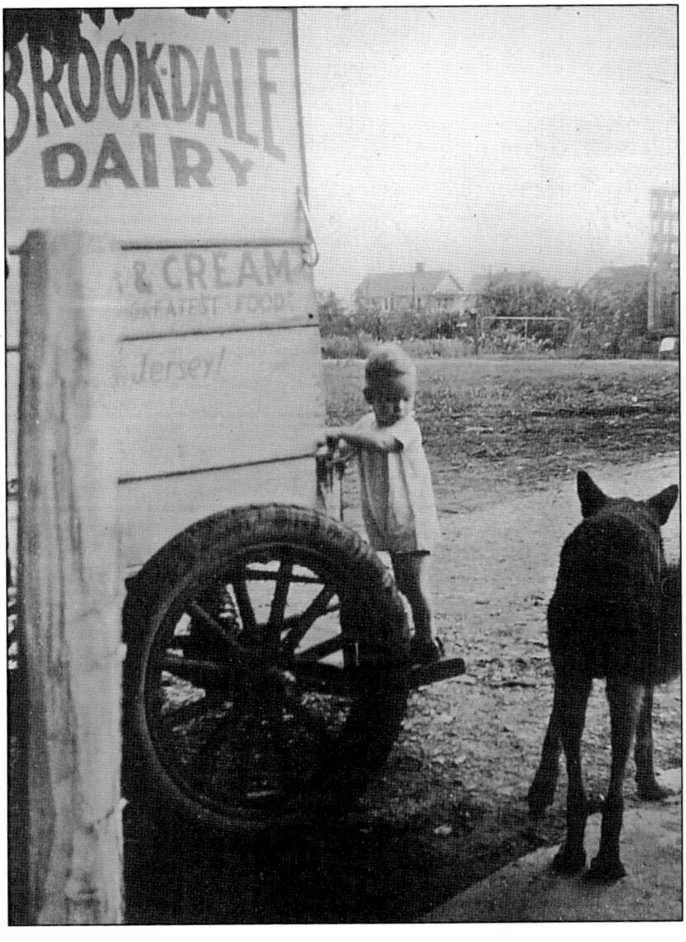

Brookdale Dairy Delivers Cream. In the 1950s, the Brookdale Dairy delivered butter and cream to the Brooksville area and surrounding villages. Pictured is one of the Kalb children riding precariously on the wooden step attached to the delivery wagon. The small child seems to be frightened by the large dog, or perhaps the dog was hoping to hitch a ride. (Courtesy of Jeannine Appelman.)

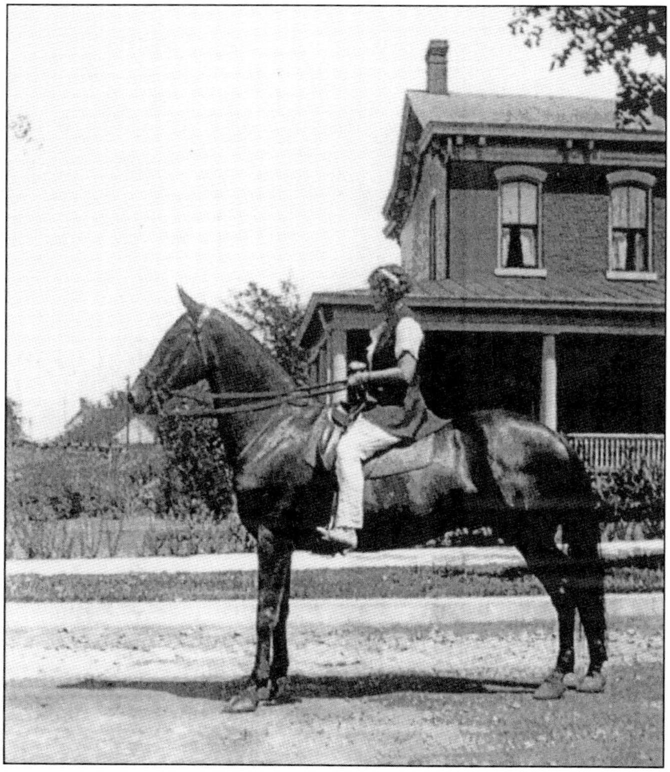

Jessie Bryant Astride Show Horse. As a young woman, Bryant was trained in how to handle show horses. "Miss Jessie," as she was fondly called by her Sunday school students, maintained Ingles Trail Stable on West Fourth Street in Augusta. She appeared on ABC's *Good Morning America* in July 1988 to discuss her weekly pastime—mowing Payne Cemetery. Jessie and her husband, Chester, operated Bryant's Drugstore. (Courtesy of Marilyn Bryant.)

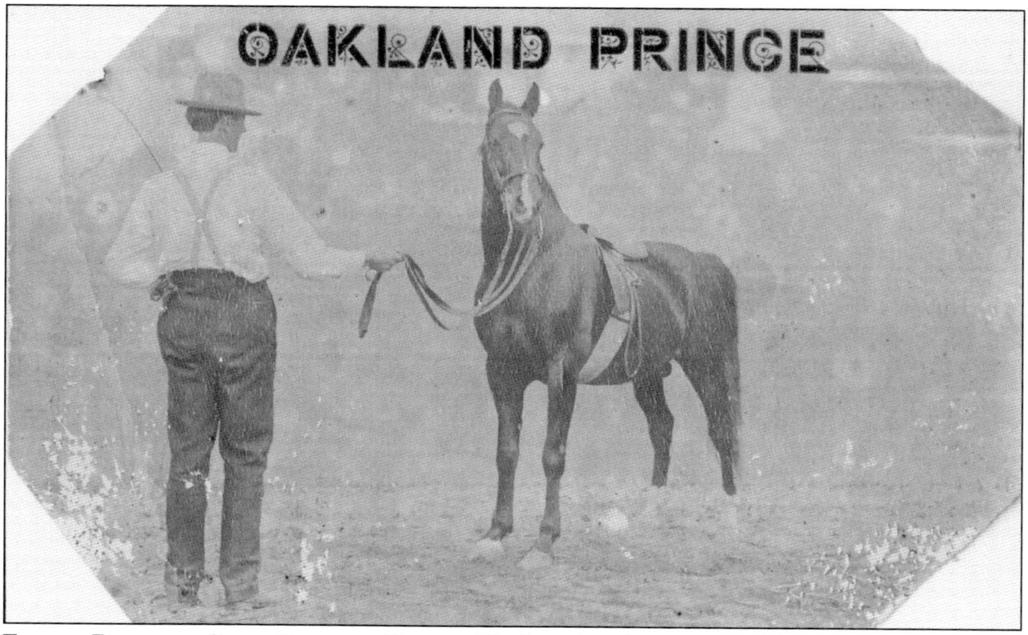

Feagan Brothers Show Oakland Prince. The breeding history of Oakland Prince was written on this postcard. He was sired by Bracken Chief; he, by Harrison Chief; he, by Clark Chief; first dam by Macey's Hambletonian, an excellent brood mare; and he spent the season of 1910 on Rock Spring Pike. He was permitted to serve mares at $10 to insure a living colt. (Courtesy of Bracken County Historical Society.)

Postman and a Neighborhood Youth. Bradford postmaster Jack Miller and John Lenox are sitting by Charles Case's mail boat in this 1942 picture. The mail was delivered by motorboat or canoe from the train station in Bradford to Chilo, Ohio, seen in the background. Miller motored across the Ohio River twice each day. (Courtesy of John Lenox.)

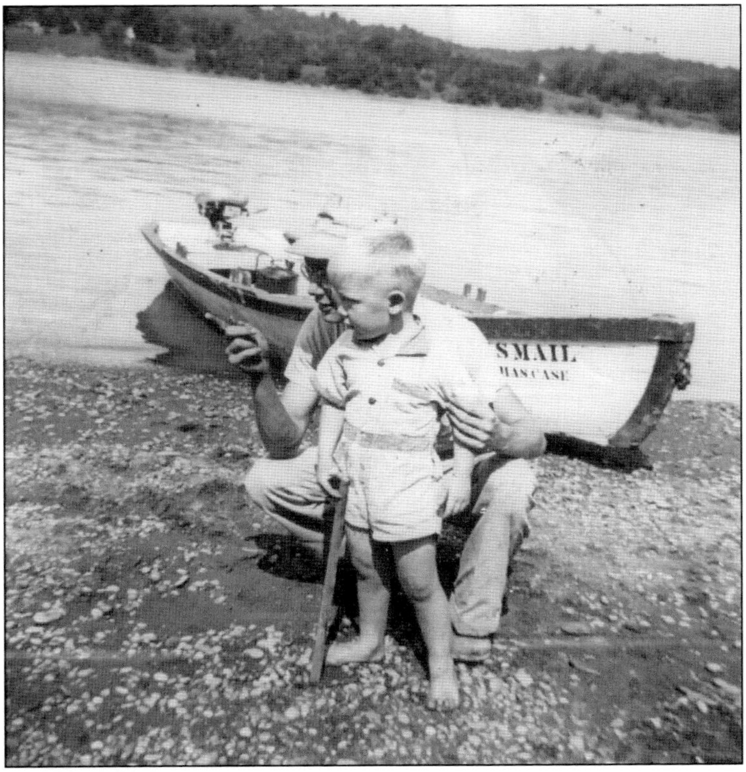

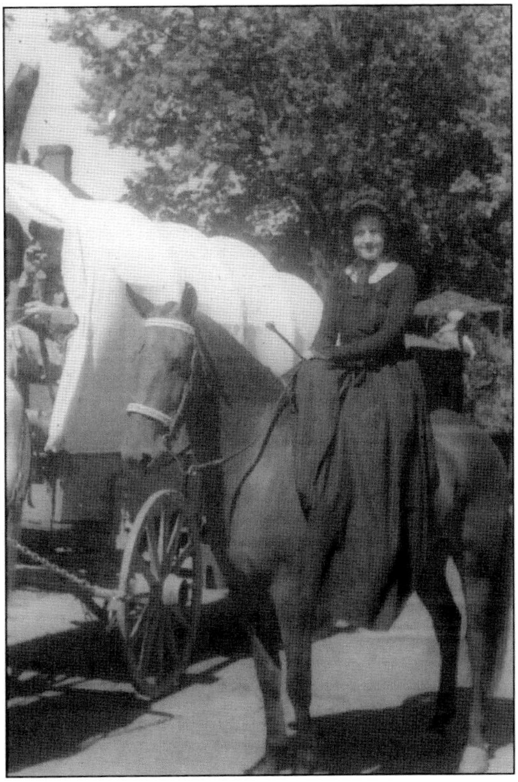

Jess McClanahan Rides Sidesaddle. Volunteering her efforts for a Chautauqua in 1942, Jess Poage McClanahan of Brooksville rode her horse in the parade. McClanahan's period costume is reminiscent of the 1800s, when the main mode of transportation was by horseback or behind the reins of a horse-drawn carriage. (Courtesy of Carol Wallin Boney.)

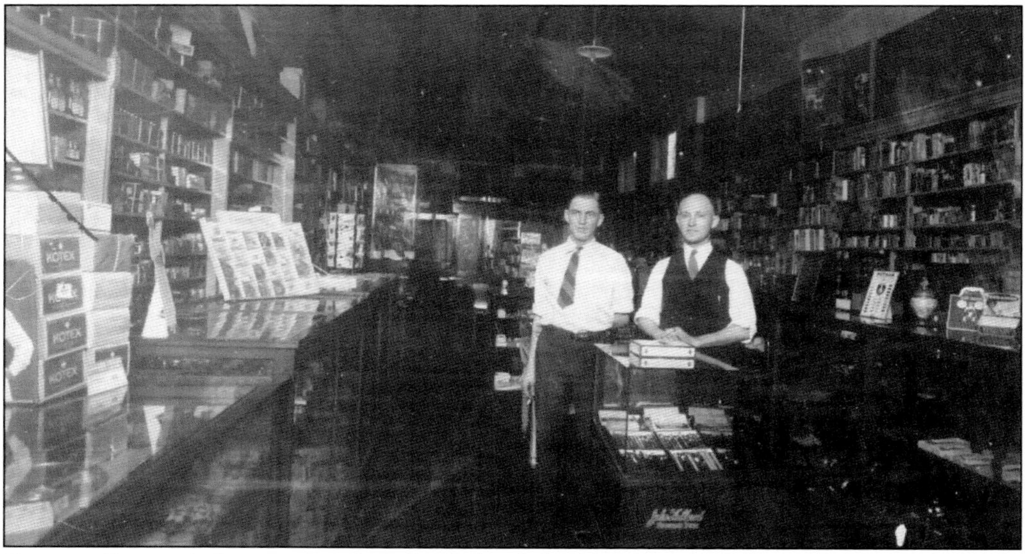

CHESTER BRYANT'S DRUGSTORE. Standing behind the drugstore counter is Chester Bryant, owner of the only drugstore in Augusta, located on West Main Street in Augusta. The gentleman leaning on the counter top is unidentified. The shelves were completely stocked with supplies and other items that Augusta residents might need to purchase. The marble counter, which customers sat at while sipping their phosphates, was later converted into a coffee table top and remains with the Bryant family. The Special Tax Stamp was issued in 1947 to Bryant so he could administer opium and coca leaves for medicinal purposes. Bryant had to pay a fee of $3 each year for the right to carry these narcotics. (Both, courtesy of Marilyn Bryant.)

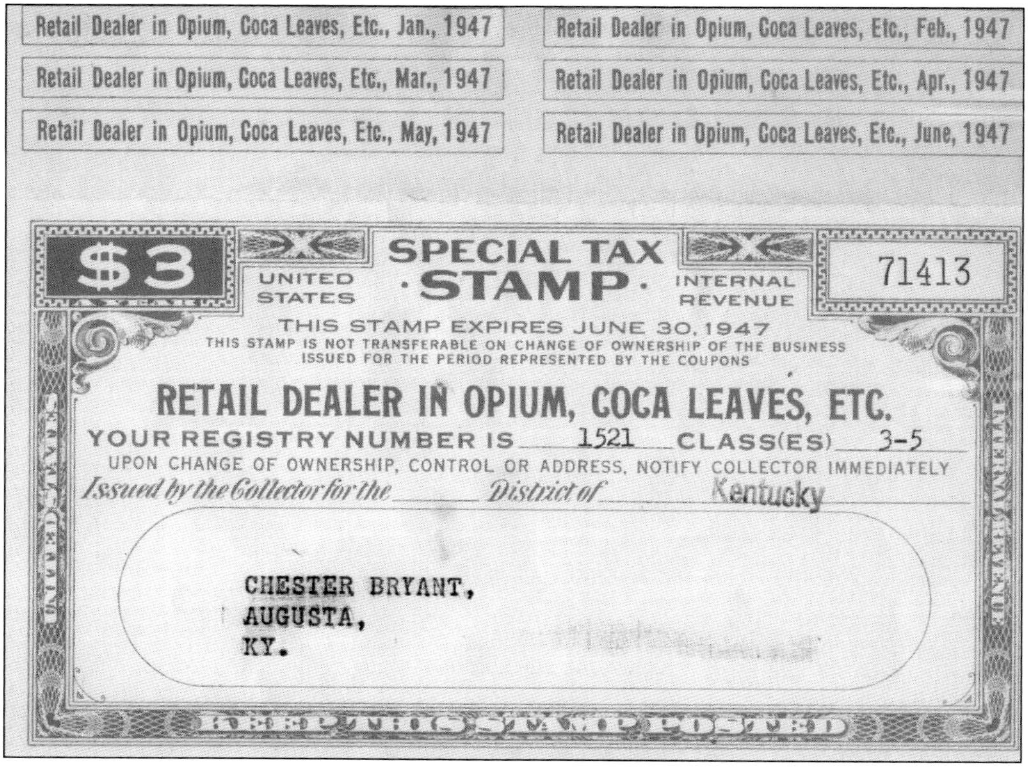

Retail Dealer in Opium, Coca Leaves, Etc., Jan., 1947
Retail Dealer in Opium, Coca Leaves, Etc., Feb., 1947
Retail Dealer in Opium, Coca Leaves, Etc., Mar., 1947
Retail Dealer in Opium, Coca Leaves, Etc., Apr., 1947
Retail Dealer in Opium, Coca Leaves, Etc., May, 1947
Retail Dealer in Opium, Coca Leaves, Etc., June, 1947

$3 A YEAR
UNITED STATES SPECIAL TAX STAMP INTERNAL REVENUE
71413
THIS STAMP EXPIRES JUNE 30, 1947
THIS STAMP IS NOT TRANSFERABLE ON CHANGE OF OWNERSHIP OF THE BUSINESS ISSUED FOR THE PERIOD REPRESENTED BY THE COUPONS
RETAIL DEALER IN OPIUM, COCA LEAVES, ETC.
YOUR REGISTRY NUMBER IS 1521 CLASS(ES) 3-5
UPON CHANGE OF OWNERSHIP, CONTROL OR ADDRESS, NOTIFY COLLECTOR IMMEDIATELY
Issued by the Collector for the District of Kentucky

CHESTER BRYANT,
AUGUSTA,
KY.

UNITED STATES INTERNAL REVENUE
KEEP THIS STAMP POSTED

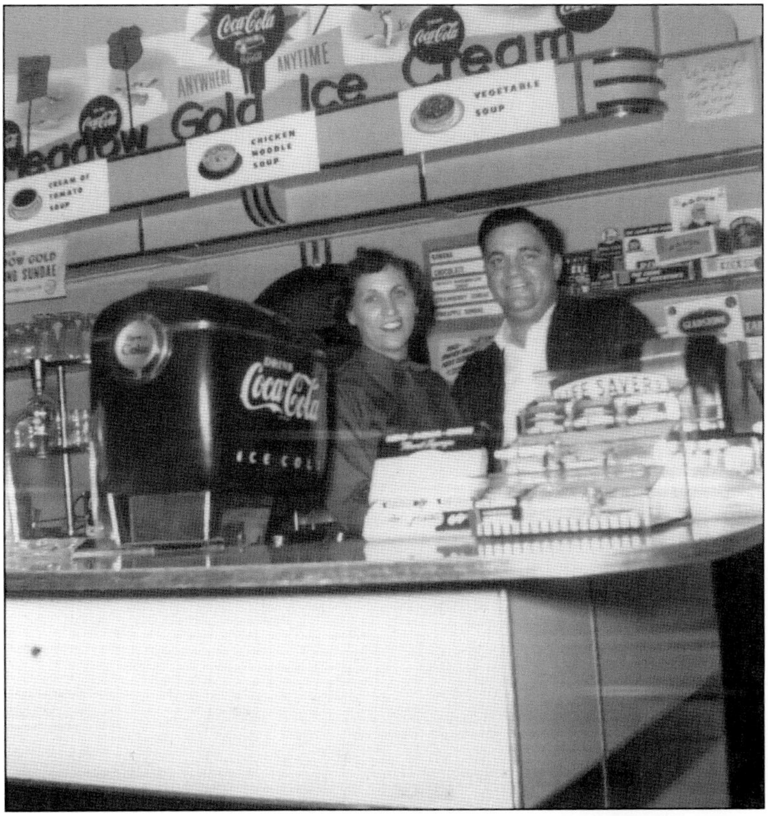

Burke's Drugstore. Ralph and Edith Burke operated the only drugstore and soda shop in Brooksville in the 1950s. The store was located on the east side of Locust Street. Most local residents remember drinking their first soda at the counter and listening to the jukebox with their favorite rock and roll song. (Courtesy of Roberta Shepherd.)

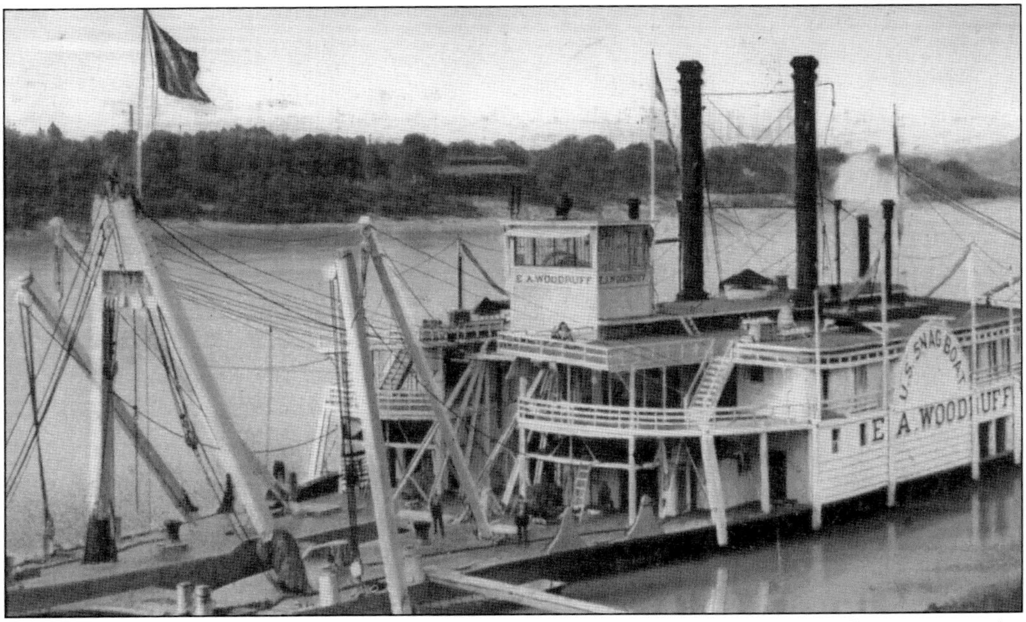

E. A. Woodruff Performs Service. Boats similar to this one provided smaller ports on the Ohio River with assistance in clearing their docks from the constant buildup of trash and logs. These boats have been replaced by larger dredge boats, which can dig out sediment and remove unwanted debris. (Courtesy of Caroline Miller.)

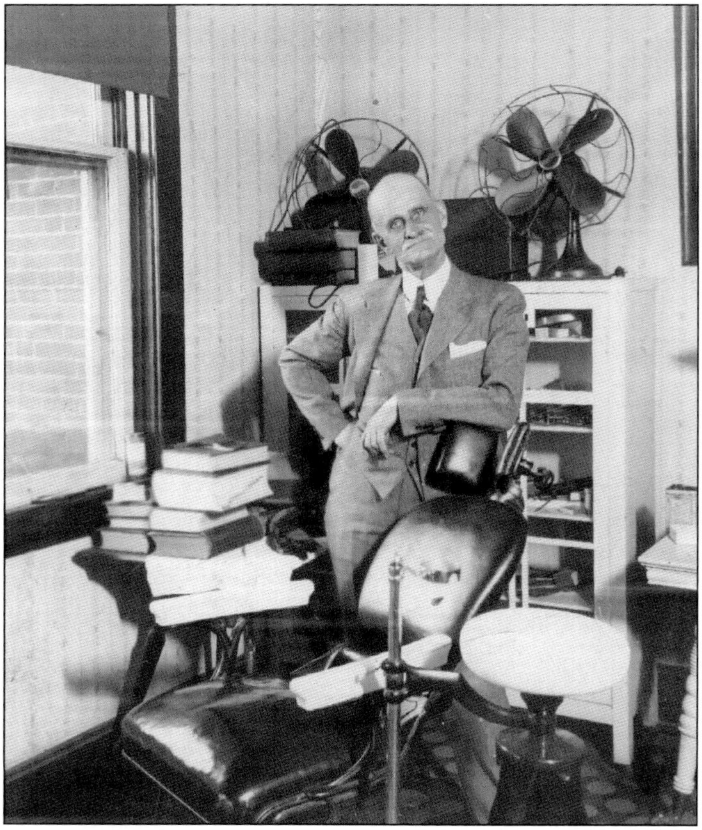

Dr. W. B. Wallin. Dr. W. B. Wallin is photographed standing next to his patient's chair. Local dentists have pointed out that the chair in the picture is actually a dentist's chair, as Wallin did have the undesirable reputation of occasionally pulling out his patients' teeth. On "Dr. Wallin Day," he was honored to have thousands sign their names to a list of babies delivered by him. (Courtesy of Carol Boney.)

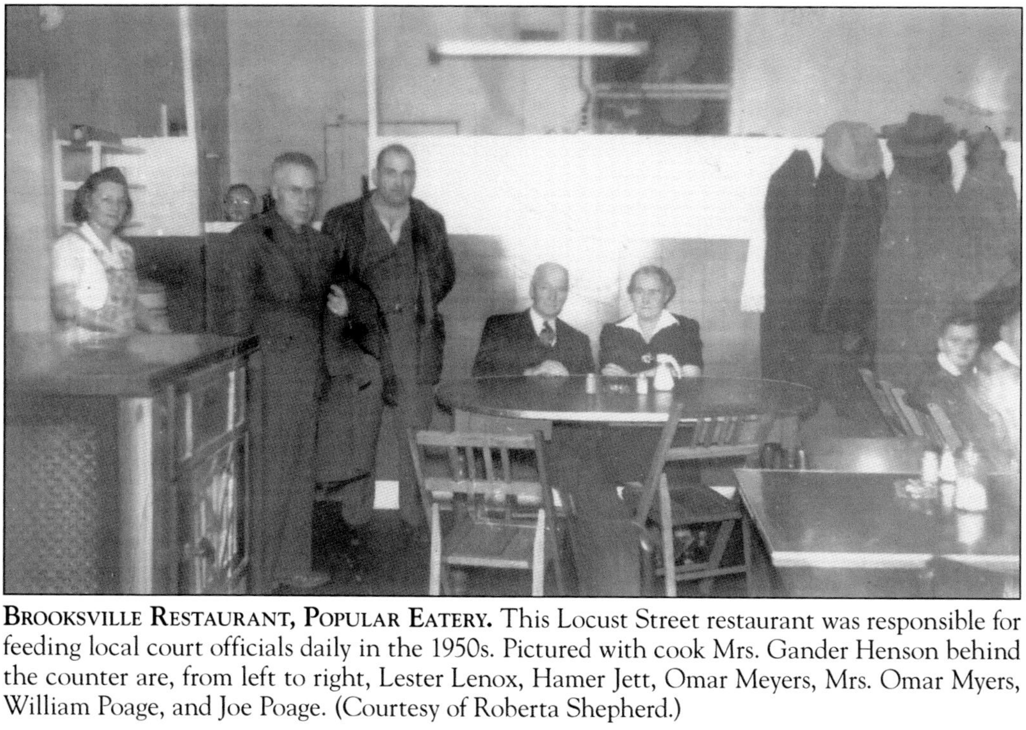

Brooksville Restaurant, Popular Eatery. This Locust Street restaurant was responsible for feeding local court officials daily in the 1950s. Pictured with cook Mrs. Gander Henson behind the counter are, from left to right, Lester Lenox, Hamer Jett, Omar Meyers, Mrs. Omar Myers, William Poage, and Joe Poage. (Courtesy of Roberta Shepherd.)

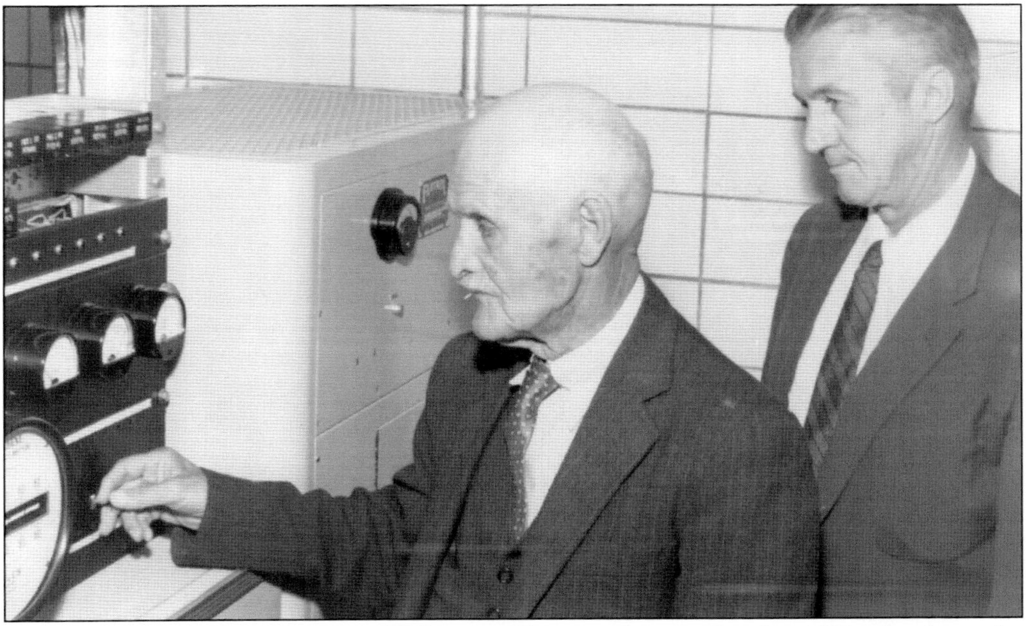

THROWING THE SWITCH. Dr. W. B. Wallin, age 87, is seen here in October 1957 as he threw the switch starting modern dial telephone service in Bracken County. With Wallin is H. S. "Scotty" Poage, manager of the northern division of Northeastern Telephone Corporation. In August 1898, the Brooksville and Milford Telephone Line began operations, and in 1903, Bracken County Telephone Company was established. (Courtesy of Carol Wallin Boney.)

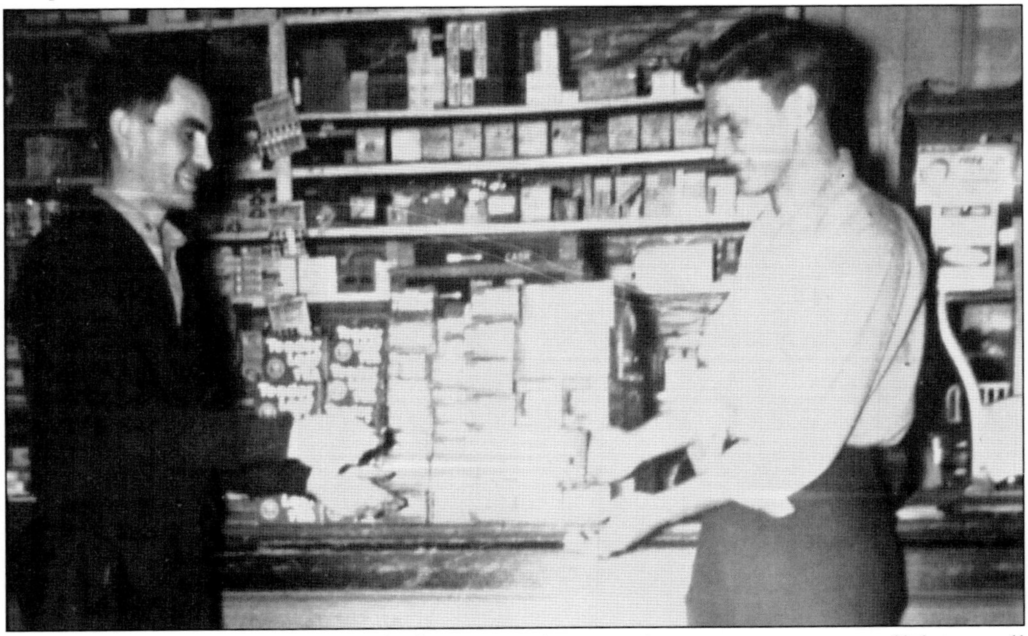

FRANK HILL AND "JIGGS" BESS. In the late 1940s, the general store was a necessity of life in small communities. Frank Hill, standing in front of the counter, operated this store in Germantown. The employee in the photograph is Raymond "Jiggs" Bess, another future entrepreneur who went on to run his own general store in nearby Highland Heights for several decades. (Courtesy of John H. Henderson.)

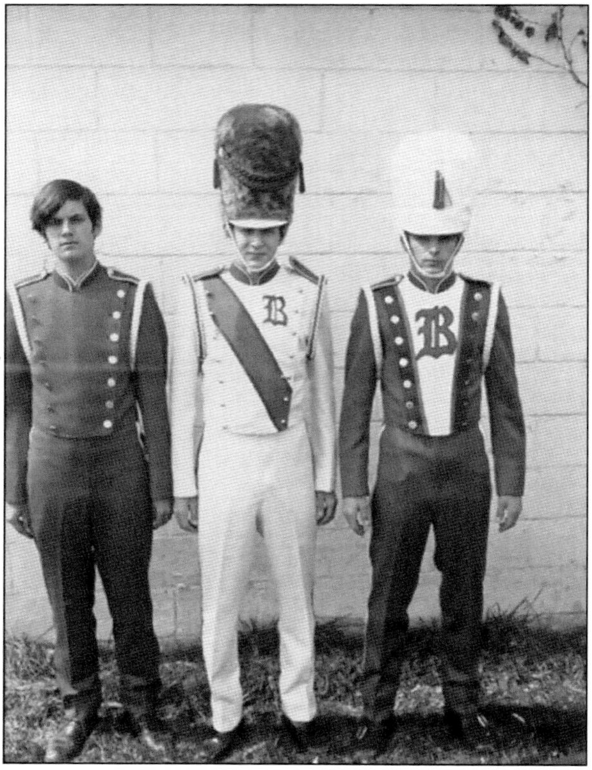

Bracken County Band Drum Majors. Pictured here are William Wilson (left), Jeff Metzger (center), and David Hay. These men were responsible for the movements of 60 members of their precision marching band in the early 1970s. The Bracken County High School marching band was under the instruction of John Wallingford. At the time, marching bands were gaining popularity, as they stood in formations and marched to an exaggerated drum cadence. (Courtesy of *Bracken County News.*)

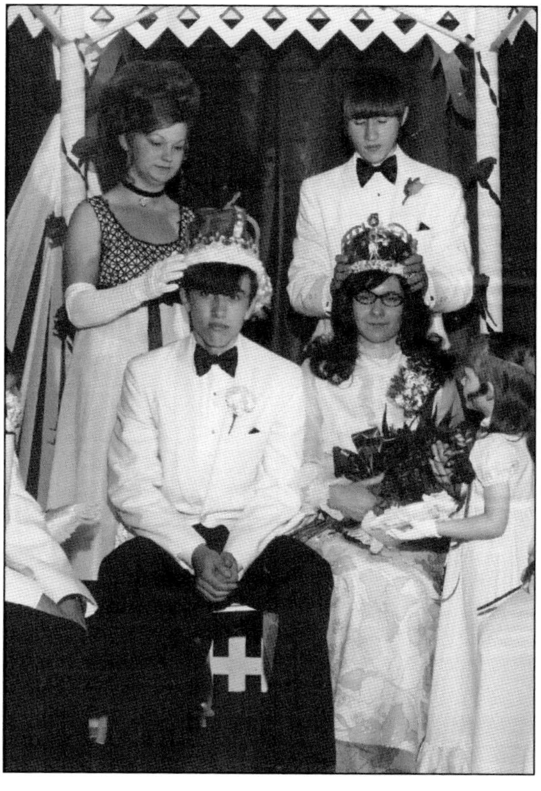

Augusta High School Prom. A ritual held each spring in area high schools is the election of a prom queen and king to be crowned at the formal dance. In 1972, Jerry Dale Thornsbury was elected king and Sara Kelsch received her crown as queen of the prom. Crowning them were the previous year's king and queen, Anita Claypool and Philip White. (Courtesy of *Bracken County News.*)

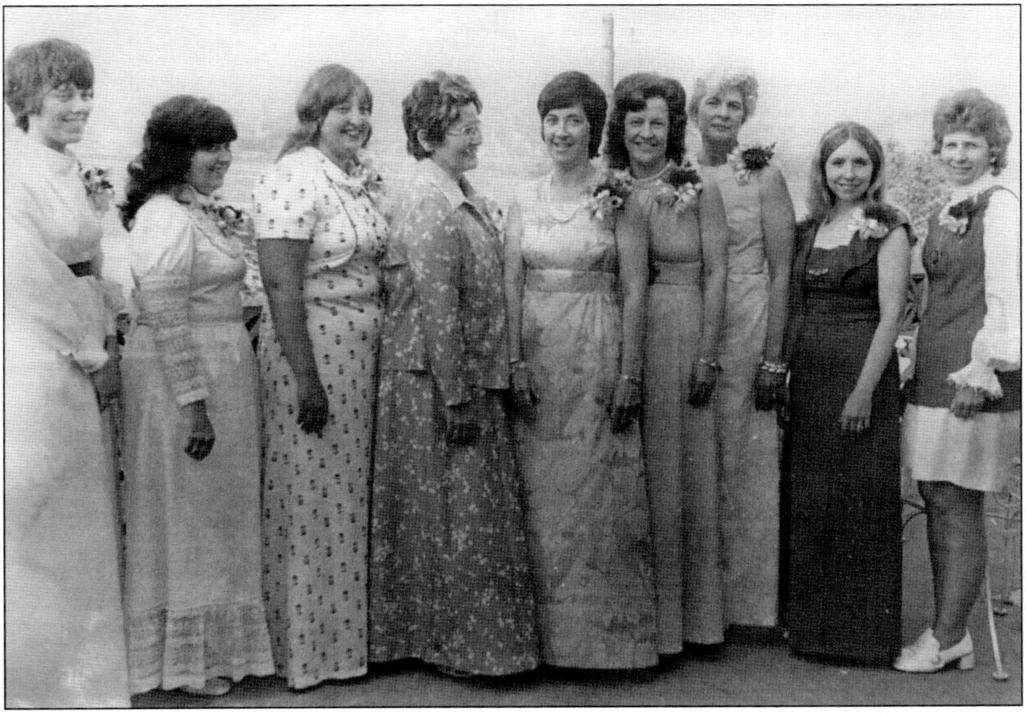

Woman's Club Officers Inducted. Some time in the 1970s, these community-minded women were being installed as officers of the Augusta Woman's Club by Maude Teegarden, president of Town and Country Woman's Club. Standing are, from left to right, Charlene Johnson, Karen Smithers, Carolyn Bradbury, Norma Faye Thornsbury, Maude Teegarden, Virginia Poe, Martha Kelsch, Shirley Tucker, and Genna Lou Murray. (Courtesy of *Bracken County News.*)

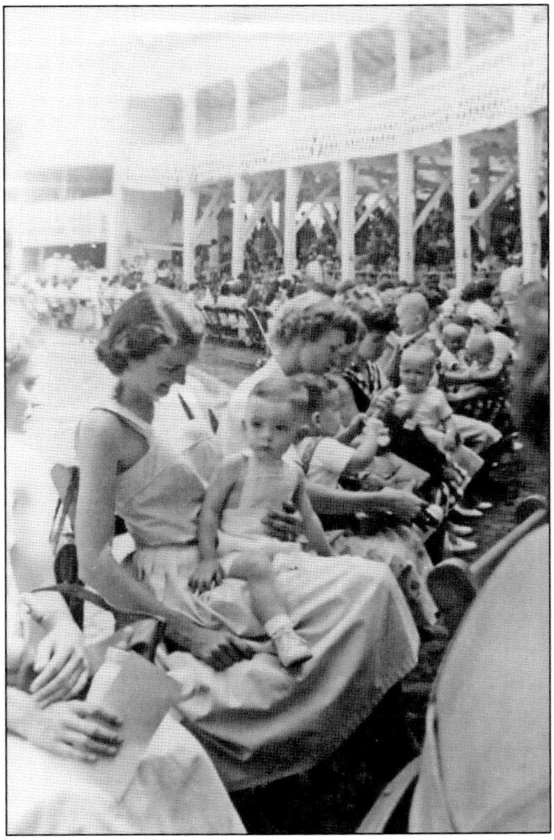

Germantown Fair Baby Show. When the heat of August was bearing down on the Germantown Fair horse ring, young ladies and grandmothers would sit with babies on their laps, hoping to claim first place. Pictured are several unidentified women with their infants dressed in pristine clothes. The children were being distracted so they would not cry, which could spoil their chances for the first place trophy. (Courtesy of *Bracken County News.*)

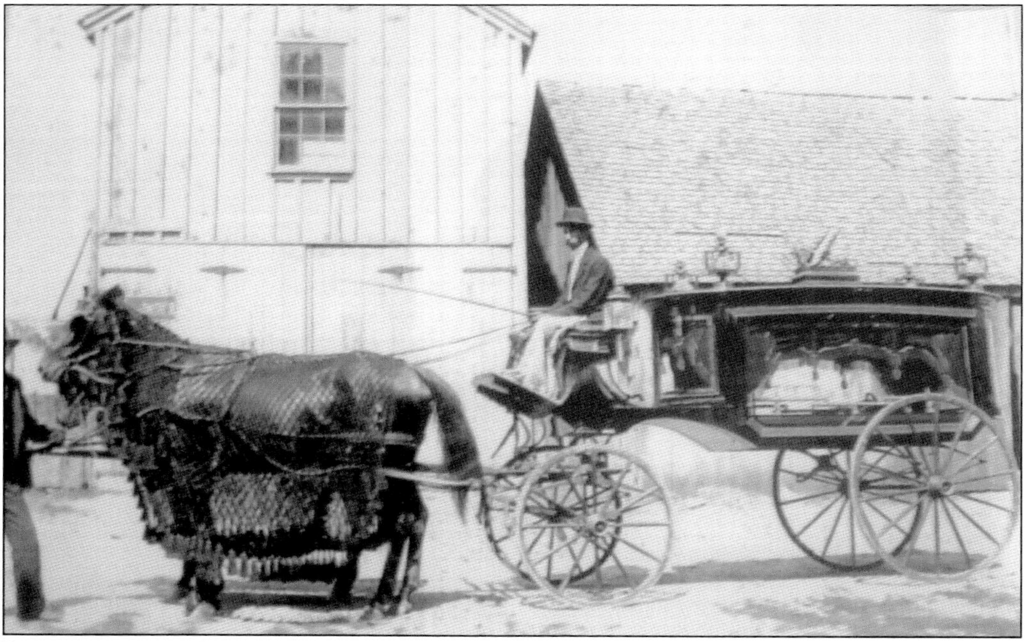

Pepper Funeral Carriage. Prior to 1938, the only funeral home in Germantown was operated by H. L. Pepper. Pictured above is H. L. Pepper driving the team of horses pulling the hearse. The windows or open areas on each side allowed viewing of the coffin. Walter Tucker is the footman seen in the photograph. Pepper's motto, printed in local papers was, "As Good as the Best." (Courtesy of Mark Litzinger and John Patterson.)

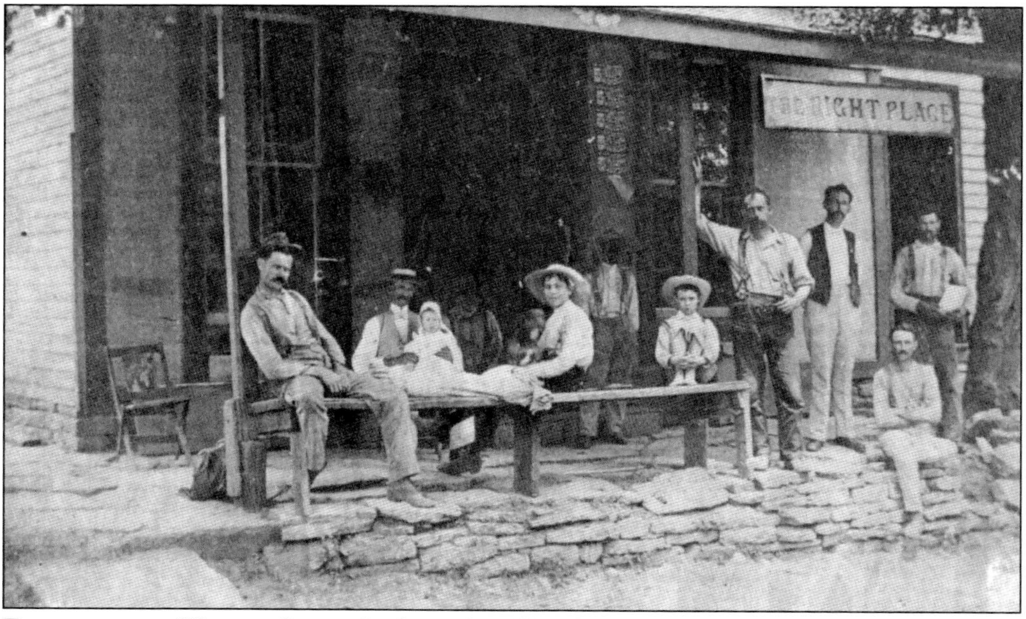

Thompson and Walton Store. In the early 1900s, Germantown men wiled away the summer days in the comfort of shade and a nearby water well. The Right Place provided the bench and the community provided the men. Pictured are, from left to right, E. Pollock, Joe Walton, John Walton Jr., Harry Tucker, Harvey Pinckard, George Bradbury, Ed Thompson, Walter Pollock, and George Case. (Courtesy of John H. Henderson.)

Six

Arts Personified Brilliance

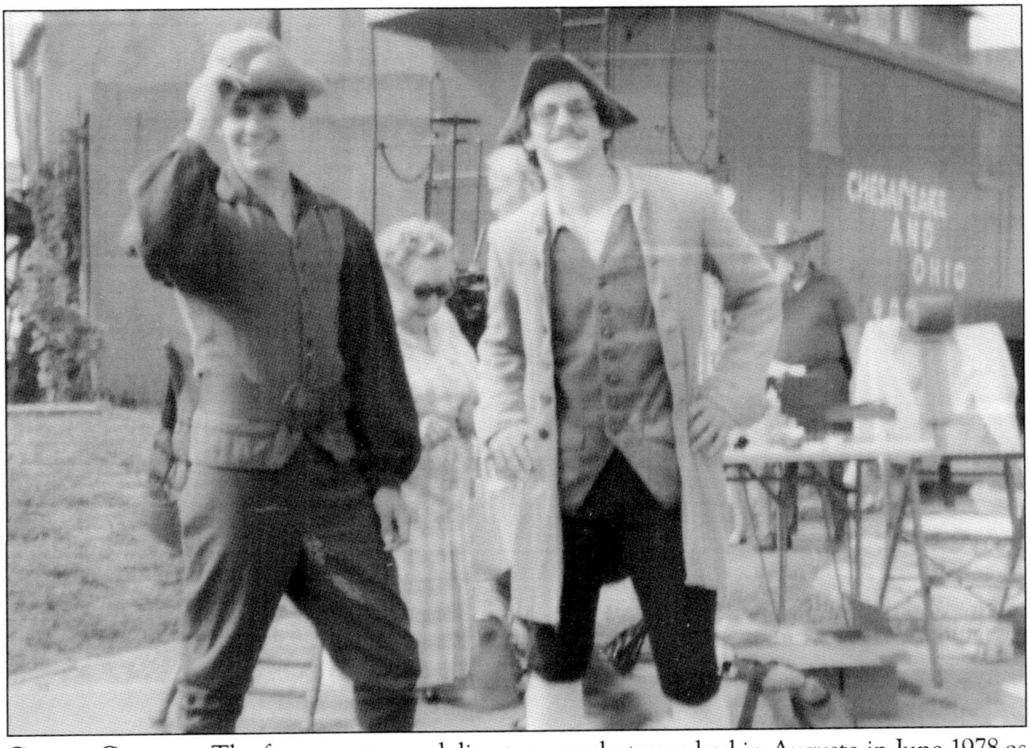

George Clooney. The famous actor and director was photographed in Augusta in June 1978 as a nonspeaking extra on the set of the television epic *Centennial*, produced by Universal Studios. Clooney (left) and his high school friend, Lee Kelsch, were clothed in townsman garb typical of early 1800s as worn in St. Louis, Missouri. Clooney, Kelsch, and Clooney's sister, Ada, were paid $25 a day for rubbing elbows with Hollywood actors. Lining the waterfront were whiskey barrels, cotton bales, and fake storefronts advertising potable spirits and rooms for muleskinners. Roaming the crowded sets were Richard Chamberlain, Clint Walker, Chad Everett, Raymond Burr, Robert Conrad, Sally Kellerman, and Robert Walden. (Courtesy of Ron and Diana French.)

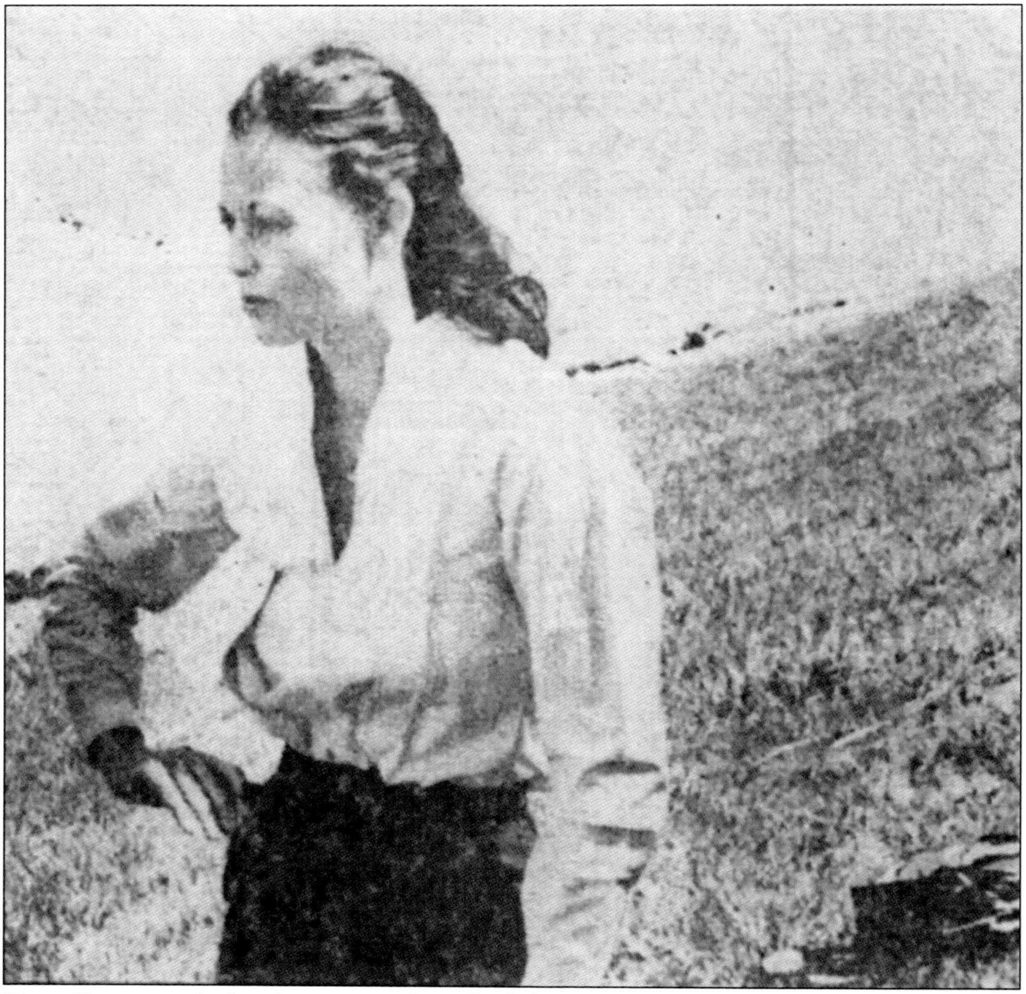

Nina Clooney. As local townspeople walked down Riverside Drive in Augusta in the late 1970s, they witnessed run-down row houses undergoing face-lifts under direction of well-known local citizen Nina Clooney. John Stone, props manager for Universal Studios, gave Clooney a prop list for the film *Centennial* ranging from camelback trunks, whiskey barrels, a doctor's desk, buggies, and champagne glasses to pewter mugs. Some of the props were weatherized to appear extremely old, while others were obtained from local museums by Clooney, who had diligently researched the proper time era for her selections. In order to make the storefronts take on the appearance of 1796 St. Louis, signs advertised a carpenter shop, a dentist's office, a bank, and a tavern, later used for staging a barroom brawl. Foam-rubber rocks covered the lower portions of some buildings, and board sidewalks were installed. Clooney was also in charge of collecting essential information from hopeful actors. Clothing sizes and special talent information were obtained from hundreds who stood in line for a chance to walk alongside the famous performers. (Courtesy of *Bracken County News*.)

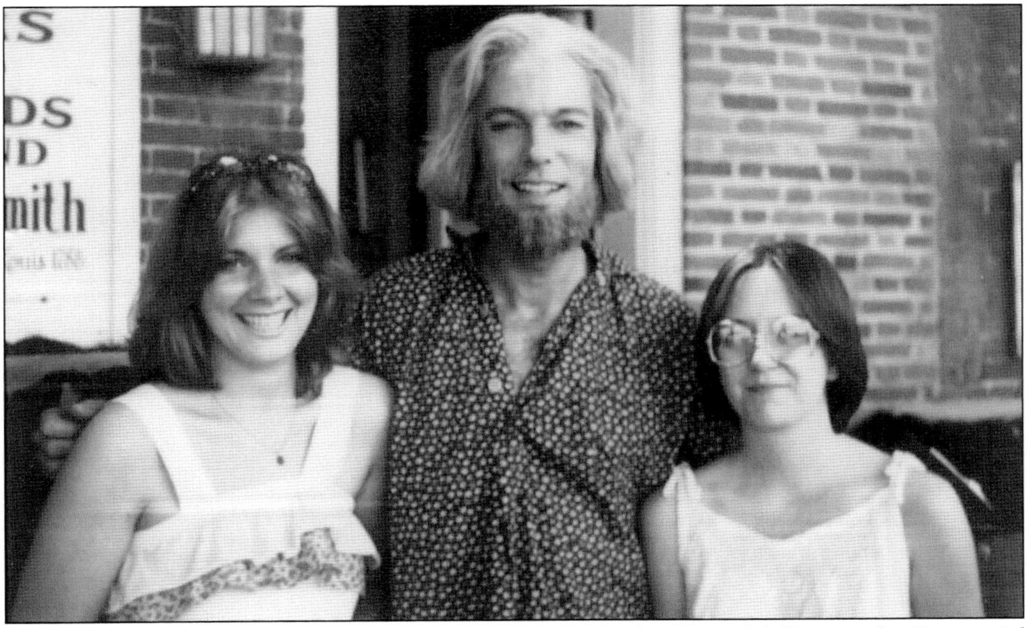

Richard Chamberlain and Raymond Burr. Known as Scotsman McKeag in the *Centennial* miniseries, Chamberlain (above) displayed his acting brilliance when he portrayed the partner of Pasquinel, played by Robert Conrad. Conrad previously performed the lead role in *The Wild, Wild West* and *Black Sheep Squadron*. Chamberlain had already gained instant fame on the television series *Dr. Kildare*. Chamberlain was the most approachable Hollywood actor and often posed for pictures with local citizens. Augusta kindergarten teacher Lisa Gardner and Talia Miller are shown receiving a playful hug from Chamberlain, and Miller (below right) is pictured with Raymond Burr. Burr, along with Bracken County native Don Galloway, starred in the hit television series *Ironside*. (Both, courtesy of Talia Thomas.)

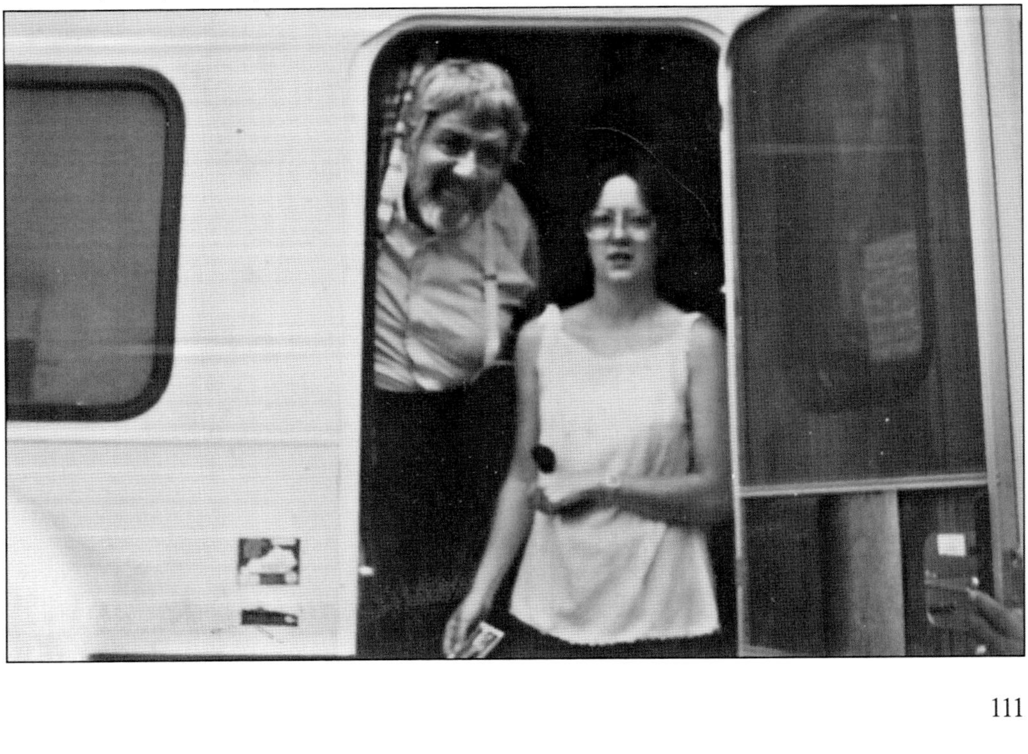

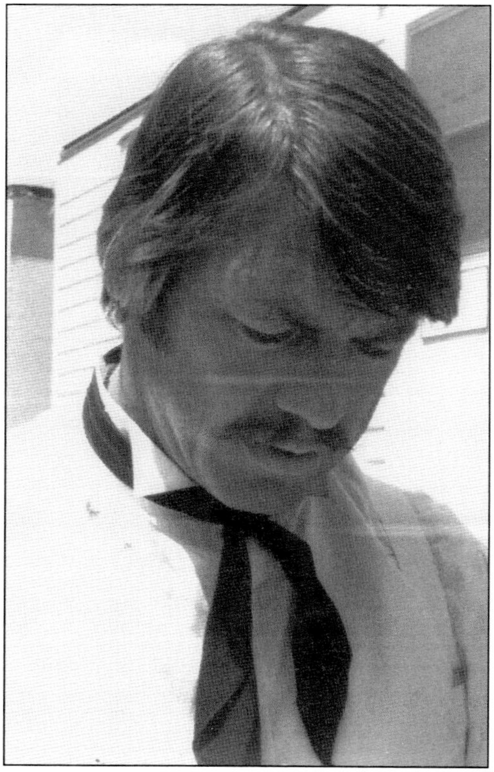

CENTENNIAL TRANSFORMED AUGUSTA. Chad Everett is photographed in this pensive pose as he portrayed Maxwell Mercy in the 25-hour NBC miniseries *Centennial*, which was televised in early 1979. Everett was most well known as the character Dr. Joe Gannon in the television series *Medical Center*. This two-story log cabin located on Riverside Drive and Williams Street became the H. Grott and Son ship building office. (Left, courtesy of Suzanne Cooper Weaver; below, courtesy of Mary Watson.)

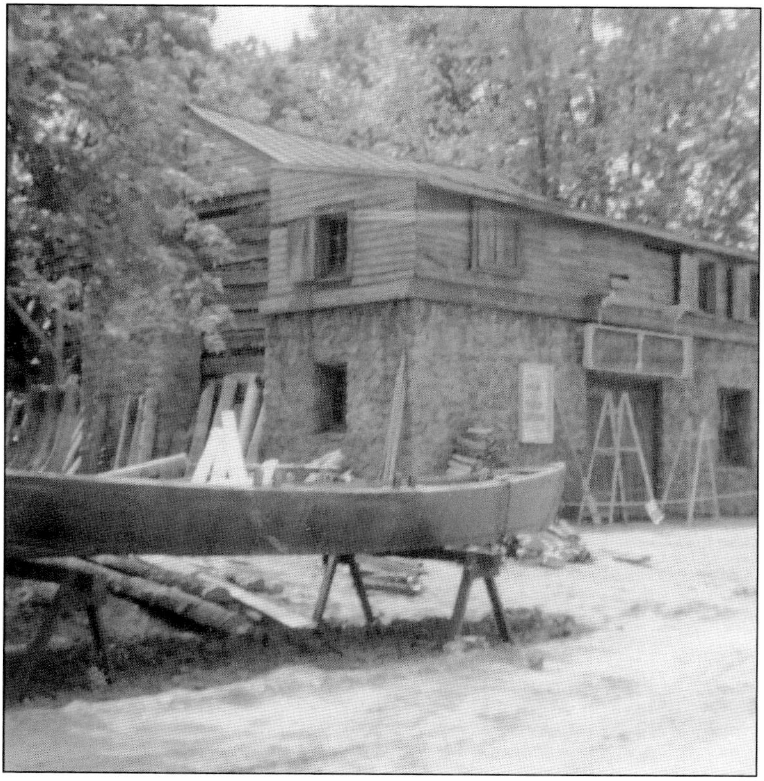

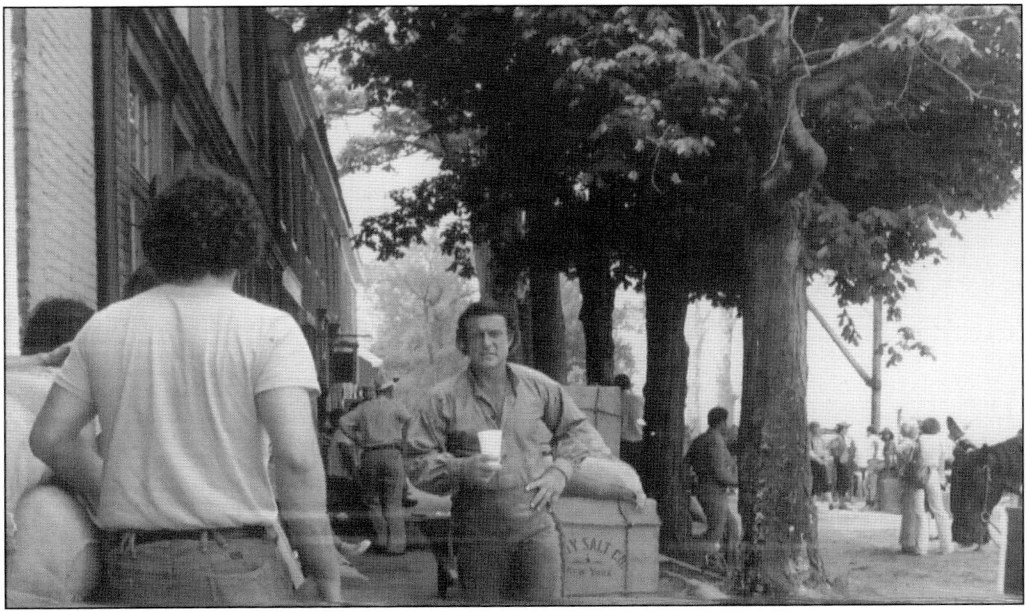

Conrad and Walker. With sweltering heat bearing down, Robert Conrad is seen enjoying a beverage on the dirt-covered sidewalk in Augusta while props are being arranged for a following scene. Below is Clint Walker, with his wife, Gigi, signing autographs in his spare time for local women who posed with them. Walker was a favorite of locals, as they hoped to catch a glimpse of this famous cowboy from the television series *Cheyenne*. Known as "Cheyenne Bodie," Walker was seen on the screen for eight seasons as well as appearing in *Dirty Dozen* and *Kodiak*. (Above, courtesy of Mary M. Watson; below, courtesy of Suzanne Cooper Weaver.)

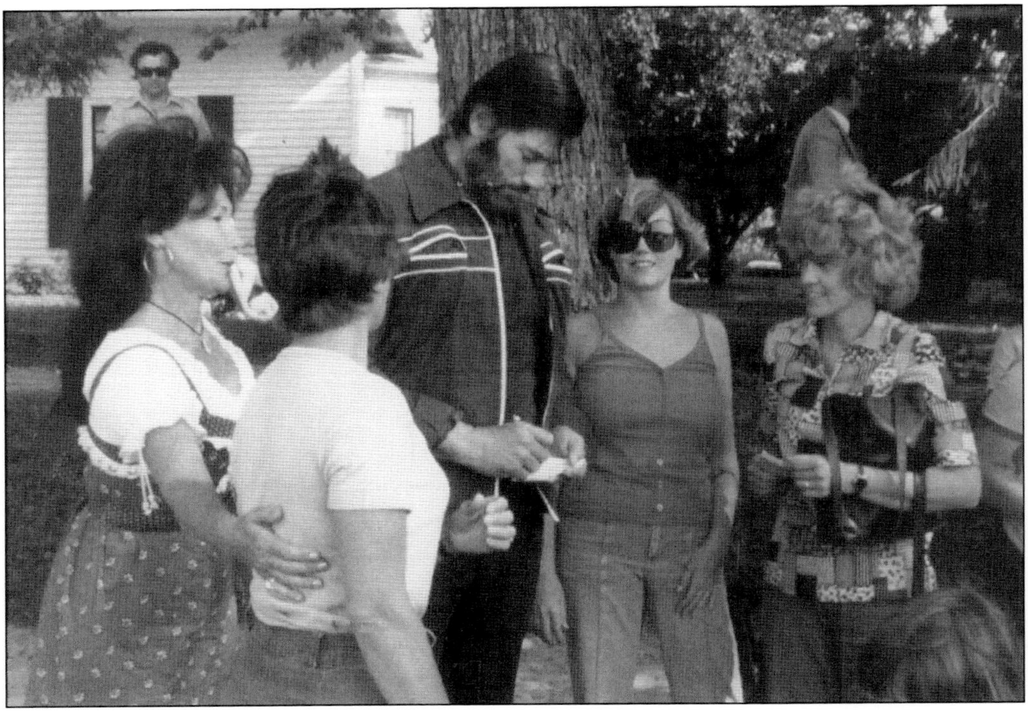

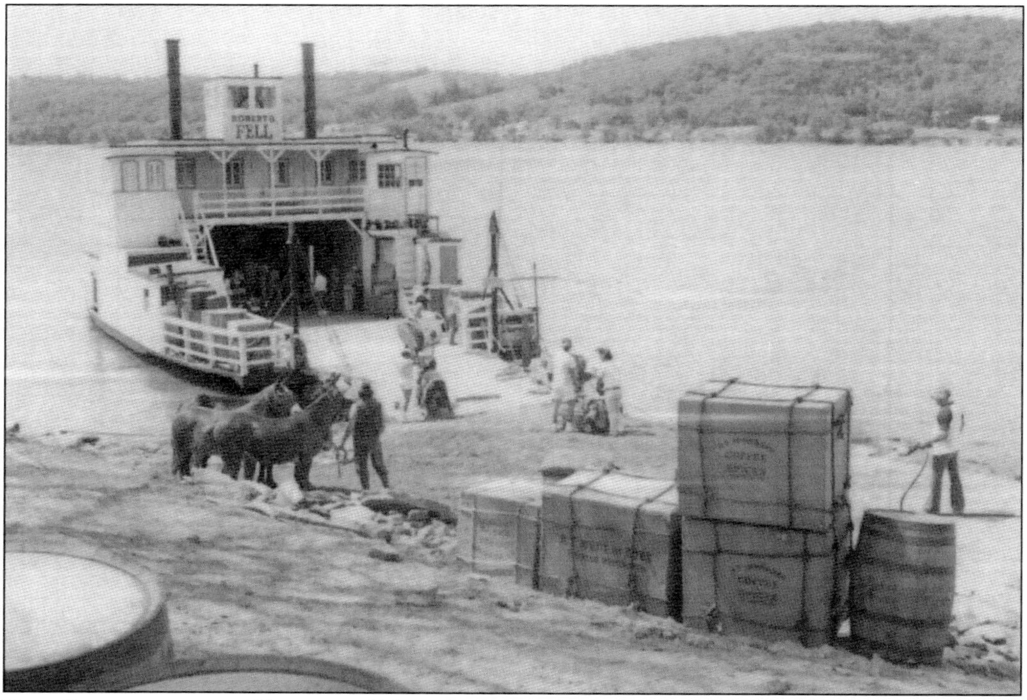

Fell Steamboat and Huckster Wagon. Augusta's ferry, *Mr. Hanes*, was converted into the packet boat *Robert O. Fell.* Crates containing coffee and spices, as well as barrels, were placed on Augusta's landing. Local citizens stood with their horses in the steamy weather for hours to complete the necessary scenes. Below is a huckster carriage used in filming *Centennial.* Master Haskell was advertising a gigantic elephant, as well as other outrageous looking animals. (Above, courtesy of Nina Clooney; below, courtesy of Mary M. Watson.)

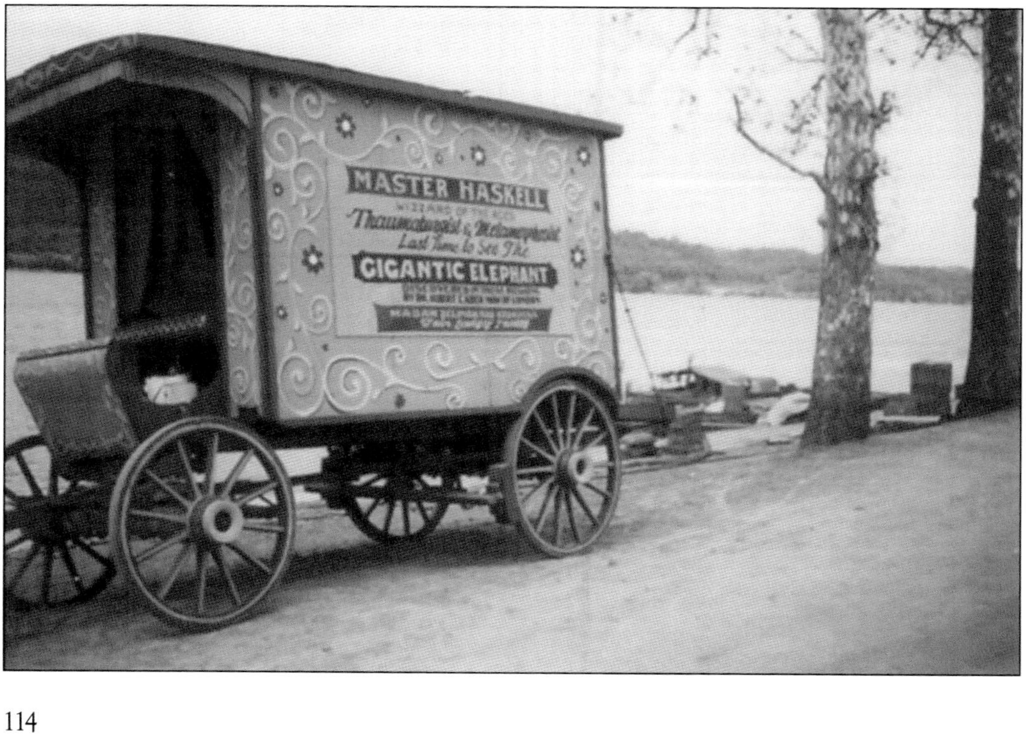

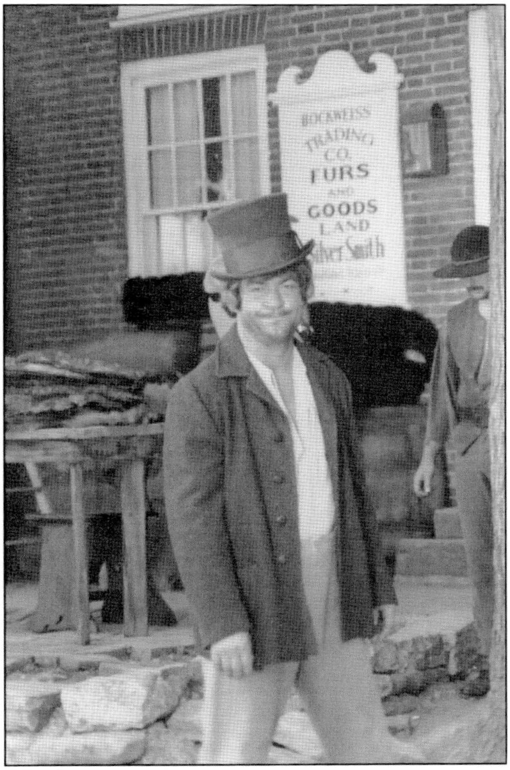

Locals Utilized in Background. Tony Taylor (right) appeared in multiple scenes in *Centennial*, changing outfits in the dressing room trailer, which contained hundreds of costumes to fit the times of an unsettled frontier. In this image, Taylor assumed the role of a wealthy buyer in search of furs to be shipped down the Mississippi to New Orleans. While not on set, the extras found themselves bolting down Main Street to gulp down an iced tea before returning to await their call. Looking amazingly like the characters from *The Three Musketeers*, Augusta residents Tim Scribner (left), Tony Taylor (center) and Lee Kelsch appeared too polished for their barroom brawl scene. (Both, courtesy of Ron and Diana French.)

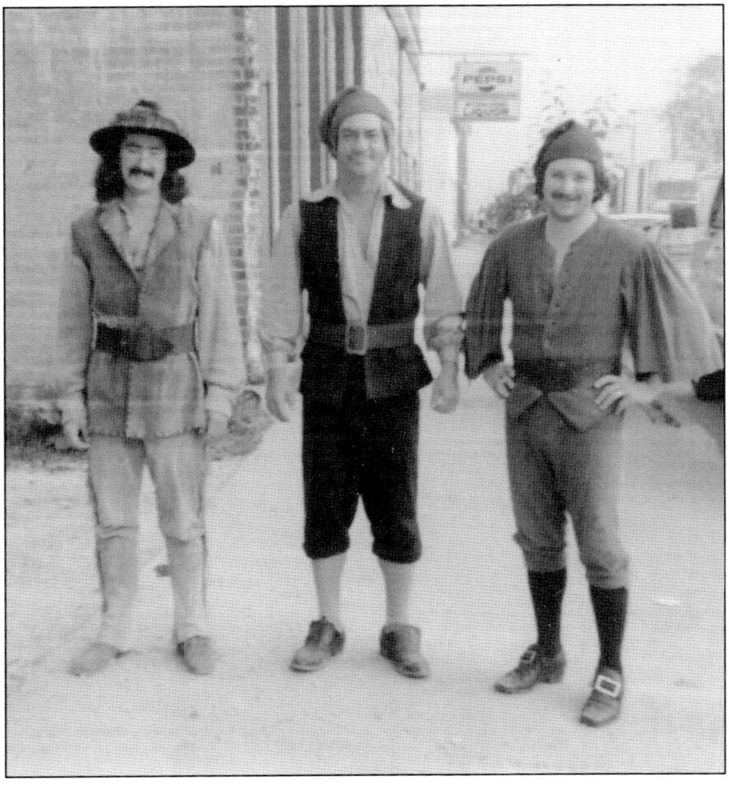

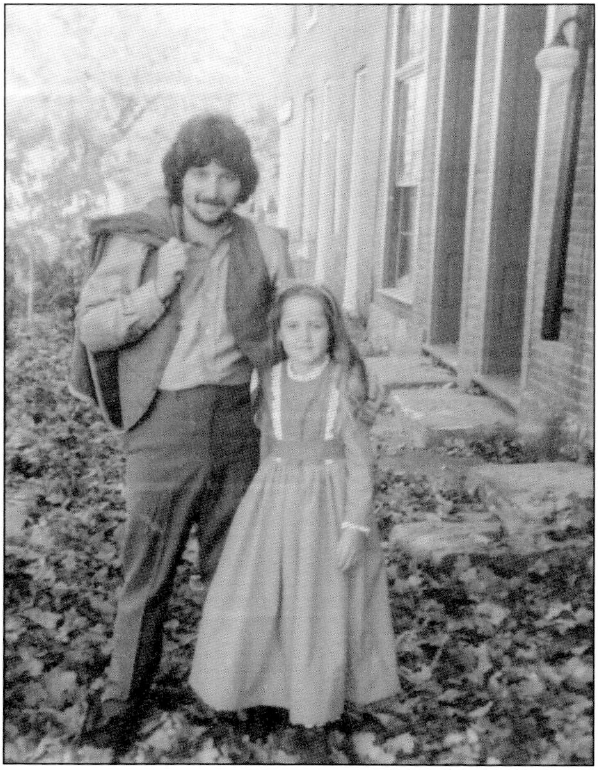

LOCAL GIRLS APPEARED IN FILM. At left, Ronald French and his oldest daughter, Gretchen, position themselves for a picture while they were appearing on the set of *This Other Eden*. This short film was sponsored by Kentucky Educational Television in Augusta in November 1978. Shown below in period clothing, Gretchen and Elizabeth Gibbs's picture was snapped on Riverside Drive, where the majority of filming took place. The series *This Other Eden* first appeared on television featuring Patricia Neal, a Whitley County, Kentucky-born actress. (Both, courtesy of Ron and Diana French.)

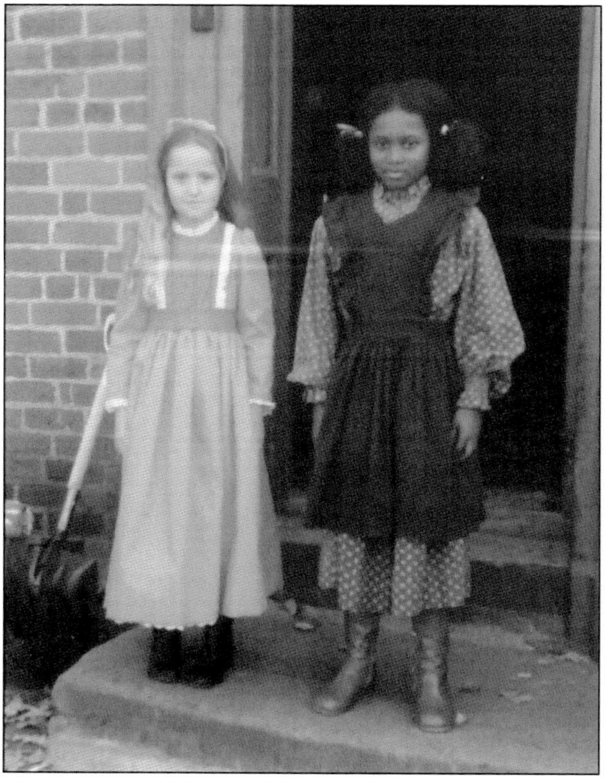

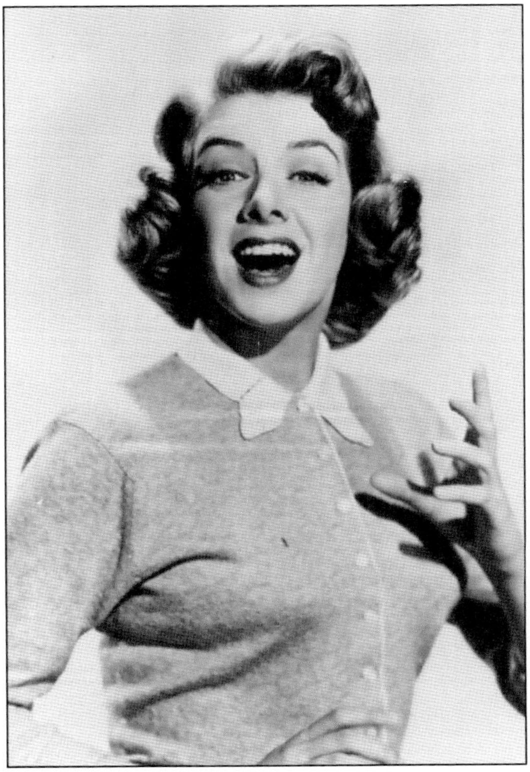

Come On-A My House. Bracken County residents opened their arms for the return of nationally acclaimed singer Rosemary Clooney. Clooney was born in 1928 in nearby Maysville, as was her singing partner and sister, Betty, and brother, Nick. After a few years in Cincinnati, she and Betty joined the Tony Pastor Band and traveled the nation. Fame was inevitable after Clooney appeared in *The Stars Are Singing*, which premiered in Maysville in 1953. Most moviegoers recognize *White Christmas* as her pivotal film, thrusting her into superstardom. After the death of her first husband, José Ferrer, she married her longtime friend, Dante DiPaolo. The Rosemary Clooney Museum, established by Heather Renee French (Miss America 2000) and her husband, Steve Henry, is open daily on Riverside Drive. (Right, courtesy of John H. Henderson; below, courtesy of *Bracken County News*.)

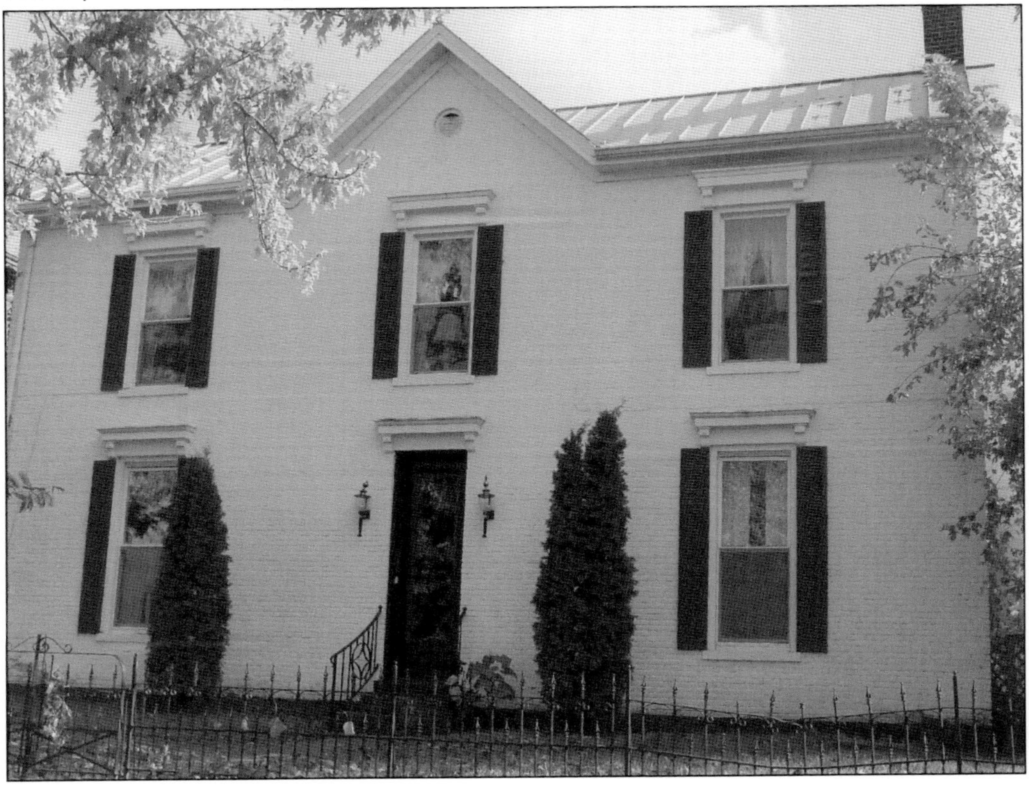

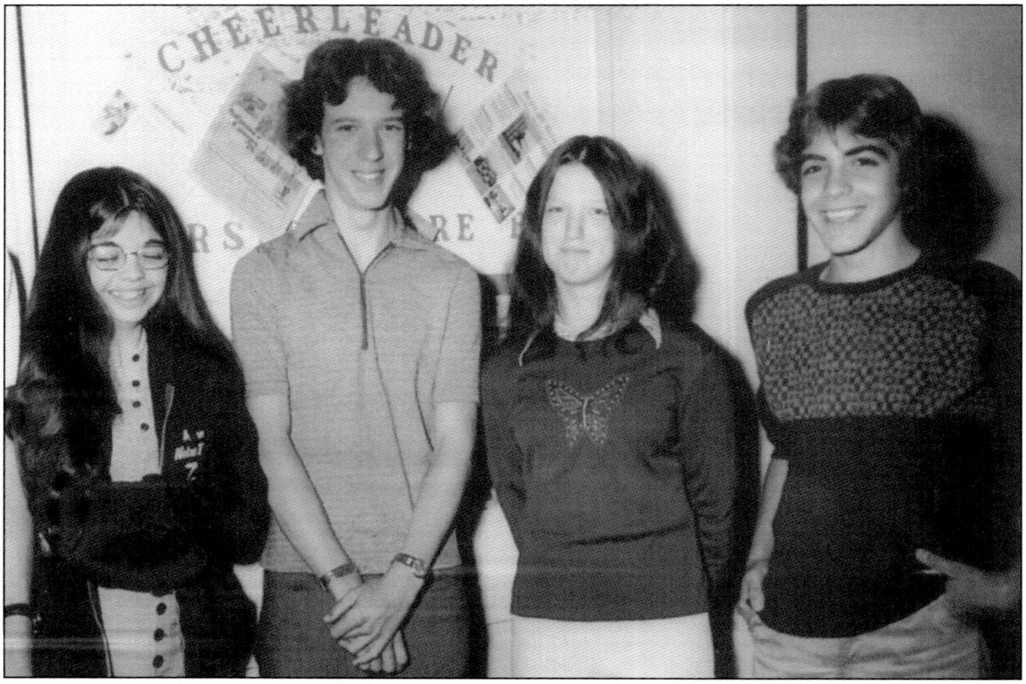

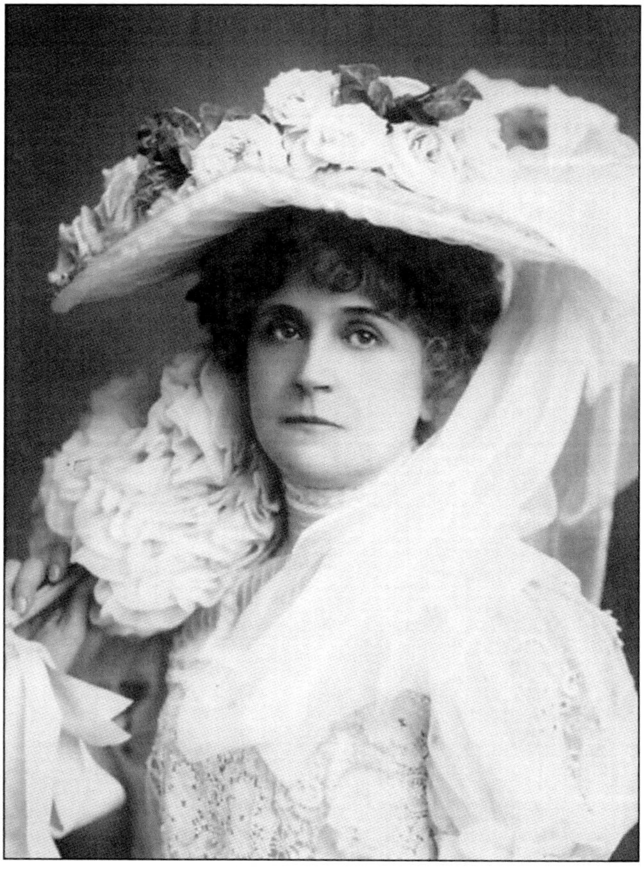

George and Ada Clooney. George Clooney and his sister, Ada, are shown on the left and right of two Augusta students. George graduated from Augusta High School in 1979 and Ada in 1978. Ada attended Northern Kentucky University, married Norman Zeidler, and is the mother of two children, Allison and Nicholas. Like both parents, Ada is also a writer. (Courtesy of Caroline R. Miller.)

Henrietta Crossman, Silent Screen Star. Henrietta Crossman is listed on some media biography sites as born in Augusta. What is accurately known is that she was a niece of Stephen Collins Foster, author of *My Old Kentucky Home*, the Kentucky state song. Foster's uncles were residents of Augusta in the 1830s. Letters in the Foster archives clearly refer to Stephen's visits to Augusta with his mother. (Courtesy of *Bracken County News*.)

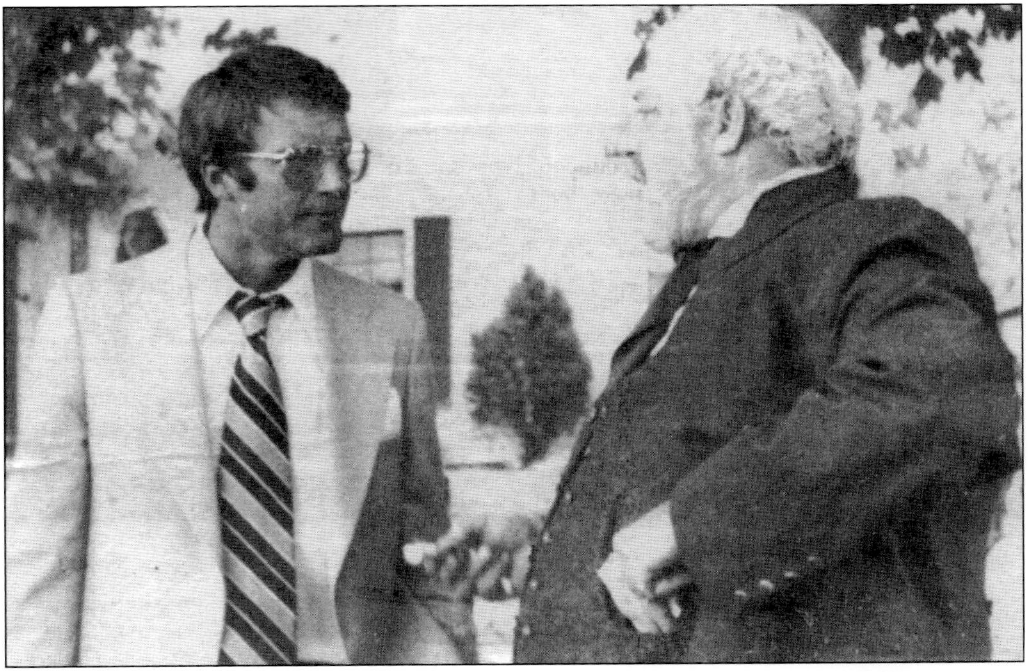

DON GALLOWAY'S FRIENDS. Pictured above is Galloway with costar Raymond Burr on the 1978 set of *Centennial*. Although Galloway did not have a role in the movie, he made the trip to Bracken County to visit his old friend. Galloway portrayed the character Kip Rysdale on the long-running soap opera *Secret Storm* and later Buzz Stryker on *General Hospital* in 1985. Shown at right are Galloway and a former local resident, Audrey Jean Cooper, on one of Galloway's return trips to Brooksville. Sadly, in January 2009, his friends attended his memorial service at the Concord Methodist Church in Bladeston. (Above, courtesy of Mary M. Watson; right, courtesy of Suzanne Cooper Weaver.)

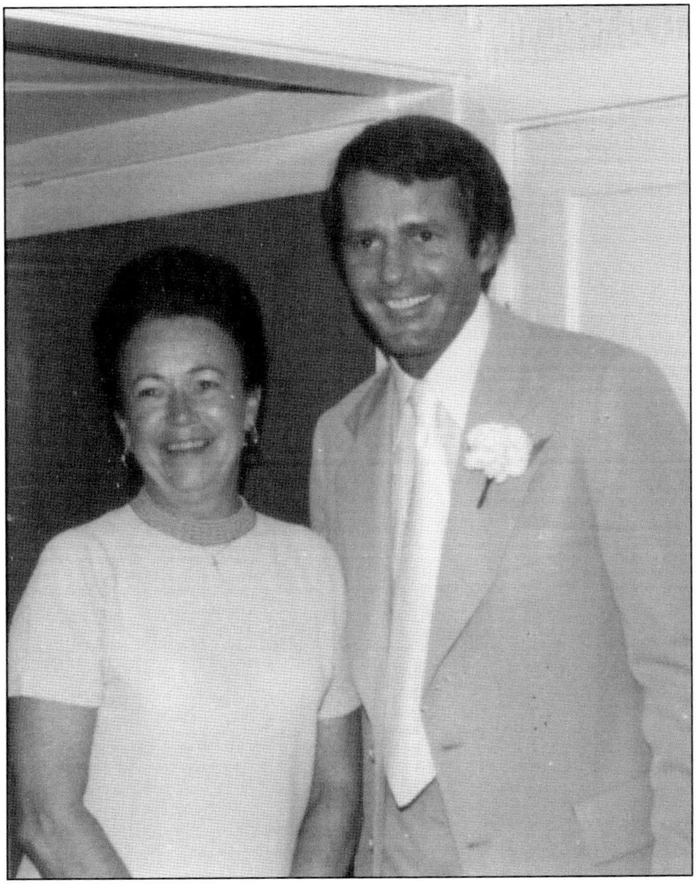

Stuart Walker's

Portmanteau Theatre

Juvenile Performance in Brooklyn
For the Benefit of the
BROOKLYN FREE KINDERGARTEN SOCIETY

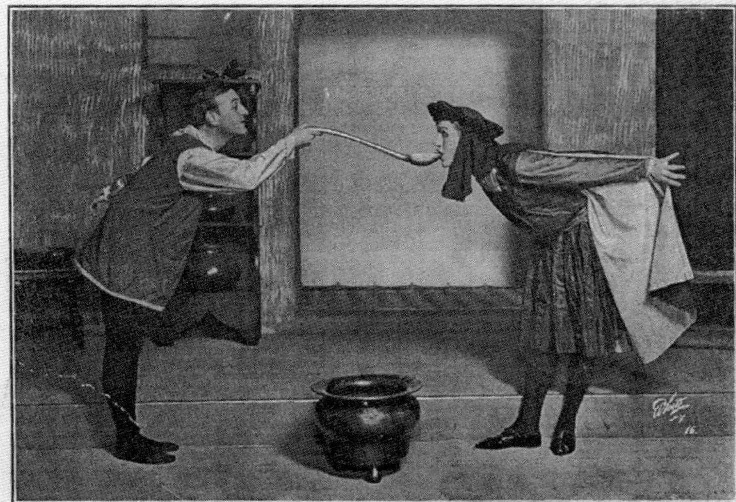

Scene from "Six Who Pass While the Lentils Boil"

Brooklyn Academy of Music

SATURDAY AFTERNOON, FEBRUARY 19, 1916

AT HALF AFTER TWO

STUART WALKER'S PORTMANTEAU THEATRE. Stuart Walker (1880–1941) was born in Augusta and lived on Front Street. While living in or visiting Augusta, he most likely attended the Russell Opera House, listed in Julius Cahn's *Official Theatrical Guide* in 1902. Walker's life has been recounted in Jo Ann Yeoman's recent biography, *Dream Dealer: Stuart Walker and the American Theater.* His interest in theater and stage began during his youth, putting on a production of *Bohemian Girl* at the age of six for neighborhood children. In the first decade of the 20th century, Walker and his family moved to Covington, where he furthered his education at the University of Cincinnati. Walker arrived in New York City in 1908 and became a student at Academy of Dramatic Arts. His invention, the portable theater, became a success, as it was small enough for convention rooms, weighing only 3,000 pounds, complete with four stand lights and a mirror reflector. (Courtesy of Jo Ann Yeoman-Tongret.)

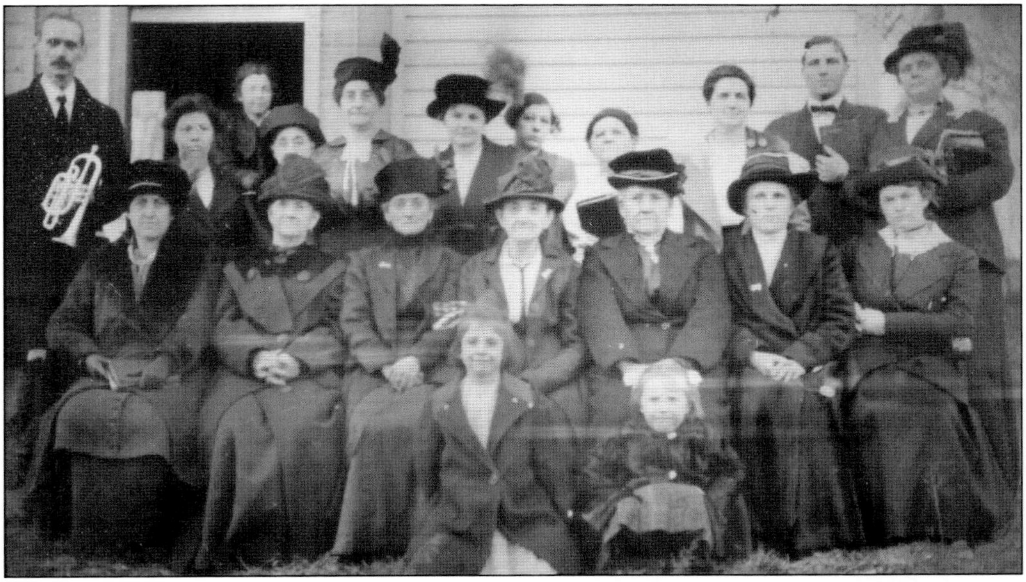

Germantown's Community Musicians. In the 1920s, several communities had bands with adult musicians who were able to afford instruments and lessons. Since only two men and one cornet player appear in the photograph, it is assumed the ladies were members of a singing group. A popular spot for performing was in the gazebo in the center ring of the annual Germantown Fair. (Courtesy of John H. Henderson.)

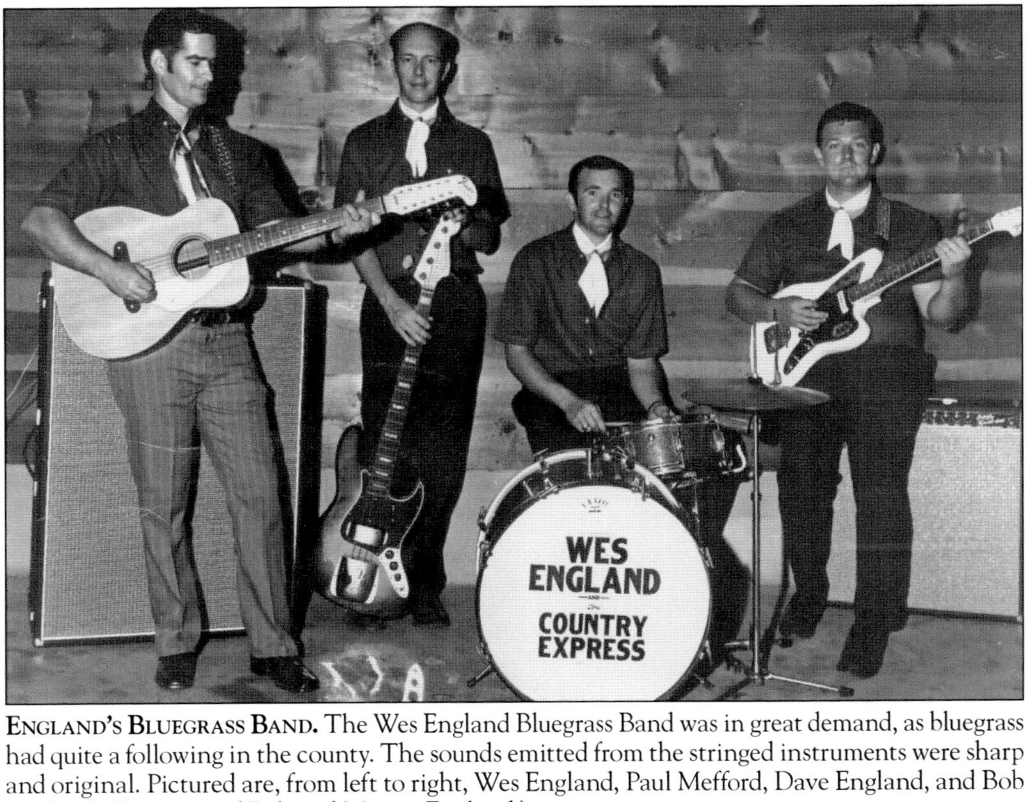

England's Bluegrass Band. The Wes England Bluegrass Band was in great demand, as bluegrass had quite a following in the county. The sounds emitted from the stringed instruments were sharp and original. Pictured are, from left to right, Wes England, Paul Mefford, Dave England, and Bob England. (Courtesy of Bob and Margie England.)

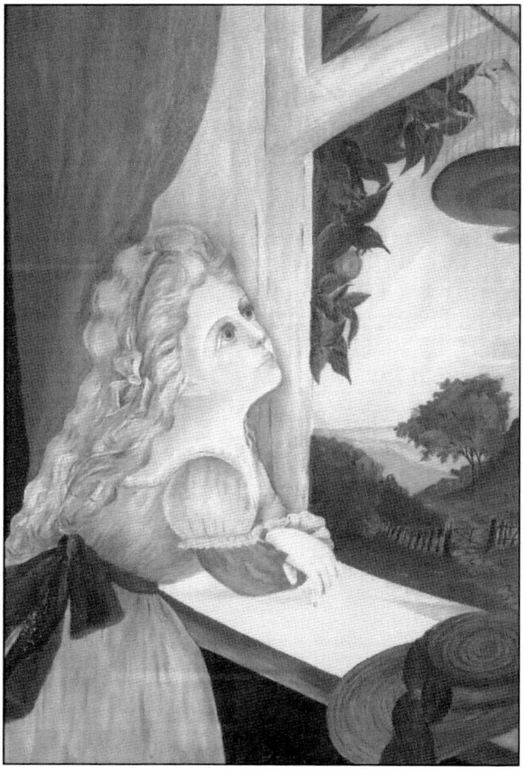

Girl Watching a Canary. Sylvia Thomas of Willow Grove, shown below in 1888, had an interest in the finer activity of painting as a young woman. Thomas's large oil painting of a young girl wistfully starring at a caged canary possesses brilliant color and detail. Other Bracken County female artists at that time were Emma Weldon, a Ms. Eldridge, Tensie Reynolds, Sallie Bradford, Sallie Lee Armstrong, Carrie Dietz, and Carrie Pribble. Their works ranged from delicate angels to a moonlit scene suggestive of Shakespeare's *A Midsummer Night's Dream*. The beautiful sunsets in Augusta were the subject of several paintings by these ladies. (Both, courtesy of William E. Miller.)

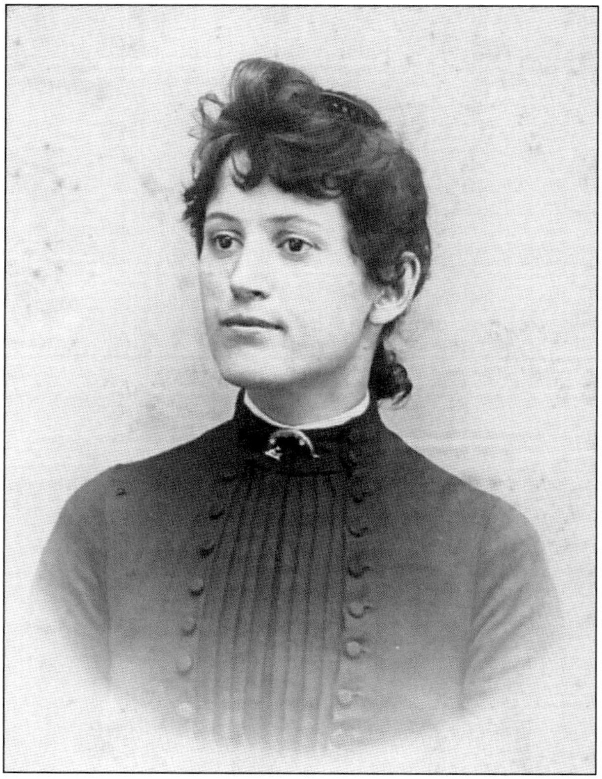

MIKE GRISWOLD, ACTOR AND PUPPETEER. Mike Griswold was a character actor in Hollywood for several decades. When he retired to Augusta, he brought with him his favorite puppets and continued performing his ventriloquist act for his fellow residents. Griswold appeared in television and film favorites, including *Incredible Hulk*, *B. J. and the Bear*, *Eight Is Enough*, *Dallas*, and *NYPD Blue*. (Courtesy of Mike Griswold.)

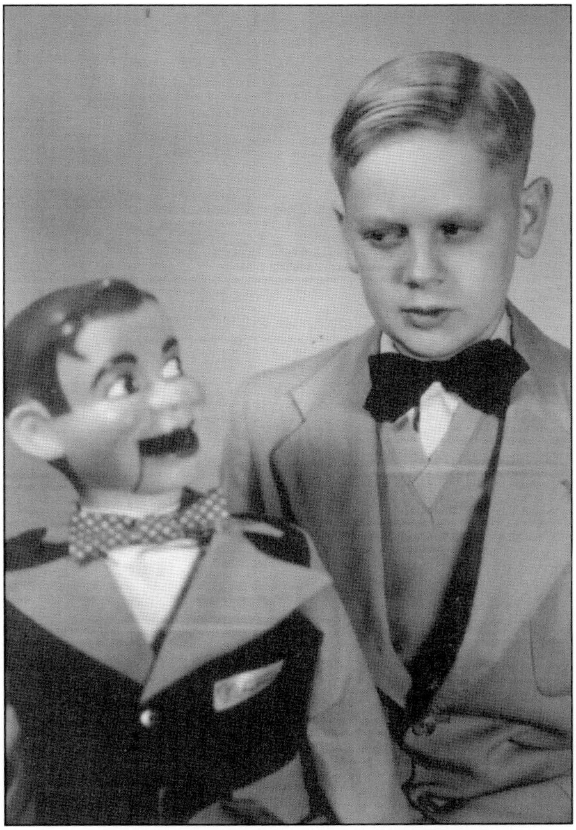

ED MCCLANAHAN, HOMETOWN AUTHOR. When searching for characters to fill his books, McClanahan looks no further than the residents of his home, Bracken County. His bestselling works included *The Natural Man* (set in Needmore), *A Congress of Wonders* (set at the Germantown Fair), and a collection of nonfiction essays, *Famous People I Have Known*. (Courtesy of *Bracken County News*.)

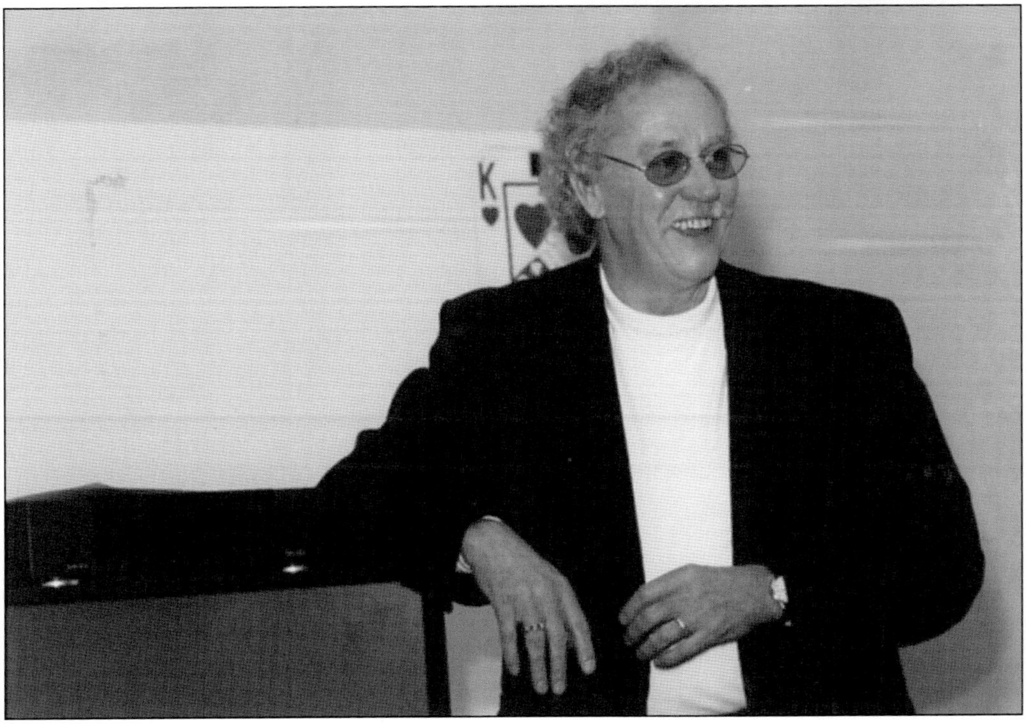

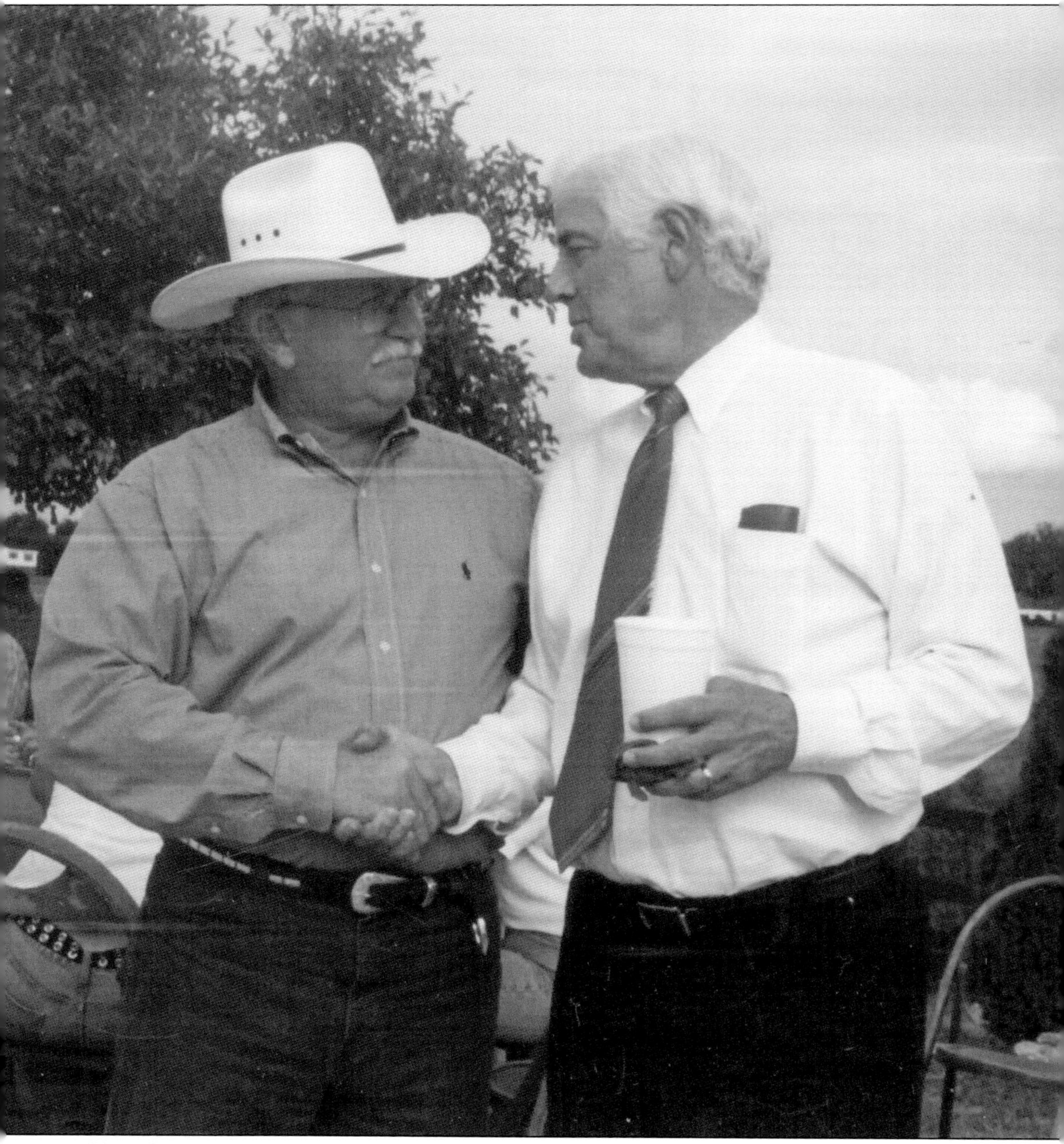

Nick Clooney, a Masterful Gentleman. Clooney (right) was born in 1934 in Maysville and has resided in Augusta since 1973. He is pictured with Gene Clabes, formerly of Old Oakland Road. As a youth, Clooney's voice was heard on the WFTM radio waves in Maysville. His broadcasting career led him to Lexington and Cincinnati, where his sisters also had their start on the radio and in television. During his later years, Clooney became a news anchor in Salt Lake City, Buffalo, and Los Angeles. An outstanding journalist and anchor for Cincinnati news stations, Clooney retired from broadcasting only to become a spokesperson and writer for *American Movie Classics* for the next five years. He also contributed a column to the *Kentucky Post* and penned three books. In 2008, Clooney became a professor at American University in Washington, D.C. (Courtesy of *Bracken County News*.)

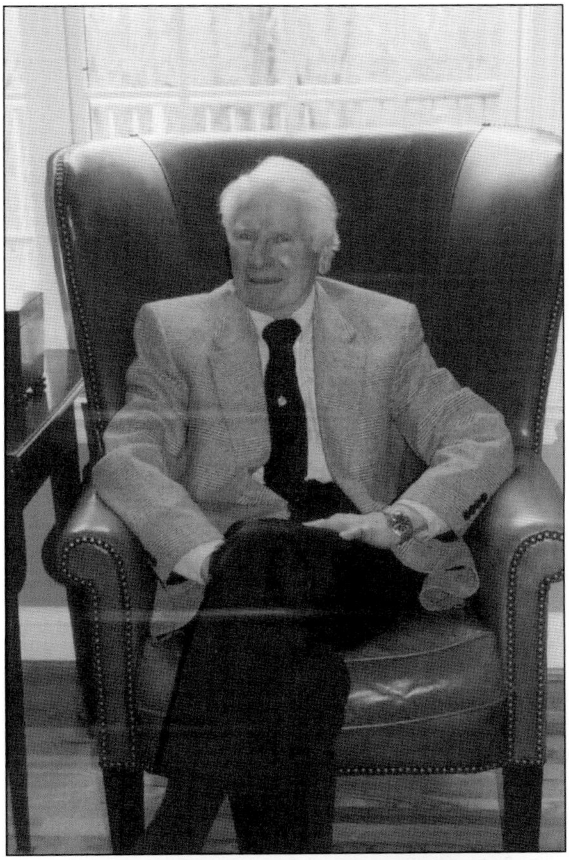

Tongret Reclaimed Augusta's Character. Over the last four decades, Charles Tongret, along with his wife, sons, and daughter, actively set out to renovate dilapidated structures into worthwhile homes and businesses. The family's journey was chronicled in Alan Tongret's book, *Inn of a Thousand Days: A Memoir of a Country B&B.* (Courtesy of *Bracken County News.*)

Luciano Moral, Singer and Chef. Moral is pictured here in his Augusta restaurant, Beehive Tavern, alongside his valued employee Carolyn Johnson Gibbs. Moral was born in Cuba but was airlifted off the island with other children. Beehive Tavern has been in operation at the corner of Riverside Drive and Main Street for nearly 25 years. (Courtesy of *Bracken County News.*)

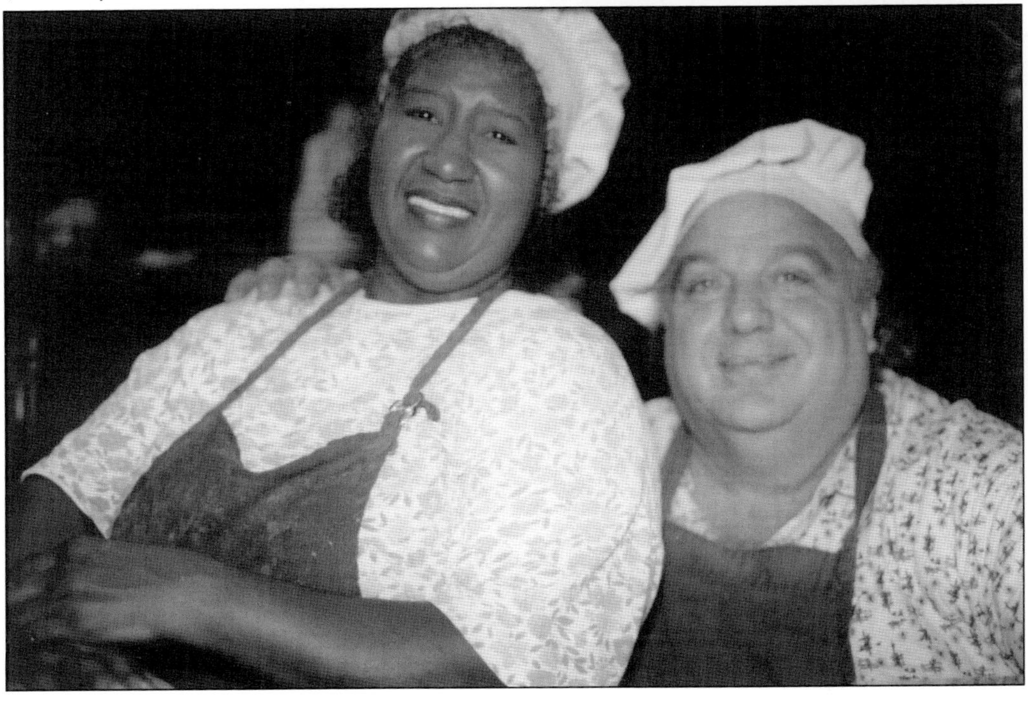

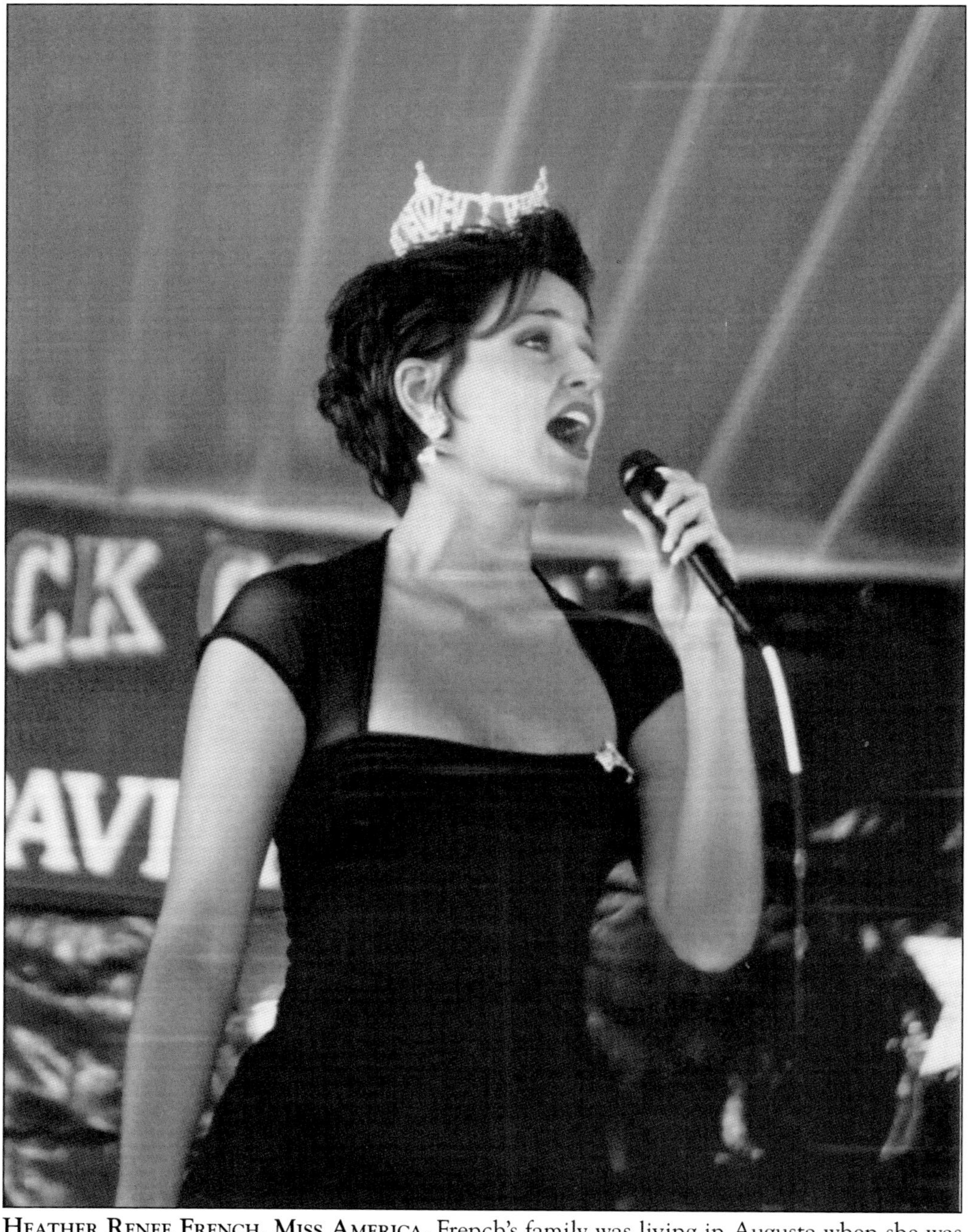

Heather Renee French, Miss America. French's family was living in Augusta when she was born in 1974, later moving to Maysville. At University of Cincinnati, French studied fashion design and illustration and instructed illustration courses. Her reign as Miss America 2000 was spent advocating for homeless veterans. After her reign, she began broadcasting and advertising careers in Louisville as co-anchor of *Fox in the Morning*. She has written several children's books and is the mother of two daughters, Harper and Taylor. She and her husband, Steve Henry, are the cofounders of the Rosemary Clooney Museum in Augusta. Recently, Heather has designed and developed several lines of fashionable dresses, which are flying off the shelves. (Courtesy of *Bracken County News*.)

INDEX OF SETTLEMENTS

These names and locations of villages and cities represent current and former locations where residents joined to found the history of what has become modern-day Bracken County.

Augusta: platted December 1797, largest city, port on the Ohio River, ferry landing
Berlin: formerly Pleasant Ridge and Hagensville, located on old buffalo trace
Bladeston: high atop a ridge where Concord Methodist Church and cemetery sit
Bradford: Metcalf's Landing, where Laban Bradford shipped tobacco and grapes
Bridgeville: located in the extreme southeastern corner of the county
Brooksville: formerly Woodward's Cross Road, county seat, second-largest city
Browningsville: located on Little Willow Creek, once home to the Browning family
Chatham: area known for fertile bluegrass soil and plantation homes on Asbury Road
Cumminsville: originated in 1880s at the site of Joseph Cummins's saw mill
Foster: former river port, site of Native American raid on nearby Holt's Creek
Germantown: settled as Buchanan Station by immigrants in log fort, platted in 1794
Gertrude: sits high atop a ridge to the west of Augusta
Johnsville: settled around 1790, often called Fairview for its spectacular views
Lenoxburg: named for Samuel B. Lenox, home of Lenoxburg Academy
Milford: on North Fork of Licking River, much destroyed by fires in 1889 and 1956
Mount Hor: formerly on Belmont Road, noted for Dr. Jonothan Haley's office
Mount Zion: generally known for brick Methodist church and lovely cemetery
Neave: originally Holton's Corner, parts destroyed by tornadoes in 1923, 1927, and 1948
Needmore: once location of tollhouse for plank Dutch Ridge Road; Baker-Bird Winery
Oakland: reputed site of old stills and Native American burial grounds
Petra: known for Porter Haley Distillery and where Duke's raiders stopped for breakfast
Powersville: established 1833, home of Phillip Buckner's hunting lodge and grave site
Rock Spring/Tietzville: site of large barn distillery and Chalfont stone house
Sante Fe: former village where the Doyle slave escape and capture occurred in 1848
South Higginsport: formerly 1 mile east of Augusta on Kentucky Route 8 and Ohio River
Stoney Point: known as Dietz Landing, site of railroad pumping station
Stonewall: located halfway between Germantown and Bridgeville
Walcott: home of covered bridge, owned by Murray family from 1832 to 2000
Wellsburg: site of former brickyard and distillery, practically destroyed by 1937 flood
Willow Grove: former site of Native American burial grounds, site of Meldahl Dam